Shepherding
OUTDOORS
– THREE DOG DAYS –

A COLLECTION
OF SHORT STORIES
from a
SOUTHERN FATHER

by WALT MERRELL

83 Press
2323 2nd Avenue North
Birmingham, AL 35203
83press.com

ISBN: 979-8-9874820-2-5
Printed in U.S.A.

This book is dedicated to my dad . . .
WALTER MARVIN MERRELL, JR.
Everyone has a father. We all need a dad.

CONTENTS

Chapter One: More of the Early Years.................................6

A True Christmas Story 8
Banks was a Blessing Baby... 12
Dueling Rattlesnakes.. 17
Horse Mafia... 21
Smith & Wesson and a Rattlesnake................................ 29
Christmas Parades 37
The Look of Love 41
Ferris Wheels... 46

Chapter Two: The Fork in the River 52

My Grandfather Died of a Heart Attack 54
The Best I Ever Had... 57
I Want to Know What Love Is 66
The Cross Between the Lakes 72

Chapter Three: Creeks, Streams, and Rivers.................... 86

Neighbors... 88
Old Jeeps, Pretty Smiles, and a Good, Good Father............ 94
Sometimes You Just Have to Be Still............................... 98
The Thunder Rolls 102
Good Dirt 116

Chapter Four: A Father's Outdoor Journal 120

Busted Plans 122
Aliens, Astronauts, and the Perfect Picture............................... 128
It Will All Come Together in the End 133
Ole Betsy 139
Shimmer in the Current.. 144
The Wild Life 147
Wild Cats 152
Zebco 33s 158

Chapter Five: A Good, Good Father................................... 162

Warm and Washed 164
This Day, I Choose to Follow 167
Paddling Through the Pain 170
Just One More Mile 175
Friends in Low Places... 179

Chapter Six: By the Campfire................................... 190

Freezers and Nakedness 192
Memory Lane 198
No Smoke, No Fire... 204
There are Plenty of Rocks on This Mountain 211
The American Spirit... 216
Tough Nuts 234
Warmth in a Cold World.. 251

Chapter ONE

MORE OF THE EARLY YEARS

—— A TRUE CHRISTMAS ——
STORY

I heard the most dreadful sound this morning . . . the sound of the garbage truck coming up the street, made especially dreadful by the fact that I knew that, last week, I forgot to put the garbage out, and, in just a few days, there would be wrapping paper galore.

With my sincerest apologies to the garbage man and to any neighbors who may have witnessed this unsightly event, here is a festive recount of the morning's events!

'Twas the day before Christmas,
and all through the house,
cans overflowed,
to the joy of a mouse.

The cans were full, with no room to spare,
In hopes that the garbage man soon would be there.

The children were nestled all snug in their beds,
While visions of Oscar the Grouch danced in their heads.
And Momma in her 'kerchief, and I in my cap,
Had just settled on the couch for our morning coffee recap.

When out on the road there arose such a rumble,
I sprang from the couch to see what made the grumble.

Away to the window I flew like a flash,
Tore open the shutters and threw up the sash.

The big blue blur on the road, not nearly too slow,
Made my heart skip a beat and my head sink low.
When, what to my wondering ears should I hear,
But my wife saying, "You better make it, my dear!"

With a young stout driver, so lively and spry,
I knew in a moment it must be BFI.

More rapid than eagles my legs did they go,
And I whistled, and shouted, and called him, "Hey, Joe!"

Now, I'm dashing! Now, dancing! Now, prancing and sprinting!
I think I might vomit! I'm stupid! I'll be in a coma . . . I'm dizzy!

To the top of the hill! To the top of the driveway!
I grabbed the can before he could dash away! Dash away all!

And then, in a twinkling, I realized my spoof,
The tingling and chilling of cold on my tush.
As I drew in my head, wishing for a gown,
There was no saving me . . . he was waiting to peddle down.

I wasn't dressed all in fur from head to foot,
You see, my clothes were inside . . . there I stood in my undies and boots.
A bundle of trash he had flung in the back,
And I looked like a peddler just looking for a snack.

My fingers, how they tingled! My tail wasn't merry!
My cheeks were like roses, my nose like a cherry!
My arms wrapped around me like a present with a bow,
And I shivered and shook like I was standing in the snow.

The grit of my jaw held tight against my teeth,
And there in my boxers, I shook like a thief.
With skin exposed from my face to my belly,
Cold and alone and, from the haste of my chore, a little bit smelly!

My sweats and my jeans all sat on the shelf,
And all I could do was simply laugh at myself!
Thank God, he gave me no wink of his eye nor a nod with his head,
Soon he drove off leaving me no more to dread.

He spoke not a word, but went on about his work,
And I scurried back to put on a shirt.
And laying my hand on the door to go back inside,

Hannah loves Christmas ornaments. Everywhere we travel, I'll always buy her one or two. This one, though, is special. Our sweet friend Brenda Gouge gave this to us. She knows what a patriotic person I am, and she knows of Hannah's love for ornaments . . . so it was the perfect gift. Thank you, Brenda.

I hoped I would avoid the laughter from my bride!

As I went on in and straight to find clothes,
Hannah sprang to her feet with applause, as she'd enjoyed the show.
And with coffee in hand, I sat panting and cold, knowing I did it, victory was bold!
Then I heard her exclaim, "'Ere what a sight!"
"Happy Christmas to all," she said. "I hope I see that tonight!"

BAY WAS A BLESSING BABY

Banks was a surprise baby. We are often asked about the girls' names . . . Bay, Cape, and Banks. The short version is that I wanted to name our first girl Maggie May, but Hannah pointed out the potential ramifications of naming your daughter after a Rod Stewart vixen . . . so, "May" eventually converted into "Bay." Fitting, since I am a nautical dreamer, and the water is my second home. "Cape" was suggested to us by Hannah's grandmother. Banks came as an obvious choice . . . because that is, after all, where the water ends.

Even as a surprise, she has been a blessing. Hannah and I laugh from time to time about how God knows more of our needs than we do, and He knew we needed her. Banks was born in October of 2009.

That first Christmas was tough for us. We were about to announce a campaign to run for district attorney, and a considerable amount of planning had gone into what was to be. A baby was never part of the original plan . . . of course, we had to adjust. At the same time, we were building a house. For those of you who don't know, when we build a house, I literally mean *we* build it. Hannah and I have slung many a hammer. Of course, we hire professionals along the way, but we work side by side with them.

That year, the Christmas tree fell . . . bulbs and ornaments shattered everywhere on the hardwood floors. Nothing will wake you quicker than the sound of breaking glass during the night! Santa came, of course, but our Christmas was sparse . . . we were pouring most of our money into construction, and what was left over was being saved for campaign expenses. And new babies aren't free!

Hannah had a rough pregnancy with Banks. It was certainly her hardest, and it did not get any easier when Banks was born. Hannah had insisted for a few years that I get a vasectomy . . . but I had resisted. She was a month or two away from resuming her career when we realized she was pregnant. To put it mildly . . . nothing was going right.

Hannah was depressed; I didn't know how to "fix it." We were broke; I didn't know how to "fix it." We were sleep deprived from the new baby and from working nights on the new house; I didn't know how to "fix it." We were under the stress of the campaign; I didn't know how to "fix it." It all seemed just a bit too much, and it was Christmas. Oh, and did I mention the tree fell?

I stood that tree back up and then we cleaned all the brokenness out from underneath it. The girls helped hang or rearrange the ornaments . . . and we were left with a great story to tell. Sometimes the stories that rise out of the ashes of calamity are the best. This one is one of my favorites . . .

A child's eyes, and a woman's smile.

I've always loved to see Hannah smile. She has a beautiful smile to me . . . and pictures of her broadly shining bright always warm my heart. I do think she is beautiful when she smiles, but I think these pictures draw me in because I see how happy she is . . . and that makes me happy, too.

And as for Banks . . . I pray her eyes always stay bright and focused on whatever lay ahead. And I pray that, just like in this picture, she always keeps them focused on Jesus.

Silent Night, Holy Night.
All is calm, all is bright.

Christmas came and went, but our troubles had not ceased. Our little farmhouse was a little more than 1,200 square feet with two real bedrooms, and our family of five was about to burst through the walls. I was now working on the new house even more because of the pressure to move. That created a cycle. I wasn't home, and Hannah was lonely, which contributed to her emotional state. We spent more money on construction, which added to the financial burden. I worked more, which added to the sleep deprivation, and Banks liked to get up most all hours of the night to nurse . . . to play . . . to poop . . . to whatever.

Then, one February morning, it started to snow. The weatherman warned that we would see below-freezing daytime highs, and he hinted that we might see some flurries. It kept snowing and kept snowing and kept snowing. Before it was all said and done, God laid a swatch of snow about seven-inches deep on top of our little farm. And there was nothing I could do. I couldn't "fix it."

That swatch of snow, I'm convinced, was just for me. You'll recall that it was only about 25-miles wide, from north to south. It was a curious meteorological event, where a highly concentrated amount of snow fell along a very small path. Our farm was right smack dab in the middle, and I couldn't "fix it."

And it stayed cold . . . for days, it stayed cold. The first day was fun. I played in the snow with the older girls. We made a snowman or two. We had snowball fights. We did it all. The second day, the new was wearing off, and, by the third day, I felt trapped. For months now, I had been running eighteen hours a day, nonstop . . . and suddenly, I was stuck there with a crying baby, and I couldn't get to anything I needed to be doing.

Wait a minute. What I "needed to be doing," I thought to myself in an epiphany . . . in an embarrassing, lonely, gut-wrenching epiphany. What I "needed to be doing." Wow, when God deals with us, He can level us flat in a heartbeat. There I stood, devastated that I had spent months neglecting my wife who desperately needed me, neglecting a newborn daughter who barely knew me, and fretting over "fixing" all of these "things" that were never within my control.

I turned and went and picked Banks up and held her close, realizing she was not even comfortable in my arms. My precious child . . . a child I brought into the world and am responsible for protecting and providing for, responsible for loving and caring for . . . this precious child was not comfortable in her daddy's arms.

The snow held us there for a few days, and we soaked up every minute. I came out of the other side with a new perspective on life. God told me during that snow to "Be still," and I was reminded that He is Lord. He had to get me still so that I could regain my focus . . . so that I would see what my family needed from me . . . so that I would see what a gift this precious baby was . . . so that I could see my efforts to "fix" were doing more harm than good, and that these things are best left to Him.

I spent the next year refocused. I focused more on my wife than I did the construction. I held her hand instead of a hammer. Banks went with me to campaign functions. We played on the floor, I held her while she slept, and she even threw up on me a time or two. No matter . . . it was all about her being comfortable in my arms and knowing I was her daddy. She was a gift. Unexpected, maybe, but a precious gift nonetheless. And I had to be trapped in a snow globe to see it.

With all that said, though . . . this story isn't really about that Christmas. As you can see from the picture, it is about the awesome bond I share with this little angel and my beautiful, smiling bride.

Thank you, Lord, for shaking me up in that snow globe, and thank you, Lord, for every wonderful Christmas season since.

DUELING
RATTLESNAKES

The two rattlesnakes twisted and danced in a rhythmic interlocking motion that seemed beautiful and fiercely dangerous at the same time. Their heads intertwined as their bodies wrapped around one another in what seemed like a never-ending spiral. A blend of browns and grays and blacks swirled as each snake made every effort to pin the other's head to the ground. The thick Bahia grass and tall sage made their presence even more ominous, as each time one pinned the other, the entirety of their bodies fell out of sight into the thick, lush, green grass.

Out of sight, and standing in knee-deep grass himself, Lincoln eased closer to the *WWF* match that was taking place in front of him. Both snakes rattled, almost in unison, as if the chorus line of a marching band . . . they seemed to play with and off of each other as they rattled. Lincoln took two curious steps toward the wrestling match only to jerk backward when the twisted tornado of rattlesnakes reemerged above the tall grasses . . . their heads reach as high toward the sky as their bodies could lift . . . at times nearly meeting Lincoln's eyes.

Each of the two snakes were huge . . . I couldn't see how long they were because most of their bodies lay wound tightly together in the secrecy of the grass, but their heads! The bigger of the two . . . well, his head must have been nearly as big as my hand, with my fingers folded over at the middle knuckle. When he flickered his tongue, it ran out at least two inches, and it was as wide as the biggest blade of grass that surrounded us. The other was no slouch either . . . her head was nearly as large as the bigger snake, though she was not nearly as thick. At his fattest . . . or at least the fattest that I could see of him . . . he was wide enough that I could not wrap my fingers around his body.

"I've never seen a rattlesnake that big in all my life, girls." They both just stared, with gaped mouths and wide eyes. Bay held Cape's right hand, and I held her left. Neither of them paid the slightest attention to their next step, for they were enchanted by the weave, dance, and song of the rattlers.

I could tell that Lincoln understood the danger. He growled and almost foamed at his mouth. I considered giving him commands to get away and back up, but I knew that he was in full instinct mode . . . nothing I said to him at this point would have much effect.

He edged to and fro, a step forward and then back, all the while swiveling his head between the girls and the snakes. His eyes peered at the two snakes for a few seconds, and then he would reposition himself so as to stay directly between the snakes and Bay and Cape. With each step we all took, walking in a semi-circle around the dueling rattlesnakes, Lincoln moved, too. Ever the barrier, he was intent on making sure that those snakes never made their way towards the girls.

Of course, the snakes barely paid Lincoln any attention. Locked in a mating ritual, they could hardly be bothered by an ill-tempered coon dog. They continued their dance, undeterred . . . with the male hoping to pin the female so he could have his way.

"Come here, boy," I said in a soft tone, so as to not let him know that I sensed danger. I feared that my tone might heighten his own . . . so I tried to convey calm amongst the chaos. I ushered Bay and Cape behind me . . . with my arm sweeping them along. Like Lincoln, I positioned myself in between the girls and the snakes. "They'll have to get through you and me both," I reminded Lincoln with an assuring tone.

He bounced his head back and forth between us and the snakes . . . still tangled in their twisted tails, the snakes' heads bobbed up and down. Both girls kept their heads swiveled, and I doubt they ever even blinked as we shuffled on past. Certainly, it was a spectacle to behold, and, given our pre-disposition to panic at the sight of snakes, the spectacle was made bolder by the fear factor. As we made our way, Lincoln began a slow and gradual retreat . . . he knew enough to know that he wasn't going to take on two rattlesnakes. Shortly, he trailed right behind us as we made our way through the field and on toward the house. Occasionally he'd stop and look back over his shoulder as if to make sure we weren't being followed. "Come on, boy," I called. Fearful he might turn back, I insisted he stay at pace with us as we weaved around the clumps of sage grass in the field.

"Will one of the snakes kill the other one, Daddy?" Bay's tone was one of curiosity.

"I don't think so, baby girl. I think they are trying to become boyfriend and girlfriend."

Her facial expression shifted as she furled her eyebrows and crinkled her nose . . . "Huh?" The notion that rattlesnakes might have boyfriends confounded her. But she was only about eight years old . . . "What do you mean?" she inquired further.

"I mean . . ." I stuttered. "Sometimes boy snakes and girl snakes like to be friends and dance with each other."

Cape waddled next to Bay, seemingly oblivious to our conversation. She couldn't have been more than five years old . . . if that. Bay held her hand, as any "good" big sister would, in reassurance that the danger had passed. We weaved around a few more waist-high sage bushels, and the old one-laned dirt road that led to our house was well within sight. I relaxed slightly, for both the danger of the rattlesnakes and the curiosity of the mating habits of rattlesnakes seemed to have passed.

"Do you mean they are going to make babies?" Bay's inquisition continued.

"Babies?" Cape asked on the heels of Bay's question. "You mean snakes make babies?"

That's a see-saw behind us and to the right of the frame. It looks more like a bench in the picture, but it is a see-saw. With 6x6 posts sunk in the ground, and a 2x12 board for a seat, I think it would have withstood a tornado. The girls played on it for hours and hours, and it was a great source of warm weather fun . . . and it was the first playground "thing" I ever built for the girls. I still drive by the old farm every once in a while . . . the see-saw is gone. I wish I had pulled it up when we moved. Who knows . . . I might go sit on it every once in a while, if we still had it.

I'd almost prefer to wrestle both snakes at one time than to have this conversation go much deeper . . . "Wonder where the goats are," I diverted. Bay wasn't biting . . . and that's always been her nature. She has a bulldog mentality—once she gets hold of something, she won't let go.

"What about the babies?"

"Yes," I said with exasperation. I couldn't lie to them because I knew that would only foster confusion, but I really didn't want to explain the birds and bees with thoughts of rattlesnakes at the forefront. "But I don't know anything else about it. You'll have to ask your momma . . . she can tell you all about it. She knows way more about rattlesnakes than I do. Now come on . . . let's go feed the goats."

Still clutching hands, the girls followed me through the lush green grass of the back yard . . . the fallen dead leaves of winter had mostly given way to the new growth of spring grasses, and we made our way to the chicken coops first. The chickens all ran to greet us but were quickly disinterested when they realized we had no scratch to offer . . . but the goats, seeing the bucket in my hand . . . began to "bahhhahahahaha."

As I heaved the bucket over the top of the fence and poured the feed down into the trough, the goats swarmed all around, jockeying for the best feeding position. The girls watched and talked of who was the cutest . . . and it seemed that all concern for rattlesnakes and mating habits had disappeared.

Later than evening, Hannah and I sat on the porch enjoying a cup of coffee. The sun was setting on the horizon, and the warmth from its orange glow offset the chill of the still cool, early spring evening air. The coffee was warm to my lips as I held the cup close . . . it was quiet. Neither of us talked. The only noise came from a few songbirds making their last melodies of the day, accompanied by the crickets chattering with excitement about the night that was to come.

"So," Hannah said with a soft whisper . . . careful not to disrupt the tranquility of the moment. "Bay says you told her all of my ex-boyfriends were rattlesnakes?"

I took a sip of my coffee and recollected my comments from earlier in the day.

"Something like that," I chuckled . . . and took another sip of the brew.

HORSE MAFIA

My middle daughter, Cape, is the adventurous sort. I used to refer to her as my tomboy. However, what was once a cute nickname for an elementary-aged schoolgirl quickly disappeared as she matured. She now stands 5'10 ½", is a starting varsity volleyball and basketball player, and is no longer a tomboy. She is, however . . . still very adventurous.

Perhaps her spirit comes from being the middle child. She often complains that she is the red-headed stepchild of the family . . . a label she sometimes earns. For, she is sometimes not simply adventurous, but also rebellious.

We had to work through some of her rebellious issues as she matured through middle school and then high school. Curfews, for example, she supposed . . . were negotiable. Of course, she knew otherwise, but James Dean whispered in her ear that she was a rebel and she had a cause. But even the worthiest of causes will quickly dissipate in their urgency when confronted with the notion of restriction and a wooden spoon. Quite frankly, I am pretty thankful that she gave up her pursuit, because at 5'10 ½", I was somewhat skeptical as to whether or not I could pull off the wooden spoon bit!

But that, too, speaks to her spirit. And that is what she has . . . we can call it rebellious; we can call it adventurous; but what she truly is, is spirited. And while I want to keep her corralled, so to speak, I never want to squelch her spirit.

She's always wanted a horse. We are country folks, but we are not horse people. I was raised in Baldwin County, Alabama. What once was my dad's rolling pastureland and pecan orchard is now an expanse of mini-storage buildings. Where his cows and horses once roamed now sit endless rows of garage doors flanked by metal siding, gravel parking lots . . . and bay upon bay of frivolous excess, so valuable that it must be kept . . . but so worthless, it must be placed in storage.

Such an ironic transition . . . America's heartland lost to America's new heart.

In any event, I grew up, a child of divorce, on my dad's farm and at my mom's house. I do not mean to suggest that I am a cowboy. I am not. The fact of the matter is, I've never met a horse that did not try to kill me. Or at least, that's my impression of it. Yes, I'm well aware that the horses respond to my anxiety. Unfortunately, that well-understood fact does little to soothe my feelings about the matter. They still tried to kill me.

Perhaps, though, it does have something to do with their instinctive knowledge of my maltreatment of one of their brethren. And while I am truly innocent of any wrongdoing, my innocence doesn't change the outcome of this story.

You see, my wife, Hannah, and I were visiting a friend in Honduras. He lived on the coast, and the staple and mainstay of his diet was shellfish and seafood. Unfortunately, I am allergic to shellfish and consequently don't eat any seafood. While there, Hannah and I had not long been married, and this was a honeymoon of sorts for us . . . Hannah dined on exquisite fresh seafood caught daily from just outside our front door. I, on the other hand, ate what could pass for ham. And, on occasion . . . something that could pass for green eggs.

Ham. Ham. Ham. Ham sandwiches, fried ham, ham giblets and hash, ham and potatoes, ham and pineapple sandwiches . . . one of the better menu options because the pineapple was fresh . . . but nonetheless, eventually you just get sick of ham. And to make matters worse, at some point, your digestive tract rebels against ham. I didn't complain, though. Hannah surely enjoyed her hogfish . . . the irony was irresistible. Thick and tender white flakes of meat, garnished with fresh Honduran jungle herbs— the likes of which none of us had any idea what they were—some plantain, and a cactus leaf that had been split open and cooked . . . sort of like we might cook a twice baked potato. Her plate looked like it had fallen off the pages of *Taste of the South* magazine. Mine, on the other hand, looked like it had fallen on the floor at Holman Prison in Atmore, Alabama.

On our last night abroad, my friend grinned from ear to ear, telling me he had a surprise. His lady friend, a Honduran native, emerged from the kitchen carrying a piping hot casserole dish. She sat it on the table in front of me, and her grin was twice as big as his. Her English was broken, at best, so I didn't understand what she was trying to tell me when she said cheese and noodles. "Cheese and noodles," I thought to myself. It obviously was not macaroni and cheese, for the entire top of the casserole dish was covered with cheese. I took the spatula that she handed to me and cut out a square, as if I were cutting a brownie. Then it became more obvious . . . this was lasagna!

I'd never had lasagna cooked by a Hispanic woman. This would certainly be a welcome reprieve from ham, and it was also especially appreciated because I knew she cooked it just for me. Us Southern boys appreciate the value of a home-cooked meal. Señora stood eagerly over me, and I could sense that she was disappointed by my portion size . . . so, without giving it a second thought, I went ahead and got another piece.

"She has never made lasagna before," my friend offered. "She did this just for you."

I scooped a huge portion with my fork . . . my mouth salivated in anticipation, for I like lasagna almost as much as mashed potatoes and gravy. It is one of my favorites, right behind meatloaf. I blew a few times on the piping hot pasta and cheese and meat medley before I engulfed it. Mouth wide open, I conjured an image of Hannah's hogfish, wide mouthed, eating that baited hook . . . and I fear our reactions were probably similar, too. Though, something tells me the hogfish was more receptive to the hook in his mouth than my taste buds were to Señora's lasagna.

I almost involuntarily threw up. I cut my eyes over to Hannah, and she could tell that I was in torment. Señora beckoned some response, and my Southern hospitality dictated that I could not let her down . . . so I gulped and exclaimed, "It's delicious!" and forced myself to eat the rest of my serving.

The next morning as we packed up to leave, Señora brought me the remnants of the lasagna. Of course, I sheepishly nodded, thanked her, complimented her once again, and graciously took the dish. On the boat ride over to the airport, I finally broke down and confessed to my buddy . . . "That was the worst lasagna I've ever had in my mouth!" He started howling with laughter and agreed, adding, "Though I'll never confess that to her."

"I think what threw the taste off was the meat," he suggested.

"I agree. That had to be the worst beef I have ever put in my mouth."

My buddy bellowed again, but this time, his laugh had a sinister tone to it. "That wasn't beef. Our neighbor up the road had a horse die yesterday." My stomach almost convulsed from my throat. Needless to say, the fish ate the rest of Señora's lasagna.

But I digress. My point in telling you "The Lasagna Story" is simply to speculate that maybe the horses I've met have all tried to kill me because I unknowingly ate their distant cousin. Maybe through the underground horse whisperers' network, they all heard of my lasagna smorgasbord, and because I ate one of their brethren, they are out to get me. And, through their plan to get rid of me, they also somehow managed to convince my middle daughter that she wanted to be a horse person . . . so I have suspected, from time to time, that she is a co-conspirator. She is . . . after all . . . rebellious and spirited.

Be that as it may, her love affair with horses started many years ago. Aside from the almost predictable letter to Santa Claus every year.

"Dear Santa,

All I want for Christmas this year is a horse. I don't want dolls or toys. Just a horse, please. Amen."

Aside from that letter itself, she talked, ad nauseum, throughout the year about asking Santa for a horse.

I was never quite sure why she closed the letter with "Amen," but I figured we could

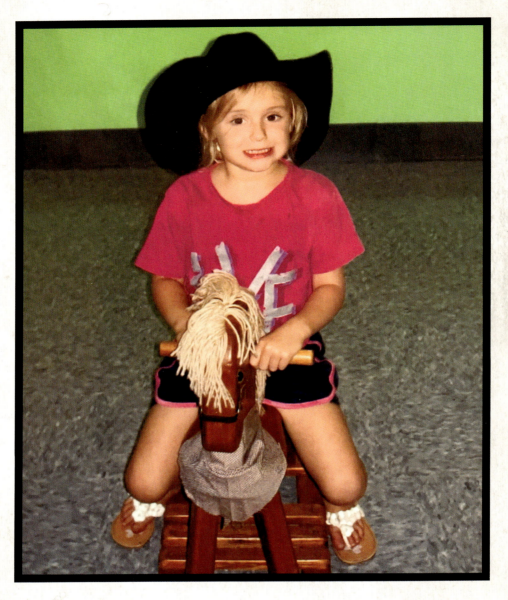

Hannah and I bought this rocking horse from a kind fellow from North Alabama. We first met him at a flea market around Birmingham and bought a black rocking horse for Bay. She named it Beauty Shop. A few years later, we found the same man at another market and bought this one, Apple Pie, for Cape. Poor Banks . . . she never got a rocking horse because, at some point, the stable was full. Hannah said, "I am not putting another horse out to pasture in the living room." I wasn't arguing . . ."Yes, ma'am," was all I needed to say. Those two rocking horses still sit in our living room to this day!

sort that out later. It didn't matter how much she prayed . . . Santa was never bringing her a horse. Every year, I wrote Santa a letter, too . . . after I talked about shooting his reindeer if he left a horse at my house, we had an understanding.

But I did search for compromise, because the truth was . . . we didn't have the means or the ability to provide her with or tend to the needs of a horse. And, as for her . . . well, she wasn't much for tending to things. She had a rabbit named Mr. Wiggles. He quit wiggling one day, and I am pretty sure he would have much preferred to have lived somewhere else. A horse simply was not an option.

So, we searched for compromise.

When she was about 8-years-old, we ventured off to the Little River Canyon for a camping trip during spring break. The park was beautiful. We spent several days hiking and fishing. We even went swimming on the warmest day . . . well, they went swimming. Because it was only in the mid-60s, I did a good job of saying, "I will in a few minutes," over and over again. And on the fourth day of the trip, we had made arrangements to go for a horseback ride in the peaks and valleys around the park.

On that fourth morning, the sky was grey and overcast. The forecast called for a mixture of sleet and rain . . . perhaps a few snow flurries, too. It was one of those cold mornings where nothing really warms you, and I hesitated to part from the warmth of the truck when we pulled up to the weathered old barn. The horses were saddled and tied up to a watering trough. Walking up, I noticed the water in the trough was frozen over. I picked up a nearby board and spent a few minutes busting the ice. Mid-bust, one of the hands came out and introduced himself.

"Colder than I realized last night, I guess," he offered, gesturing to the ice. I agreed, and we shook hands and made small talk as we walked inside the barn. "It's supposed to start raining . . . or sleeting . . . or something here in a bit, but I think we will be okay. We will stick to the wooded roads and stay out of the fields. That should keep us pretty well protected."

Cape was giddy with excitement. She was already petting the horses and talking to them. Bay, our oldest daughter was, too, but she was a little more contained. Cape was grinning from ear to ear as she rubbed a particularly spry Appaloosa on the nose.

I thought back to "Dollar Bill," a white and brown and grey Appaloosa that tried to kill me once. He was wild . . . had been in a pasture for three years, and nobody had ridden him at all. My daddy thought I was just the teenaged boy to break that horse. "Get up there on him. He won't buck but for just a minute. Then he'll settle down and remember what it's like to ride." Daddy was right. He quit bucking in less than a minute . . . as soon as there was no more weight on his back. My stepbrother ended up breaking the horse . . . for the horse broke me.

Cape looked at me with wide eyes, "This is the horse I want to ride, Daddy." As long as our host didn't mind, I didn't either. And so it was, Cape mounted up, and she rode tall in the saddle. Pretty as a peach, she was on Cloud Nine sitting atop that horse.

I was, too . . . for every daddy treasures his daughter's smile more than anything else on God's green earth.

We rode down a dirt road lane about a quarter of a mile and came to a blacktop where we were to cross over and take to the woods. Snow was already falling, and I could feel the temperature dropping. As beautiful as it was to ride horses with big, puffy snowflakes falling all around, it was also something we had not planned for, and I was a bit concerned about the girls getting too cold or too wet. The woods would be welcomed . . . but as we approached the blacktop, a distraction began to unfold.

Apparently, it was garbage day in Fort Payne, Alabama, and the big blue garbage truck came barreling down the blacktop about the time we neared. He was in a lower gear, and that big diesel engine roared as he approached. The horses all pranced with uneasiness . . . particularly that Appaloosa. Cape seemed unsure of how to handle the horse. Our host gave her instructions in a reassuring tone, and Cape did well to follow them. She and the horse both managed pretty well . . . until the driver stopped and put the truck in reverse. Apparently, he missed a can.

"Beeep—Beeep—Beeep . . ." The engine revved even higher as he backed up the blacktop toward us. Cape's Appaloosa danced in a circle two times, and everybody but Cape knew what was coming next. Bending his front knees, that horse dug in hard with his front feet, and then bolted. Cape hung on to the reins and grabbed the saddle horn all in one swift motion, and her torso and head rocked back, nearly lying flat across the back of the horse, until she could right herself. Her horse had two strides on me already . . . I dug in hard to the ribs of the big quarter horse I was riding . . . "Let's get it!" I hollered, slapping his flank as I went.

The race was on . . . my buddy, our host, was right behind me . . . and Cape's Appaloosa was headed straight to the barn. Trouble was, there were a few fences and a few closed gates along the way . . . but I never stood a chance. That Appaloosa was Speedy Gonzales to my quarter horse, Fat Albert. And would you believe that in the midst of all of that chaos, even at a full gallop, I could hear Cape laughing? . . . and it was a sweet, sweet sound . . . and her laugh made me smile.

Forty-five seconds later, and we were back at the barn. Cape was sitting proudly on her mount, grinning from ear to ear. I was already tired and winded . . . as was my steed . . . for neither of us was cut out for that kind of work. "Are you okay?" I asked, as my buddy rode up behind us. "I'm great!" Cape exclaimed, "This is the exact horse I want." And then she turned to my buddy and asked, "How much?"

Now, as a dad, I've always tried to recognize my own fears and limitations, and I have worked hard not to teach my children those same hang-ups. I'm scared of heights; I'm allergic to seafood; I don't like cats; and then there are horses . . . Cape jumped off the highest cliff at Lake Martin; her favorite pet was a stray cat that looked like a dinosaur furball; she loves crab claws; and she still asks Santa Claus for a horse every year . . . even at 16.

"As for me . . . well, I got down off that old quarter horse, and we parted ways as friends. And I've ridden horses a few more times with Cape, not for the love of the horse, but for the love of my daughter. That's why I go . . . shepherding outdoors."

As for me . . . well, I got down off that old quarter horse, and we parted ways as friends. And I've ridden horses a few more times with Cape, not for the love of the horse, but for the love of my daughter.

That's why I go . . . shepherding outdoors.

— S M I T H   &   W E S S O N —
A N D   A   R A T T L E S N A K E

Hannah and I were married September 26, 1998. Although . . . she might argue with me about that when she reads this. She will likely insist that it was the 28th. Truth be told . . . I wasn't entirely sure which was correct until I did a little research this morning. One of the beauties of modern technology is the availability of information . . . my research revealed that September 28, 1998, was, in fact, a Monday. Since I am certain that we married on a Saturday, and I am certain that we married in September of 1998, then I am left with only the confirmation that the 26th is, in fact, the correct day of the month to celebrate our anniversary.

The confusion came from our honeymoon. Walking Beale Street in Memphis, Tennessee, we encountered a caricature artist. And though there are likely more sophisticated ways to commemorate your wedding, we found some appeal in the sketch artist's work. Twenty-five minutes later and $50 lighter, we had our first family portrait . . . "Walking in Memphis." I don't remember the artist's name or even what he looked like. I can't tell you if he was Black or if he was White. I can't recall if he was pleasant or rude. I can't recall if he had a mustache or not. But I do know for certain that he dated the sketch . . . "September 28, 1998." And therein lies the problem . . .

For years, Hannah and I mistakenly celebrated our anniversary based upon the date on that sketch. One of the two of us recalled that we asked him to date the sketch to commemorate our wedding date, and thus, the sketch became the Ebenezer stone that marked our anniversary. For at least a dozen years, we celebrated our anniversary on September 28 every year. Then, for one reason or another, we needed a copy of our marriage certificate for some official documentation. Only then did we discover our error.

Now, due to the fact that we mistakenly celebrated the wrong date for so many years, there is always confusion about whether it is the 26th or the 28th. I suppose we're old enough now that remembering the correct date as opposed to the incorrect one has become very tricky . . . after all, it only happens once a year.

So, this morning, I set about to research the issue once again because today is September 21. I knew that, inside of a week, we would celebrate our anniversary . . . I just couldn't remember which day it was to be.

Now you know . . . and so do I.

On one of our very early anniversaries, Hannah gave me a particularly special gift. I know it was early because we were living in the Valley of Shiloh, north of Gantt, Alabama. And I know that's where we were living because of the story I am about to tell you. We lived in that house when Bay was born, and thus, it was a very early anniversary . . .

I was a little bit embarrassed when Hannah handed me the wrapped gift. We were still very young and very poor. We had sunk everything, down to our last spare nickel or dime, into the construction of that house. Built around the turn of the 1900s, we moved the house from downtown Gantt and restored it to its former grandeur. We did most of the work ourselves.

Point is, we were broke, and so when Hannah handed me that gift, I was embarrassed because I had not spent much at all on her anniversary present. In fact, I had picked her a bouquet of flowers, written her a letter, and planned to take her out to dinner one night later that week. This gift, though, exceeded what I expected from her. Of course, then pride and ego kicked in, and I was tempted to decline the gift without even opening it. But I ultimately reasoned in those few seconds that gifts are not from the ego, but from the heart. Had I declined it based on my ego, I simply would've hurt her heart.

As is the custom in our house, the first thing I did was shake the gift. It was very heavy, and it certainly did not rattle or jangle or jiggle. Given the shape of the box and its hard exterior, combined with the weight, I knew what it had to be. Either Hannah had picked up a box-shaped rock from the river and wrapped it as a gag gift . . . or she had given me . . .

"A pistol!" I exclaimed as I tore back the paper to reveal the "Smith & Wesson" logo on the outside of the gun case. I grinned from ear to ear, and she did, too. I could tell that seeing me smile was all the thanks she needed. She gave me the gun as a gift from her heart, and my smile and reaction told her that my heart was very appreciative.

And I was.

A stainless-steel 357 magnum with a 6-inch barrel . . . this was a *Dirty Harry* gun. I already felt taller just holding it in my hand. The metal was cold against my skin, but the black rubber grip felt comfortable and warm in my palm. I checked the revolver's cylinder just to make certain it was not loaded, and then for the next few minutes as Hannah and I talked about how much I liked it, I jockeyed it in my hands. I was growing comfortable with the gun and getting used to its balance and feel.

I knew that Hannah had given me this gun as a means to offer protection for our family. That served my ego well . . . as I believed all men should be the protectors of their families. And new to husbandry, I was still feeling my way through the various roles that I played in our marriage. This gift from her gave me the knowledge that she relied on me for protection. And, with the good Lord's help, we have made it this far . . . some 25 years in the making.

*The Andalusia Junior Women's League hosted the Red Garter
Revue for many years. Monte Morgan was kind enough to send
us this picture . . . Hannah and I were emcee-ing the event
that year . . . the year "Stars Fell on Alabama." Hannah
certainly is the consummate Southern Belle. As for me . . . well,
I am no Atticus Finch, but I do try to write like Mark Twain!*

A day or two later, I bought a holster for this 6-inch smoke wagon, and, in my immaturity and youthful exuberance, I wore that dragon slayer on my side while out and about tending to chores on the property. Why, I even wore it to town a few times . . . taking it off my hip before going into any of the stores but keeping it on my side as I traveled. I was trying to grow comfortable with the presence of the gun, and at the same time . . . it sort of felt "cool" to have the gun on my side.

Immature. Yes, I know. But I've never been one to write of myself in any light other than the truth . . . that is the point, after all, of my writing . . . to describe my folly so that others might benefit...

Three or four days later, Hannah and I loaded up in the truck to head to town. My trusty six shooter on my side, we were headed to the hardware store and the grocery store. I wasn't sure what evil villain I expected to encounter in either one of those locations, but I was "walking tall."

Our driveway rounded the back of our house, ventured out through the woods a hundred yards or so, and emptied out onto the paved road. Halfway around the semi-circle, I spied what I thought to be a heinous and vile villain of the worst sort. As I stopped the truck, Hannah saw the villain, too, and yelled, "Rattlesnake!" The nearly 4-foot-long rattlesnake was as thick as my forearm and had a head the size of a can of Copenhagen. He was one of the largest rattlesnakes I had ever seen up until that point in my life. And here he was, less than 50 yards from our back door. We didn't have children yet, but we both knew that this was not an acceptable neighbor to have this close to our house. He must be dispatched.

In her excitement, Hannah yelled, "Run over him, quick!"

If only I had been wearing a cowboy hat . . . I looked over at her, and with a slightly exaggerated country twang, I said, "Don't worry, ma'am. I'll protect you." Now, my wife sometimes has a facial expression that tells all, and this was one of those moments. She looked at me with eyes that said, "Why are you talking like that, and what are you doing?" With the confidence of a Greek god, I put the truck in park and winked at Hannah. Her mouth gaped slightly in disbelief at my actions . . . bewildered as to why I was not running over the rattlesnake.

I opened the door of the truck and stepped down out of the cab. A gentle breeze blew hot Alabama heat across my face. Leaning back in so that she could hear me, I assured her that I would dispatch this heinous invader with my new pistol. "Just run over him," she insisted. "You better not let him get away!"

"Don't worry, ma'am," I reassured her. "Everything's under control," I said as I steadied my hand above the holster, ever ready for the quickest of draws. If ever I felt like a cowboy . . . this was the moment. I knew I was headed to a shoot-out at the O.K. Corral, and this would be a story that my wife would celebrate for years to come . . . as the day that I rescued her from sure death at the fangs of what must be a gigantic rattlesnake . . .

My fingers on my right hand twitched as they hovered above my pistol. Its new luster of stainless steel glinted in the afternoon sun. Turning back briefly, I found the rattlesnake still lying motionless in his sunbath in the middle of the driveway. So big was he that he hardly felt threatened by the encroachment of the truck. I took two steps away from the open door of the truck, and I reached down with my left hand to pull a piece of sedge brush from the ground. Stripping most of its husk away, I put the last remnant in the corner of my mouth, turned back to Hannah, tipped the brim of my imaginary hat, and winked at her. She rolled her eyes and shook her head . . . giggling the entire time . . . and then yelled, "Kill that snake, and quit goofing off."

Turning back to my nemesis, our eyes met, and I saw him squint as he tracked my every move. I heard the wind blow through the trees with a slight flash of air so hot I thought the devil may have just breathed across the back of my neck. My gait was wide and waddled . . . inexplicably so . . . and I thought I heard the clank of stirrup clatter with each new step I took. My trigger finger danced with anticipation as I kept my gaze transfixed on the devilish foe.

Clank . . . clank . . . clank. I took three steps and curiously considered why I could still hear stirrups, but then regained my focus and honed back in. The snake slithered ever so slightly with nervous anticipation as I drew closer and closer. His brown and gray and white tones blended so well with the leaves that were lightly scattered on the ground. He turned his neck ever so slightly so as to position his head more properly in my direction. Now, he had a better position from which to strike. I paused my advance . . . so as to let him settle back down before I made my last few steps and settled this score.

The snake drew his body up, not entirely into a coil, but perhaps what we might consider a pre-coil. What once was an elongated stretch across the sunbaked driveway was now a retracted series of curves, spring-loaded such that any provocation would likely cause the snake to launch. These next few moments would be crucial and could very well be fatal.

I looked back to the truck, only to find Hannah now wearing a big frilly, lace hat, a corset, and some of the brightest, fire-engine red lipstick you have ever seen! "What are you lookin' at?" she inquired with an air of confusion. Her question rattled my reality, and the saloon girl attire that she wore just a moment ago gave way to the t-shirt and shorts she was actually wearing. Disgruntled, I turned back to the snake, and we locked eyes again.

I heard a faint whistle in the distance . . . a whistle identical to that which always sounded out just before Clint Eastwood drew down on a Bandido in *The Good, The Bad, and The Ugly*. The devil's breath blew across my face one last time as I heard Hannah exclaim, "You come back to me, Walt Merrell. Don't you go getting yourself killed." In true cowboy fashion, I never looked back . . . because real cowboys don't.

My feet were spread out six inches wider than my shoulders on each side. My right hand danced and hovered above the pistol which lay on my right hip. With my

Seeing this picture still breaks my heart. It so epitomizes what Lincoln was . . . a protector. Standing between us and the fellow taking the picture, Lincoln would have died before he let something happen to us, and especially to one of the girls. He was "the best dog I ever had." And I miss him so . . .

left hand, I pulled the sedge brush from the corner of my mouth and slowly lowered my hand back to my side. Then, I waited for the snake to make the first move. After what seemed like minutes . . . but was likely only an intense few seconds . . . the snake flickered his tongue.

With lightning-fast reflexes, I drew my pistol with such speed that the Duke himself would have been envious. I'm sure that, to Hannah, the pistol, moving so fast through the air as it shed the light of the sun off its mirrored surface, appeared to be nothing short of a shooting star. No doubt, with such speed and agility, she would be overcome with assurances of her own safety in this harrowing moment, and she would know that this cowboy would save her and come home.

"Kerrr-ploowwwww!" The first shot rang out in eardrum-rupturing fashion! The rattler began rattling with the intensity of a thousand locusts swarming the air and coiled up into an aggressive last-man-standing posture. Furiously, I searched his body for blood or holes . . . I had seen, after all, in the wake of the muzzle blast, a fury of sand explode up from the ground. Being the sure shot that I am, I was confident the bullet had gone completely through the soon-to-be-retired beast and pushed sand from the ground.

Yet he appeared unscathed. "Must be these new sights," I thought to myself as I used my thumbnail to pick meticulously at the gun sight on the end of the barrel. The snake's buzz permeated my every thought as his chatter overcame every other sound in the wilderness of the driveway . . . save Hannah asking me repetitively, "Did you get it? Did you get it? Did you get it?"

"You have to fire a few shots to break in the gun," I offered without answering her questions.

"Kerrr-ploowwwww!" The second shot rang out with almost a predictably identical result. The snake now raised his head six inches above his coil, and his mouth gaped wide open, bearing his fangs and daring me to take one more step toward him.

"Did you get him? Just get in the truck and run over him!" Her voice rang out with the clarity of a church bell on the Sunday morning prairie.

"Look here, little lady, you better just leave the man stuff to the cowboys," I said with my best twang. I cut my eyes at her, as if to suggest that she "ought not give me any more lip." Perhaps, it was the lack of sedge brush in the corner of my mouth . . . I considered. Grabbing another piece, I stripped it down to a suitable size and wedged it back in the corner of my mouth. "What are you doing?" Hannah asked with curious frustration in her voice.

"Kerrr-ploowwwww!" The third shot rang out with deafening results as my ears began to ring so loudly that I could barely hear the rattlesnake's song. Sand went everywhere as the rattlesnake flinched back. No doubt, unnerved by the near fatal accuracy of my shots, the rattlesnake thought better of the confrontation and opted to retreat. Despite what you see in the movies, us real cowboys know that shooting a moving target . . . especially at point blank range . . . is exceptionally difficult. As the rattlesnake zigged and zagged, I fired my last three remaining shots and, regrettably, none of them found their mark.

Moseying back to the truck, fairly well satisfied that I had held off the attack and forced the enemy to retreat back into the hills, I reached into the console so that I could reload just in case they came back at nightfall. Hannah looked at me as if I had just shot her dog.

"What in the sam-hill was that, you wanna-be Josey Wales?" With that devilish grin across her face, her sarcasm was unmistakable. I pulled the sedge brush from my mouth, locked eyes with her, and then my lowest, raspiest voice, I offered a perfectly logical explanation for the result . . .

"Well . . . I guess it really was that punk's lucky day."

Hannah scoffed and howled at my retort, and then scolded me for the next five minutes about how that rattlesnake should be wearing a Goodyear tattoo across its neck . . . and instead, it was still lurking in the shadows.

Funny thing is . . . we never saw another rattlesnake the whole time we lived there. I still maintain to this day that he was so scared of the crazy man who thought he was a cowboy that he left town and never came back.

A few weeks later, George and I went out into the field, and he taught me how to shoot a pistol. Truth was, prior to that day, I had only shot a pistol three or four times in my life. There's no shame in not knowing, and there is certainly no shame in practicing. I learned a few valuable lessons that day . . . especially about humility and practicality . . . and even though Hannah and I look back on that moment and laugh at the absurdity of it all, the lessons learned still linger with great importance today.

I still believe a man should protect his family, but he should be prepared to do so. Most foes that confront and attack the family don't rattle before they strike . . . nor do they sit idly by while men act like buffoons trying to show off in front of their wives. Instead, those foes come into the family in the most obvious of ways and attack with subtlety. The slow erosion of morality that is taught through television programming; the decline of civility that is replicated through the cowardice of keyboard warriors; internet bullies and trolls; child predators who lurk in the dark places of the Internet; and so much more . . . those are the rattlesnakes I fear most.

Maybe I should have named this story "Smith . . . and Wesson . . . and a long-haired Cowboy Named Jesus," for He is the one who will ward off any attack. Teach your children well, my friends, for the enemy lurks.

— CHRISTMAS PARADES —

I was never asked to drive the firetruck in the Centreville Christmas Parade . . . and, perhaps, for good reason.

Hannah and I had not been married but a few weeks when Mickey Barton came knocking on our door. At the time, I had never met him, but looking through the glass in the front door, I summed up pretty quickly that, "He ain't a Jehovah's Witness."

"Who is it?" Hannah yelled from the kitchen sink. She was washing dishes left over from Saturday lunch, and she was trying to decide whether to dry her hands to welcome a guest or keep washing because I was going to shoo whoever it was away.

"Don't know yet," I said, cracking open the door. Mickey was wearing a Centreville VFD shirt. I was not in the FBI, but even I recognized that as a "clue."

"Afternoon, sir," I offered as I stepped out on the porch. I had yet to determine if I was going to invite him in or not . . . after all, we'd only lived there for a few weeks, and we didn't know anyone except the Murphy family up the street and the next-door neighbors with all of the dogs. Mickey smiled and stuck out his hand to introduce himself. We shook hands and exchanged pleasantries, and he welcomed us to town.

Not big on small talk, Mickey got down to business quicker than a Pentecostal evangelist at a tent revival. "You ever been a volunteer firefighter?" he asked, leaning in with an expression of curiosity on his face.

The question caught me off guard . . . my words fell over each other as my mind searched for the very simple response. I expected an invitation to the church two blocks away or a complaint about my dog . . . I never expected to be asked if I was a firefighter. Some seconds later, I finally managed to chuckle through a "noooo." Perhaps uncertain as to why I was giggling, Mickey laughed a little, too.

"Well, have you ever thought about joining the fire department?" Mickey smiled all the way through the question. What kid has not daydreamed about being a firefighter? I couldn't possibly deny that I had thought about it . . . but thinking about it in some fantastical fashion and actually being asked to do it are two entirely different things.

"Do what?" Hannah's voice echoed down the hall and jumped over my shoulder. I could tell from the tone that she was completely opposed to the idea of me running into any burning house . . . and who could blame her? We were newlyweds, and she had not signed up to be the wife of a firefighter. I was in law school at the time, and outside of the time I spent working on a small farm in Shelby County, my life did not involve much risk. "Oh, no! You aren't playing hero and leaving me a widow!"

Hannah was still down the hall and had yet to come and properly welcome our guest, and I could see that the conversation was going to digress quickly. So, I gestured up the hall to Hannah and pulled the door shut so that "us men folk" could finish our conversation. Looking back through the glass, I saw Hannah stop her march down the hall, throw the dish towel over her shoulder, put both of her hands onto her hips, and turn and sashay back into the kitchen.

"Something tells me she doesn't like the idea very much," Mickey said with a grin on his face.

"I reckon she doesn't," I agreed. "But tell me more."

For the next twenty minutes, we sat on the front porch steps and then migrated into the living room. Of course, Hannah was hospitably Southern, as her momma raised her to be, welcoming him into our home with a wide smile and a pitcher of lemonade. The more Mickey talked about what being a volunteer firefighter meant to him, the more it meant to me, too . . . and the more Hannah softened to the idea.

"You'd be the closest firefighter to the station if you joined us," Mickey offered. "The station is right there . . ." He pointed through the window and down the street. "You're only a few houses away." I looked, knowing his effort was simply for demonstration, but I knew where the station was.

"That's one of the reasons we decided on this house," I offered. "Because it was so close to the fire station. Figured it would mean we'd be better protected."

Without missing a beat, Mickey chirped up, "You'd sure be protected if you were driving the firetruck."

Another fifteen minutes or so, and Mickey left as pleasantly as he'd come. I assured him we would pray and talk about it, and I invited Mickey to give me a call in a few days. And Hannah and I did . . . talk and pray about it, that is. Then we rented the movie, *Backdraft*, a 1991 blockbuster about life as a Chicago firefighter. The movie did it for me . . . "Those guys were heroes . . . who wouldn't want to serve like that?!?!"

The movie did it for Hannah, too . . . "Those guys were nuts! Who would want to die like that?!?!"

So, we prayed about it . . . discussed it some more . . . and ultimately, I won a two-out-of-three game of rock-paper-scissors . . . and so, the decision was made.

I called Mickey and shared my excitement. Mickey, celebrating with me, suggested we do some training as soon as possible. I was eager to oblige, so the next Saturday, I spent most of the day at the fire station, learning how to run the pumps for Centerville Engine No. 1. It was not an overly complicated process, but very important nonetheless. And, given the fact that Engine No. 1 may have actually seen service time in World War II, knowing her subtle finesses was a delicate matter indeed.

Perhaps I exaggerate . . . she was a mid '50s or early '60s one-ton Chevrolet truck with dual rear wheels and a three-speed manual transmission. Engine No. 1 had definitely been surpassed by the department's other trucks when it came to modern conveniences, but she made up for it in consistent reliability. She had a big round Cagney-and-Lacey-type rotating red light smack dab in the middle of the dulled red cab. She carried several hundred gallons of water and could pump out of multiple hoses, including a brush fire hose on the front of the truck. On the back of the truck were rails for men to hold on to and a platform where they could stand as sentries—though our department policy forbade any rear riders—and atop each sentry's post was another rotating red light.

By the end of the day, I could not only drive the truck, but I thoroughly understood the pumps and all of the mechanisms. I knew how to attach a hydrant hose to flow water into the truck from the nearest hydrant, and I knew how to pull and attach hoses—no more than two, for that was all the pump could handle—to the outflow valves for the men to fight fires with. "I think you pretty well got it," Mickey offered as he patted my sweat-soaked shoulder. "Next hot call we get, she's all yours."

Nervous, but brimming with machismo, I grinned and said, "I got it, L-T."

A few weeks went by, and all was quiet. Thankfully, Centreville was not a hot bed for arsonists, errant fireworks, or nuclear explosions. But unfortunately, with each quiet day that passed, I feared my muscle memory was fading, too . . . "What if I forget something?" Days passed still, and rust began to set in, so I went down to the Station a few afternoons and went back over all of the truck's working . . . but never cranked it or pulled it out of the bay.

The following week, I was in the middle of my Saturday projects when my pager sounded three tones. "That's us!" Adrenaline raced through my veins, and instantly, sweat beaded on my forehead. I consciously talked to myself about staying relaxed as I grabbed my gear, gave Hannah a hug and kiss, and raced for my truck. In hindsight, I recognize how frightful that moment was for Hannah, but in the heat of the moment . . . I neglected her. I do regret that.

Of course, I was the first one to the station! I threw my gear bag down on the concrete floor and unzipped it. Inside sat my turn-out trousers, already pre-positioned over my boots. About two seconds later, I was fully suited up. I unplugged the "Ole Girl" from the battery charger, threw open the big rolling bay door and, in one swift swoop, pulled the cab door open and launched into the seat! A second later, her big, noisy engine roared to life . . . like the fat lady at the end of a long buffet line, her growl echoed out of the block building and into the street. My mind was racing through the checklist . . . two switches flipped to the "on" position, and the sirens started screaming, too. I revved the engine . . . "Help is on the way!" I screamed out loud as I let off the clutch, and the truck pierced the veil of the bay door and blared out into the street. Goose bumps covered my entire body . . . I felt alive!

Alive, that is, until I heard metal crashing against metal and felt the truck struggle and grunt . . . "What the—" I searched both the right and left fenders. "I didn't run over anything." Then the sound of more crashing filled the confines of the cab. In my side view mirror, I saw the subject of my calamity . . . the bay door dangled from the tall red light that was mounted atop the sentry post at the rear of the engine. I immediately realized that, in my haste, I failed to raise the door all the way, and now I was dragging it down Highway 82. But only for a moment . . . for about 50 feet down the highway, the door dislodged and came to rest smack dab in the middle of the road.

"Centerville Engine 1 to Dispatch."

"Dispatch, go ahead."

"Uhhh, yes ma'am. Would you ask a city police officer to report to the fire station? There is debris blocking the road."

"Chief to Centerville Engine 1."

"Go ahead, Chief."

"Engine 1, did you say, 'debris?'"

Like I said, they never asked me to drive the fire truck in the Christmas Parade . . . and I guess they never will.

THE LOOK OF LOVE

Banks came home last night from her first day of school after our spring break. Banks is 12 . . . she has a special friend at school. He is smitten with her, and her with him. It's cute and age-appropriate, and he makes her smile. And that . . . makes me smile.

She was holding a Disney bag in her hand when she came in the door. "What's that?" I asked. Her sheepish grin betrayed her . . . as I immediately knew it was something from him.

She held up the bag, and with a devilish grin, said, "You've never gotten me anything from Disney World."

And she was right . . . I had not.

"And I probably won't either, baby girl. Disney World is good for some folks, but it's not my speed." She giggled. "You see, baby girl, Disney World is just one long line that goes on for days. And eventually, you get tired enough that you just leave and go home. No one ever actually gets to ride anything." She rolled her eyes at the ridiculousness of my assertions.

We have a local charity in town that hosts a great event called "Cookies with Characters." High school kids dress up as Disney princesses and Mickey Mouse and every other character imaginable, and for ten bucks or so, younger children can have their picture taken with every one of these nearly-the-real-thing characters. The younger kids love it, and it raises a lot of money for a worthy cause. It is truly a win-win.

Bay and Cape grew up, for the most part, without television. They didn't have access to the internet, either. So, neither of them ever had much of an interest in anything Disney. But, in seventh or eighth grade, Bay made the math team at school, and most of the practice opportunities were web-based. So, Hannah and I reluctantly agreed to install internet service at the house. Well, you know how that goes . . . by the time the internet guy was done explaining the sales pitch, we had signed up for a new phone, cable television, and internet service. I think we even agreed to have the company's name tattooed on one of the girls . . . guess we'll have to play rock-paper-scissors to sort that one out.

And so, it was . . . Banks was exposed to The Disney Channel. And thus began her passionate pursuit of all things Disney. "Daddy, when are we going to go to Disney World?" My response was never hopeful.

"That would be never," I'd say.

"Why not, Daddy?"

Again, not one to build false hope, I was brutally honest. "Because I'm pretty sure hell is just a place where you stand in line all day long shoulder to shoulder with people who are allergic to deodorant. And the sign on the wall says Disney World."

Time and again, we had similar conversations . . . and each time, Banks' disappointment hurt me, too.

Fast forward a few months . . . Hannah and I were on our way out of town, the destination of which I don't rightly remember. I do recall that the girls were staying with George and Brenda, and as we drove out of town on Highway 29, I couldn't help but notice the bright pastel colored sign that alerted all passing motorists that today was "Cookies with Characters." It was being held at the county fairgrounds inside the Kiwanis Building.

So, as if ordained by the good Lord himself, I called Brenda.

"Hey, today is 'Cookies with Characters.' Can you take Banks?"

Ever the faithful grandmother, she responded without hesitation. "Sure, I will, honey. That will be fun!"

"Okay, but there's just this one thing: Don't tell her what it is called or where she is at?" Brenda took a long pause and said, "Okay . . . I guess. I'll try."

And so it was that Banks went to "Cookies with Characters" and had a phenomenal time. She took pictures with every Disney princess and droopy-eared dog there, and she especially loved the two mice . . . Minnie and What's-His-Face. A couple of days later, Hannah and I came home to a serenade of stories about all that she had seen and experienced. About how beautiful Pocahontas was and how she loved Cinderella's dress . . . on and on she went about the splendor of it all! When she was nearly done, I interjected, "That was so nice of Big Momma to take you to Disney World. She sure is sweet."

Banks' expression changed, and she paused her recollections . . . "Disney World?"

"Yes, baby. You saw all the princesses and Mickey and Minnie and all those other characters, too. Big Momma took you to Disney World!" Yes . . . I was lying to my kid . . . but I was pretty sure there was an asterisk behind "Thou shalt not bear false witness." You know . . . that little thing on the credit card application right next to the too-good-to-be-true offer . . . the * (asterisk). That means verse 16 really looks something like this:

Exodus Chapter 20, verse 16:
*"Thou shalt not bear false witness against your neighbor."**

And then Moses turned the stone tablet over:
Unless it is to avoid going to Disney World.

That's how an asterisk works. It's the exception to the rule . . . or the ultra-fine print . . . and I was firmly convinced that Disney World was the exception to Exodus 20:16.

None the wiser, Banks grinned from ear to ear . . . and I almost saw her melt with appreciation. She went straight to the phone and called Brenda . . .

And that was the last time, for a good while, that I heard Banks talk of wanting to go to Disney World. Interest was spurred again a year or so later when one of her little friends went to Disney World and came back with pictures. I'm pretty sure the little friend was demon possessed . . . an angel of darkness.

"Hey, you tricked me!" Banks demanded.

She was right. I did. The next time I saw that little girl and her parents, I threw holy water on her. Sure enough . . . she started to cry. I elbowed Hannah . . . "See, I told you so . . ." but all I got in response was an eyeroll and a huff. Then she went over and started trying to dry the little girl off. I told Hannah there wasn't any need . . . the water would evaporate soon enough under all that demon heat.

And then Banks started talking about Disney World again.

And now, all because of this beau of hers . . . and his gift bag from Walt Lucifer's Castle . . . she is talking about Disney World even more.

Before I let her open the bag, I laid hands on it and tried to expel any Disney demons. Banks knew I was just kidding, and so she played along . . . the demons fought hard against the power of the Holy Spirit, but they soon yielded . . . in the chaos of the fight, the bag landed in the trash can. "Daddyyyyy," Banks said as she laughed. I had just replaced the garbage bag in the trash can, so she knew it was clean. She pulled the Disney bag from the trash and began to open it . . . both of us laughing and smiling as she did.

Slowly, as if opening the first present of Christmas morning, she unlayered the contents . . . carefully wrapped in tissue paper of black and red. "Guess who it is," she said, as she held up a figurine on Minnie Mouse standing next to the Eiffel Tower. Banks' face glowed almost as much as Minnie's, and then she asked if I knew what the Eiffel Tower was the universal symbol for. Of course, I had no idea, but before she gave me a moment to consider the matter, she blurted out with exaggeration . . . "Looooove!" as she giggled that her beau had given her such a gift.

I studied it for a moment and gave her an appropriately complimentary remark. Then I informed her that I, too, had a gift for her. Her eyes bounced with anticipation . . . "What is it?" I retreated to the study and came back, carrying a brand-new tackle bag full of all the stuff she needs for bream fishing. She opened it up and looked somewhat confused. "Is this fishing stuff?"

"It sure is, baby girl, and it's all for you." I went on to remind her that we had to search a little for some good hooks last week. "And I only found a few. And I only had two corks left. We get a big bream that breaks that ole line, and we are in a fix." She nodded her head in agreement. "And so, I decided to buy you your very own bream box, fully equipped." She smiled and nodded again. Then she glanced over at the Eiffel Tower.

"And you know what that bream box is?" I asked her.

"What?" she responded, with a puzzled look on her face.

"It's a father's universal symbol of love for his daughter . . . and it is far greater than any Eiffel Tower." She rolled her eyes in an I'm-embarrassed way, and then grinned as she said, "Thank you, Daddy," and gave me a hug.

She may yet go to Disney World one day. But I know there will be a whole lot more fishing trips between now and then.

I can't stand the thought of standing in long lines with thousands of people to ride a whirly-gig for 38 seconds and end up throwing up when I am done. So, I don't much care for the mouse or his house. What I do long for is the peaceful quiet that comes from fishing or hunting or the great outdoors. She may want to go to the Mouse House . . . but she will never forget our time in the woods or on the water.

FERRIS WHEELS

"Well, there's a full moon in the western sky,
And there's magic in the air.
Ain't nothin' I know of, can make you fall in love,
Like a night at the county fair."
—CHRIS LEDOUX, COUNTY FAIR

It was late October in Andalusia . . . fall hinted at the horizon, though she was late that year. The sun set in the Western sky, and shades of orange and red blanketed the midway's otherwise luminescent display. The too-warm afternoon air would slowly give way to the cool of the night . . . and the county fair would slowly come to life.

Hand in hand, Hannah and I walked across the parking lot. Banks and two of her girlfriends pranced with excitement about twenty feet in front of us. They were at that age where they still hovered close for security but stayed far enough away than none of their classmates might mistake them as being dependent on us. "Girls, y'all stay together. Do not separate for any reason."

Banks looked over her shoulder and smiled, "Yes, ma'am." Zoe, one of the other girls, agreed. They hastened their pace as they drifted off into the line to get into the gate.

"Do you think next year she will be old enough to come by herself?" Hannah's question struck me . . . I hadn't considered going to the county fair by yourself as being some sort of rite of passage, but I suppose it is.

"I don't know," I muttered with hesitation. "There are still lots of folks here. All kinds of folks." She didn't respond. She knows I am jaded in some ways because of my profession.

"I know that guy right there," I added. "I put him in prison. His daddy, too." She glanced toward the fellow and surveyed him. He looked my way and nodded. I returned the gesture and cracked the corners of my mouth to show a glimpse of a smile. His face softened just a bit as his youngest son pulled at his hand. He turned his attention toward the half-pint, and we kept walking. "Meth. I sent him to rehab three or four times. He couldn't put it down, and then he started stealing."

Hannah nodded her head, "His son was cute." I nodded my head in agreement, and we continued on.

The sun reached back over the horizon. White, puffy, cotton candy clouds blanketed the skyline. They glowed pink and orange, white and red. The Ferris wheel silhouette rolled through the middle of the picturesque landscape as riders stared off into the irresistible beauty of the sun's passing. "Let's go ride the Ferris wheel," Hannah offered. I didn't know if she was serious or joking.

Turning to study her face for more information, I asked, "Do you really want to?" I could see it in her eyes . . . she was serious. They had that longing look in them, as they danced back and forth from my eyes to the Ferris wheel.

"It's the sunset," she reminded me. "What's more romantic than watching the sunset from the Ferris wheel?"

"I don't know," I responded, drawing out the longest "ooooo" from my last word, so as to demonstrate my hesitation. I looked to the top of the Ferris wheel. "What is that? About 400 feet high?"

She laughed and slapped me on the arm. "Come on, it's not that high! You've done it before." I laughed, and she smiled . . . but I knew she still wanted me to get on that wheel of tension.

I had been on the Ferris wheel with her before. Bay was about five, if that gives you some perspective. As I recall, it was the first time we had been to the county fair when Bay would have actually been old enough to enjoy the rides. Before that, she would have been too small for most of the rides . . . so five years old seems about right. We started just as we always did. "Let's go ride the merry-go-round," I said to Bay . . . the lights of the midway twinkled in her eyes. She clutched my hand tight as we skipped over across to the merry-go-round. I always let her pick "her horse," and then I grabbed one nearby. She mounted a fine black steed, ordained with golden reigns and a mother of pearl saddle. "Black Beauty," she announced . . . we had not long before watched the movie by the same name. She grinned from ear to ear as the horse leapt up and down and the carousel went round and round. She held fast to the pole with two hands at first, but by the time the ride came to an end, she leaned back and let her right hand flow behind her, as if she was an accomplished saddle bronc rider.

"Let's go get on the Ferris wheel, Daddy!" Her eyes were as wide as the Mississippi River as she surveyed the wheel in the sky and all of its gloriously bright lights. "Uh . . . okay," I said.

"It all happened so fast," I thought to myself as we exited the merry-go-round. She asked, and I couldn't say no. As Hannah greeted us at the exit, I struggled to find a solution to my current predicament. I knew Hannah would gladly ride the Ferris wheel. She wasn't scared of heights. I am. "I will just use the 'I have to go to the bathroom' excuse," I reasoned to myself. But before I could intervene and rescue myself, Bay made her report to Hannah . . . "Daddy said we were going to ride the Ferris wheel next!"

Hannah's countenance changed entirely. "He did?" she asked with bewilderment.

"He sure did, Momma! Come on! You can go with us!" Bay grabbed her hand and started pulling . . . and I knew I was committed. Hannah and I exchanged a glance or two as we made our way to the Towering Inferno . . . but there was nothing more to be said.

A minute later, we were standing in line, coincidentally, with one of Bay's friends and her mom. "We can all ride together," Bay exclaimed.

"Oh yes . . . let's add even more weight to the aging bolts holding this death contraption together," I thought to myself . . . forcing a smile to my face. Of course, though, everyone else was quick to agree. I could feel sweat beads forming on my forehead. My palms were getting balmy, too, and I started feeling clammy all over. "What in the hell have you gotten yourself into?" I thought to myself . . . because an eternity in hell, for me, would surely be a perpetual ride on a Ferris wheel . . . or standing at the edge of a balcony on a high-rise building . . . or being on a blimp or a hot air balloon. "What is wrong with these people?" I thought to myself. My heart raced, and my blood pressure was, no doubt, at stroke level.

Bay tugged at my hand as the line moved forward. Her smile was a light that could pierce any darkness. "How can you resist that smile, Daddy?" Hannah knew I was full of dread, and she intuitively tried to remind me why I was willing to overcome my fear . . . and she was right . . . I did want to ride the Ferris wheel with my daughter. Doesn't every dad?

The rickety cart creaked and irked as we boarded. The metal floor echoed and moaned as the gate swung shut and the latch clanked into place. The cold metal felt lifeless on my derriere. Bay studied the inside of the cart with curious enthusiasm. She positioned herself so she would get what she thought was the best view . . . "Daddy, will I be able to see town if I sit on this side?"

I had to orient myself before I could answer . . . and telling her, "Yes, I think so," only brought home even more the reality . . . "Oh, God. We are going to be so high that she can see downtown."

My conscience scolded myself immediately for being so flippant in calling the Lord's name . . . but in doing so, I felt compelled to pray. "Dear God, please give me strength to ride this ride for my daughter. Amen." I'm not sure God cares about Ferris wheels, but I know He cares about relationships.

The cart lurched forward as we rolled to the next station so other folks could board. The surge and then sudden stop left us swinging back and forth. Even though we were perched only a few feet off the ground, I found myself slightly nauseated . . . and highly anxious. I moved to the edge of the cold steel seat toward the center of the cart. At the time, I wasn't sure why . . . I was just acting on instincts . . . but looking back, I now realize that if I was in the center of the cart, I was less apt to fall over the railing.

We lurched again as the next cart loaded. With each lurch, Bay's smile and anticipation grew brighter and brighter . . . and my fear grew stronger and stronger. Bay's wide eyes surveyed the landscape, and she leaned her head over the rails and stood up in the cart as sure footed as if she was on solid ground . . . I was getting dizzy. I scooted closer to the middle. Two or three more carts loaded, and finally, we were underway.

Optimistic that the constant motion would be better than the lurches, I tried to relax. I focused on Bay's smiling face. Hannah held my hand. She was certainly not scared, and she quite enjoyed the ride. I kept my eyes trained to the horizon, certain that such would avoid the panic that might ensue if I ever looked down. After a few seconds, I opted to simply close my eyes. Perhaps that would be the best way to overcome this fear.

The wheel of death cracked and moaned beneath us. With my visual senses shut down, the sound of the mechanism of the wheel of misfortune was inescapable . . . each pop and tong must surely be any number of aged and decrepit bolts clearly snapping in two . . . the steel beams strained and groaned under the weight of all of these folks. I cracked my eye and realized the folks in the cart above us must have a total weigh of a thousand pounds. "What are there? Like, ten people in the cart? How many kids do they have?" I shut my eyes again. I clutched the center pole of the cart with both hands. I imagined the strain of the bolts holding that very cart over our head . . . and the chaos that would befall us when their cart fell into ours, and we all came crashing down. My imagination was overcoming the reality of the situation.

"Daddy! Look! Look! Look!" I opened my eyes to find Bay nearly hanging out of the cart. I mean, her elbow was almost over the rail as she pointed to the horizon.

"Hannah is such a bad mother," I quipped to myself, provoked by thoughts of Bay having a good eight inches of her arm over the edge of the cart. I looked up to see the buildings of downtown Andalusia . . . and though, but for a moment, I was captivated by the beauty of it all, I soon lost sight of the tranquility. "Dear Jesus," I thought to myself. "We are so high up in the air." I averted my eyes back to Bay, trying to find her smile. Bay's mouth was moving, but at this point, I lost all awareness of what she was saying. I slid off the seat and sat on the bottom of the cart.

Hannah laughed as I retreated . . . "You think you are safer down there?" she chided harmlessly. I crisscrossed my legs around the center pole. "If this sucker falls," I said through the grit of my teeth. "They will have to pry me from this pole." Hannah and the girls all laughed . . . with me . . . I think? By now, though, the family in the cart above us had taken note of my perch, and the dad—whom I knew, sort of—decided to have some fun at my expense. He howled well-intended, manly chides from on high as he challenged my manhood, my dignity, and most every other thing a man holds dear. It was all meant in good humor, but becoming the spotlight of the showcase was not what I called good fun. I wanted to ride the ride . . . not be the show. But tomfoolery is contagious . . . others joined in, and soon, everyone was laughing, including me, at my predicament. Nevertheless, I was still scared to death.

Staring straight down, I felt the cold sensation of the lifeless pressed steel coming through my pants and permeating my rear end. Surveying the floor—so as to avoid looking out—I saw gum, dirt, wood chips, dip spit, a cigarette butt, and what I thought might be vomit, or breast milk, I wasn't sure. "Ferris Wheel Gumbo" was all I could think, and I was sitting in it. "Could this get anymore humiliating?"

"Well, we walked through the midway,
the lights and the laughter,
She puts her little hand in mine
Well, she don't act like she knows what I'm after,
But t'night I'm gonna make her mine.

You know the tunnel of love, well it ain't my style,
So I take her on the Ferris wheel,
Way up in the sky, with the stars in her eyes,
I'm gonna tell her just how I feel."

—CHRIS LEDOUX, COUNTY FAIR

We passed the apex of the ride for about the third time, and my anxiety was at a fever pitch. As we neared the bottom of the ride, I hollered out to the operator. Making eye contact, he, too, was laughing at me. At this point, I had already lost whatever dignity I had . . . and I didn't care. "I'll ghls. Akkufbkbd. Kahsbdiau. Skdjdakdhf. Klkjs uwyee. Touty this ride!" The roar of the music through the speakers and the whine of the motors drowned out my words.

"Huh?" his face and eyes said.

I grabbed tighter to the center pole and leaned my face to the opening in the side of the cart. "I said . . . I'll give you twenty bucks if you stop this danged wheel of death and let me off!" And with that, the previously half-asleep operator sprang to action like Chuck Norris . . . and the whole ride came to an immediate, screeching halt.

Twenty bucks poorer . . . soiled butt . . . and without much dignity left, I stood firmly on solid ground and watched Hannah and Bay and their friends ride round and round to their hearts' content.

"I love you, baby, but I ain't getting on the Ferris wheel. We can see the sunset just fine from here."

Chapter
TWO

THE FORK IN THE RIVER

── M Y G R A N D F A T H E R ──
D I E D O F A H E A R T A T T A C K

My grandfather died of a heart attack, though he suffered from Alzheimer's for years before he finally, and mercifully, died. I was elementary-aged.

I only saw him once after he was placed in the nursing home. I remember him leaning over the side of the bed, holding his hand near the floor and rubbing his fingers together as he called, "Here, kitty, kitty, kitty." That dreadful memory of my grandfather in some delusion no doubt replaced some fonder, more productive memory of him previously stored in the recesses of my brain. I hate that memory. I am thankful my parents never took me back to the nursing home.

My other memories of him are much more precious. I cherish them . . . especially one in particular . . . one that has remained with me ever so vividly for all these years. It was a bright, sunny, summer day. He had a lake house just outside of Fayetteville, Alabama, on Lay Lake. It was a smaller, one-story house with a big sunroom at one end. It had a huge fireplace in the center of the living room, and he had an old, vinyl recliner to one side. I remember sitting in that chair with him in front of the fire during winter visits.

He built a pier out to the lake. To the shoreside of the pier was an old boat house . . . the rusted tin siding shaded the interior such that it was a spooky place for a wee lad such as myself. Mayflies were abundant on Lay Lake. When they hatched, they covered the interior walls. I wasn't so much bothered by them as I was the spiders that seemed to web in overdrive when mayfly season came around.

In that boat house, he kept an old jon boat with a small outboard motor. I don't remember the particulars about the boat or motor . . . I just know he'd be embarrassed that I have the boat I have . . . not because his wasn't good enough, but because mine is excessive. He'd be right. I'm not proud of it . . . I could learn a lesson about necessity from him, too.

I am proud, though, that I still have his tackle box, most of his lures, and several of his old Mitchell reels.

He took me out fishing that summer day. It is the only time I can ever remember him taking me fishing by myself. We were not too far from his house when I hooked a fish . . . but this was not the customary bream that I was used to catching. This fish stripped drag and pulled hard, making the gears on the reel whine as they gave way. This was a surely a bass!

For those unfamiliar, most kids learn to fish by catching bream. You graduate to "big boy" fishing when you catch a bass. It is a milestone, of sorts, for aspiring fishermen. This fish, surely a monster, ran for what must have been a mile or two . . . Paw Paw impatiently gave me instructions, which I failed miserably at following . . . and the fish swam up into the rip rap—a form of rock boulders—on the bank. The line snapped and went slack . . . as did my excitement and my confidence. Dejected, I remember thinking to myself, I wasn't a big boy . . . just a little one.

I don't remember much that happened after that. I spent the rest of the trip lamenting what could have been. I didn't catch another fish . . . and at some point, Paw Paw gave up on the idea that I might move on. We headed home.

As we walked up to the house from the boat house, I was still complaining about the fish that got away. Paw Paw was walking in front of me. I think he had simply had enough . . . and knew I was missing the moment. You see, at this point, he knew he had Alzheimer's. I did not. He knew the day would soon come when he would not be able to take me fishing . . . he knew this may be the last. He knew he wanted me to remember the good . . . not the bad.

He turned and faced me, leaned down, and looked dead into my face. He said, "Son, quit worrying about that one fish. Life is like running through a forest. If you spend all your time looking back over your shoulder, eventually you will run smack into a tree." Then he turned and walked off.

I had no idea what he was talking about. "Didn't he realize how big that fish probably was?" I thought to myself as we made our way up the path to the house.

That was the last time my Paw Paw ever took me fishing.

Twenty-five years later, I found myself on the losing end of a trial. Frustrated at the loss and convinced I should have won . . . I think I must have vented ad nauseam to Hannah. Frustrated, she turned, leaned to me, and looked straight into my face . . . and the memory of Paw Paw's advice flooded back to me. I had remembered the fish and the complaints, but not until that moment did I remember his sage words. Hannah's inadvertent reenactment triggered the memory . . . and his wisdom has stuck with me ever since.

I've made plenty of mistakes in my life. I've had my fair share of failures and certainly things I should regret. Like Jimmy Buffet, I've had moments in my life where I could relate: "I have been drunk now for over two weeks. I passed out and I rallied and I sprung a few leaks, but I've got to stop wishing, got to go fishing . . . down to rock bottom again. Just a few friends."

I don't remember the good of that last fishing trip with Paw Paw because I was so intently focused on the bad . . . on that stupid fish. I remember more about that fish on that day than I do my grandfather. But thankfully, his words lingered in the recesses . . . and they rang loudly, making their mark, when the time was right.

I don't dwell much anymore on the mistakes of my past. They helped mold me and shape me into who I am today. Likewise, I don't dwell much on others' mistakes either . . .

I sure won't dwell much on the mistakes of the future. I learn from them and move on . . . for to do otherwise would be a dishonor to that moment . . . when my Paw Paw left me the most precious thing he had left to give...

I love you, Paw Paw.

─ T H E B E S T I E V E R H A D ─

Part One

Hannah grilled hamburgers tonight. Leaner, farm-raised, Alabama ground beef that our friends the Davises raised. At least once a year, we buy a cow from them. Our thought is that perhaps, one day, we will turn some of our land into pasture and raised cattle ourselves, but for now . . . a Davis cow is more than satisfactory.

As always, the hamburgers were exceptionally good . . . but they were not, in fact, "the best" hamburgers I have ever had.

You see, whenever Cecil Hicks . . . that would be Hannah's grandfather and Brenda's father . . . enjoyed a particular item of the meal, he would lean back in his chair and yell—yes, yell— "Flo, those were the best peas I have ever had!" He would yell because he was deaf as a doorknob and could not even hear thunder. Like so many old men who've lost their hearing, he believed that if he could not hear himself, then others must not be able to hear him either. His deep, sometimes raspy, bass voice would rattle the dishes across the dining room table and find itself resting in the company of Flo's smile. She loved the praise, and as he did not offer it after every meal, she relished when he did. She'd beam like a bride who just turned the corner to begin the wedding procession. Proud and not too shy to stand in the spotlight, Flo would sheepishly brush off the compliment, but then dive headfirst into an explanation of why these peas were exceptionally good.

I always enjoyed listening to Cecil talk of Flo's cooking, because I knew how much it meant to her. As the woman of the house, Flo took great pride in her kitchen. By complimenting her as the best at anything, Cecil was making sure his wife understood just how much he appreciated her contribution and how much he loved her. She reciprocated by always making sure he had a hot meal when he came in from working nights at the Hunt Oil Refinery in Northport, and by making sure their house always felt like a home to Cecil and their children.

So now, when Hannah cooks something that is exceptionally good, I continue the tradition by telling her, "That was the best creamed corn I have ever had!" And right then and there, in that moment, they were the best I had ever had. Like Cecil, I don't give the compliment without justification, and, like Flo, Hannah is sheepish about the praise. She oftentimes rolls her eyes slightly as she turns her head and speaks some humble acknowledgment that mostly has to do with her being glad that I enjoyed the meal. Usually, she then retreats to the kitchen to begin cleaning up . . . not one to bathe in glorification, Hannah is quick to retreat when the spotlight turns to her.

She also knows and understands the significance of the compliment, as we laugh and joke on occasion about Cecil's antics at the dinner table, including his sometimes "best of" award. And Hannah appreciates the family significance in the fact that I carry on the tradition . . . though I don't rattle the dishes and yell it at her . . . but, perhaps one day, I might!

The hamburgers were perfectly charred . . . having sat just the right length of time on each side, so as to reveal the darkened pattern of the fiery hot grates of the grill. And though it was leaner meat, the butcher had used pork fat to give a little extra flavor and keep the meat juicy. The patties glistened under the sheen of pork and beef fat that had essentially melted all throughout . . . and these were not dinky meatball patties like Uncle Pickens would have patted out in fear of another Depression. No, these were large, hand-patted patties, full-meal-all-to-themselves, patties.

If there's one thing I like about a hamburger, it's the fact that it fills the entire bun. Hannah, not quick to overlook details, always pats out extra-large patties . . . just to suit my liking. And her attention never goes unnoticed. Picking up one of the largest patties, the juice coated my fingers as I laid it on the Hawaiian bun. I couldn't resist but to lick my fingers afterwards . . . and the savory flavor of smoke and charr and a hint of pork all made my mouth water even more. I reached for a piece of provolone cheese, but I was interrupted mid-swoop by the throat clearing, "Uuhhn-uhh" of Hannah's disapproval of 1) picking up food with my hands; and 2) picking up food with my hands after I licked my fingers. Seems to me that if we French kiss from time to time, a little finger licking wouldn't hurt . . . but I opted to grab a fork and comply with her wishes.

Sometimes, discretion truly is the better part of being a husband, and I oftentimes exercise my discretion in favor of my wife's preferences.

I put two pieces of provolone cheese across the top of the still-steamy-hot patty and could immediately see it melt into a drape across the top. Next, I smothered the cheese-topped castle with barbecue sauce and fresh cut pineapples. Only then was the masterpiece complete . . . and I finished it off by smashing the top of the bun down, compressing it all into one delicacy.

Joining Cape, Banks, and Hannah at the dinner table . . . I always let the ladies serve themselves first . . . we held hands, as is the custom in our family, and thanked the Lord for the blessings He had provided to us, including this meal. At the end of every blessing of the food at our table, I kiss Hannah's hand. Holding her four fingers in my hand, bending them so as to roll the top of her hand toward me, I gently kiss across the top, much like you'd expect to kiss the hand of royalty. It's just my way of saying

*I suppose many a young man will spend his older-man-days
regretting some of the things he ought to have done differently
as a younger man . . . and trying not to make the same
mistakes his father made during his older days . . . when
the young man was still young.*

I love you, Deddy.

"Thank you" and letting her know how much I appreciate her. As the girls grew to understand the significance of the gesture, I began to do the same with them . . . though, Cape has reached that time in the teenaged wasteland where she detests the idea of her father kissing her hand. So, I rarely manage to give her the same . . . but we do occasionally have an entertaining wrestling match at the dinner table. She's big enough now that she usually wins, and Hannah gets irritated with our lack of table manners . . . so I am oftentimes left without the benefit of the hand kiss to my daughter and with a scolding from my wife!

The hamburger was delicious . . . perhaps, one of the best I had ever had. Each bite was a flavor rush of sweet pineapple and tangy barbeque sauce, which perfectly complemented the juicy flavor of the meat. Honestly, the taste of the cheese was lost in all of that, but that was okay. This was enough . . . and it was delicious. This was one of those meals where I was so very tempted to make a second hamburger. So good were they, that I was willing to make myself miserable for the rest of the evening just so I could experience the pleasure of eating the second burger. Alas, though, thoughts of hiking the Appalachian Trail the following spring reminded me that I needed to lose some weight, not gain more! One was enough. Besides, I was actually full. Hannah had baked sweet potatoes to go with the burgers, so we had plenty of food on the table. The sweet potatoes were a perfect complement, too . . . all in all, it was a fine meal.

But I could not bring myself to tell Hannah that it was the best hamburger I had ever had . . . although, I was tempted. Why not? My daddy made "the best hamburger I ever had" . . . and, though it probably wasn't anywhere near as savory as any burger Hannah has ever made, it was still the best.

Part Two

My dad could not sing, that I know of, and I doubt he could dance either. Though I suspect that he fancied himself a regular Elvis Presley from time to time, he had little in common with the King . . . except that, like Elvis, Daddy would eat the same thing for meals over and over again—because he liked it. Daddy's favorite meal . . . a hamburger, instant mashed potatoes, and Le Sueur English peas . . . or at least that was his favorite during a certain time of his life, and mine.

My parents divorced when I was nine. It was the summer after my third-grade year, if memory serves. They took me on a great outdoor adventure to Fort Morgan, a Civil War era fort that guards the entrance to Mobile Bay. As beautiful as it is massive in spectacle, the Fort has been a source of awe and entertainment for many a kid for generations. Tired and weary from the long day, they sat me on the couch in the living room and broke the news . . .

Daddy moved into an apartment in Mobile, and for the next two years or so, he and I built a relationship as strong as any I had ever had. In hindsight, it seems that, perhaps, I was all he had. His sister was five hours away. His parents had both passed. Sure, he had friends and drinking buddies, but, through the eyes of my more-matured self, I suspect that those were very shallow relationships. I think that during that time in his life, I may have been the only love Daddy felt on a consistent basis.

Likewise, I needed him, too. Every child needs their daddy. And, like Forrest Gump, "That's all I have to say about that."

And as was so often the custom in divorces of the '80s and '90s, I spent every other weekend with him. It was during those years that I would have spent every day with him had I been able to . . . because every child needs a daddy. I'm tempted to divert off into a tangent about the absurdity of every-other-weekend-visitation and how such arrangements are only designed to kill a relationship between a parent and a child . . . but that is not the point of this story. I'll save that one for another day.

I will mention, though, that the enemy comes to "steal, kill, and destroy." John 10:10. The enemy will not walk through the front door of your house with a pitchfork in his hand, fire breathing from his ears, and declare, "I am here!" No . . . he is far more subtle, and he will make every effort to steal the joy from your heart, kill your spirit, and destroy your testimony without you ever even knowing it. And what better way to wage all-out-war on God than by attacking the family? Guard your hearts, friends . . . elsewise, you may leave your children slain on the battlefield of divorce.

"That's all I have to say about that."

During these weekend visits, Daddy and I were inseparable. We played football on the lawn of his apartment complex; drove down to Dauphin Island to see what the boat captains were catching; never missed an episode of the WWF; and always rooted for Hulk Hogan. We watched football on Sundays together, we made a few trips here or there, and we slept in the same bed.

He was my best friend.

I lost track of how many hamburgers we ate during those two years. It would not surprise me if the number was in the hundreds. Seemingly every night, Daddy went into the tiny kitchen . . . no bigger than what was required to provide wall space for a sink, a refrigerator, and a stove . . . and patted out hamburgers on the small countertop. With no more space than the average school desk, he had barely enough room to have the package of meat lying next to the plate where he would stack his patties.

He always patted out at least four patties. And almost every night, he made the same declaration: "Two for me, one for you, and one in case we get hungry later." He'd grin with a goofy demeanor as he said it, knowing he had said it to me a hundred times before . . . and knowing I knew neither one of us were going to eat the last one. He had a small Weber grill out on the porch of his apartment. I suppose it was more of a stoop than a porch . . . two lawn chairs and a charcoal grill made it crowded. He loved that charcoal grill, though . . . he loved the flavor, and I think he loved the unpredictability of cooking over an open and unregulated flame. More than once, he'd holler, "Bring me a glass of water . . . and hurry!"

I always watched him through the sliding glass door as he tended to the burgers. The stoop was just a little too crowded for both of us to be out there while he cooked hamburgers. So, I usually stayed inside and watched TV. I could tell it gave him great joy to cook the burgers for just the right length of time at just the right temperature . . . to him, it was a science, one which I never learned.

Just last week, Hannah and I were at small group Bible study when the subject of men cooking came up. At least two of the men in our small group are grill masters. They've honed their craft to near perfection and routinely serenade our palates with their savory preparations. "Do you cook, Walt?" The fact of the matter is, I don't. Not necessarily because I do not know how, but I do not know how to cook well. I can make great instant mashed potatoes. I can heat up a can of Le Sueur English peas. I can recall fond memories of watching my dad cook hamburgers through a sliding glass door . . . and I can make a mean can of Chef Boyardee.

Every time the subject of grilling comes up, I am encouraged to engage my girls at every level. I regret not learning from my dad, so I try not to exclude my girls. Case in point . . . Cape took the ASVAB, the Armed Services Vocational Aptitude Battery test, earlier this year and scored quite well. She remarked recently that she knew she struggled with some of the "mechanical" questions, "But, I had learned enough growing up that I understood the concepts." I may not grill much . . . and that is certainly a skill I'll never be able to teach my girls . . . but I try to expose them to life at every turn so that they will be ready for whatever comes next.

And besides, every child needs their daddy.

Daddy loved onions, too. He ate them at every meal. Even if it was simply to cut up an onion and eat raw slices as an accompaniment to whatever he was eating, he was going to eat onions. And just as often as he made his "Two for me, one for you" declaration, he also offered me onions. Every night . . . "How about I cut up some onions for you?" His smile reminded me that he knew I didn't like onions, and he thought it was funny to ask anyway—yet his eyes let me know he hoped I would say, "Okay." He loved onions so much that he wanted me to love them, too.

"No, Daddy." His request always irritated me. "I don't know why you like them nasty things."

He'd laugh and make some comment about how I just don't have good taste, and, soon enough, we'd sit down and eat our hamburger, our instant mashed potatoes, and our English peas.

One night, Daddy declared that he was making special hamburgers with a secret ingredient. He forbade me from coming into the kitchen as he worked furiously to hide his efforts. He hinted that it was a secret seasoning that was going to make the hamburger "sooooo good." The kitchen had a serving window over the sink, and I could just see the side of his elbow and shoulder as he patted the burgers out. Though I couldn't see his hands, I knew that, like always, he patted out four.

"You're gonna love this!" He beamed with pride at his new concoction, and I could tell that he was genuinely excited to see my reaction. After a few minutes, he retreated to the stoop where the charcoal grill waited patiently for him to return. I watched through the sliding glass door, and I remember how much particular care he paid to placing the patties in just the right place on the grill. Every so often, he'd turn and look at me and smile, clapping and rubbing his hands together, and then he'd rub his belly as if to indicate how good the burgers were going to be.

A few minutes later, he came back inside with four piping hot burgers still smoking from the charcoal. Admittedly, my mouth watered as I anticipated the fantastic concoction that he had conjured up, and I was eager with expectation. "I'm starving! Let's eat!" I declared, as I ran to the kitchen.

"Hold on . . . I'm going to fix yours for you," Daddy said. "I'm afraid that if you fix it, you might figure out the secret ingredient, and that will spoil the surprise."

"Fine enough," I retorted. "But hurry up," I said, with almost a hint of pouting in my voice.

Two minutes later, we were sitting at the coffee table. He was in his recliner, and I sat on the floor. He didn't touch his food. Instead, he just stared at me, waiting for me to take a bite of my hamburger. It was a bit awkward . . . I felt like the tiger at the zoo with the crowd gawking . . . waiting for me to eat the squirrel that wandered into the pen. Reluctantly, I finally took a bite.

The juice from the burger ruptured into my mouth. Complemented by just the right amount of ketchup and mayonnaise, salt and pepper, it initially tasted just like the hundreds of other burgers that Daddy had cooked nearly every night before. And they were good! However, as my mouth continued to close down on the beefy delicacy, I realized there was, in fact, something different . . . the texture changed, and then, flavor burst forth into my mouth that was completely foreign to any hamburger that I had ever enjoyed before . . .

"Auuurrrgggckkkk!" I gagged, as I rolled the wad of meat and bread out of my mouth and onto my plate. Daddy's facial expression changed completely from one of excited anticipation to one of frustration and, perhaps, even anger.

"You put onions in the hamburger meat!" I exclaimed, with frustration and disgust. He laughed nearly uncontrollably. And, not one to surrender, Daddy refused to acknowledge that I simply did not like onions and insisted that these were "the best hamburgers ever!" We argued for a few more minutes, I ate my mashed potatoes and English peas, and then, still mad, I retreated back to the depths of whatever TV show was blaring over the boob tube.

To this day, I hate onions. I don't know why. I just don't like them. Daddy thought that, because he loved them, that I should or would, too. For years after that, he joked

We always insist that the girls sit and eat with us as a family at the table. Life and busy-ness can complicate our family time together . . . but we do our best, and the girls know that it is a priority. No television. No phones at the table. Just us as a family. We may not speak a word . . . but it is still our time.

I grew up in a home where family meals were non-existent. Mostly, my parents were gone. I ate more meals alone than with family. But Hannah . . . well, she grew up with the understanding that "Lingering Around the Table" was a family ritual and not just a way to pass the time. No doubt, I learned much from her about the value of family time . . . and I am so grateful for it.

about how much I liked that hamburger he made that night and how it was "the best hamburger ever." I always disagreed and disputed his account of the events, and still do, to this day.

Except to say that, perhaps, I might now agree that I was the best hamburger ever. My daddy died a few months ago, and I would gladly sit down and eat that whole hamburger with him today.

Time is precious friends . . . don't waste it.

I WANT TO KNOW
WHAT LOVE IS

My dad bent over and gave me a hug . . . He was wearing his "fancy cologne."
I think it was Old Spice. It was thick and almost gawdy, like he had splashed
a double handful on both sides of his face. So thick, in fact, that for several
hours after he left, the smell of his cologne lingered on the left side of my face and
neck. There would come a time later in life when that smell would invoke pleasant
remembrances, but on that particular night, my dad's over-abundance of cologne did
nothing more than irritate me.

My mom gave a few last-minute instructions to my oldest brother and his wife.
I would be staying with them while my parents were away. She reminded them to
feed me and make me bathe. Looking back now, I find her reminders and instructions
humorous . . . I pretty well had raised myself up until that point, and there was little
reason for her to fear that I could not continue to do so in her absence for the week.

She also leaned down and hugged me, clutching my shoulders and telling me that
she loved me as her handbag rolled off her shoulder and sucker punched me in the gut.
And I knew that even if she did just clobber me with her oversized pleather purse,
she did love me. But her words and her eyes were clouded with anxiety. I sensed that she
would have preferred to drag out our "goodbyes" . . . and, perhaps, that she would
prefer not to even go on this trip. She hesitated before she stood up. My dad was
lingering at the door waiting on her. He grinned from ear to ear, confident that he was
about to perfect his master plan. I was eagerly reassuring . . . phrases like, "Oh, I will
be fine," and, "I can handle myself," and, "Y'all go have a great time," were rolling off
my tongue like a used car salesman promising that "this" was the best car on the lot.
Mother looked back over her shoulder at Daddy and smiled hesitantly, then she turned
to me and kissed me on the cheek and retreated out the door and into the nighttime air.

As a 9-year-old, I was flooded with emotions that I could not fully comprehend or
reconcile. Just a few weeks prior, my parents sat me down on the couch in our living
room and told me, "Daddy's going to move to Mobile." Initially, I was befuddled by
the statement . . . not using the word "divorce" had softened the blow but had also
confused me. "For how long?" I asked, not yet understanding what they were telling
me. By day's end, though, my life had been forever changed.

That same initial confusion I experienced as I struggled to understand the meaning of divorce reemerged a few weeks later when Daddy told me, "I am going to take your mother to Hawaii."

At nine, complex motivations escaped me . . . so my thought process was simple . . . "They are going to work on fixing their marriage, and maybe Daddy won't leave." I pressed Daddy for more information, but in reminding myself of the things he said, I realized he was not pumping me full of optimism with his answers. No . . . in fact, remarks of, "I don't know what this means," and, "I guess we will just have to wait and see," probably were truly offered in the same sense of befuddlement that I already had. Truth was, I don't think either one of them knew what the trip meant.

Standing at the living room window, I watched as the headlights of Daddy's charcoal grey Delta 88 backed out of the driveway and turned toward Mobile. I recalled Daddy telling me, "We'll fly all night long so we can have a full day when we get there." I stayed at the window for a solid thirty seconds . . . long after the red taillights of that Oldsmobile had drifted out of sight . . . just wondering what all of this might mean.

Of course, and despite my dad's careful responses, I had formed many 9-year-old conclusions about the trip and what it all meant. "Daddy is pulling out all the stops," I thought to myself as I stared into the darkness. "He has on his fancy cologne, and that's sure gonna impress her." I unknowingly shook my head with approval as I considered his efforts. "And he had on his fancy boots . . . and they were clean, too. He polished them himself." Again, impressed with his efforts, I shook my head in admiration for how hard he was trying to win Mother back.

Undoubtedly, in these few weeks, I had discerned that it was Mother who wanted the divorce. I don't have any specific recollections of conversations, nor do I recall the reason why I came to that conclusion, but I knew that it was Daddy who was trying to win Mother back. And, as most any 9-year-old would, I wanted him to succeed. And I would have done anything I could to have helped. Thus, all of the used car salesman reassurances . . . the smiles and hugs free of fret or dread at the thought of my parents leaving for a week without me . . . the "Yes, ma'ams" and "I promise I'll study" remarks, all designed to reassure her that everything would be fine in her absence. I was going to do my part . . . to make sure this marriage came back together.

For, in those few weeks, I had also discerned enough to know that I did not like the battle that was festering and the war that was brewing . . . nor did I enjoy being pulled at from both sides . . . and as much as my home life had been less than desirable, it was much preferred over having my parents divorced. Much preferred, indeed, so, from the instant that Daddy told me, "I am taking your mother to Hawaii," I engaged in every sort of effort that I could to foster their reconciliation. "Be sure to hold the door open for her," I reminded him. He chuckled . . . my dad was never one to not already know all the right answers, so he entertained my suggestions but had no real intentions of honoring them. "And don't fuss with her about silly stuff." He chuckled again, this time with a little less enthusiasm . . . and as much as I wanted to tell him not to drink too much . . . I knew better. He'd have to come to that conclusion on his own.

My brother, Trey, quit school when he was 14-years-old. He and his wife, Nancy, married when he was 16, and at that point in their lives . . . both in their early 20s . . . they had lived and endured several full seasons of maturity. Trey worked on tugboats . . . still does. Nancy, ever the faithful wife, stayed home during his two-week hitches and worked hard, too. They fought for everything in their marriage and overcame every hardship and obstacle that life could throw at them . . . Today, they are in their 60s—I think. If memory serves, Trey is 12 years older than me, so that makes him 60. Nancy is a little older. They still spend time together every day . . . they still work hard . . . and they still fight through the obstacles of life. I know they love each other . . . they must, for they have been through so many fires that only a bond forged in love could have endured.

Nancy nudged me away from the window, telling me, "Go get dressed for bed. You got school tomorrow!" And so, I scurried back to my room and closed the door. I wondered, with romantic fancies, what conversations Mother and Daddy might be having. How might he be wooing her with promising words of "I love you"? I wondered if he had begun to detail for her all the magical things they would see on the trip, or if he had tried to hold her hand. And then I wondered what song was playing on the radio . . . "Radio! Radio!" My minded exploded with excitement as I rolled across my bed and grabbed the big, heavy, black rotary phone off the floor.

My fingers plugged the hole of each number as I twisted my hand to the right . . . "Four," I called each number out loud as I knew them by heart, listening patiently to the spring of the rotary unload on the dial as it tick, tick, ticked back into place. "Nine," . . . tick, tick, tick, the process repeated itself seven times over.

WABB 97.5 was *the* radio station in Mobile, Alabama, at the time. Daddy and I listened to it frequently, though he sometimes betrayed our radio pact with a little country music from 95 KSJ. I knew the "request line" number for WABB by heart . . . as listening to music was one of the best ways for a bored kid to pass the time on a rainy day back in those days. But getting through on the request line was never easy. One phone line and thousands of listeners trying to get through . . . "It's a long shot, but it's worth it," I thought to myself as the last rotation ticked away.

A few seconds of silence passed. "Beep—beep—beep." The dreaded busy signal let me know that the DJ was taking requests from other callers. I hung up and began the process again. "Beep—beep—beep." Again and again, I called and called . . . because I knew I had the perfect song that would surely reignite the fires of love in my parent's marriage. Undeterred, each busy signal just gave me more determination to call again. Watching my alarm clock on my bedside table, I knew they'd be in the car for at least an hour . . . I still had 15 minutes. "Beep—beep—beep." Like a nagging mosquito that won't go away, the busy signal was likewise ever present.

Time was drawing nigh . . . it had been about fifty minutes since they left the house, and my romantic conjectures had given way to anxiety about getting through to the DJ. I knew that if they heard "this" song, everything would be alright . . . my mind was frantic . . .

"WABB, what's your request?" The voice answered the phone without even a hint of a ring. So expectant to hear the busy signal, my hand was already moving towards the two buttons that had to be pressed to reset the phone. I was taken aback and caught off guard . . . "Uh . . . " I said with childish hesitation, "I Want to Know What Love Is."

I heard the DJ take a draw on a cigarette and slowly exhale. Both my parents smoked for most of my life up and to that point . . . I knew that sound. As he finished exhaling, his deep, slow, almost defeated voice said, "Me, too, kid. Me, too." And he hung up.

A few minutes later, "We Built This City," by Starship came to its climactic conclusion, and the DJ broke the airwaves to introduce the next song . . . "This one goes out by request for all of you out there searching for answers." . . . and that now-famous Foreigner song began to play . . .

"I've gotta take a little time,
A little time to think things over.
I better read between the lines,
In case I need it when I'm older.
This mountain, I must climb,
Feels like a world upon my shoulders.
Through the clouds, I see love shine,
Keeps me warm as life grows colder.
In my life, there's been heartache and pain,
I don't know if I can face it again,
Can't stop now, I've traveled so far,
To change this lonely life.

I wanna know what love is,
I want you to show me.
I wanna feel what love is,
I know you can show me."

Driving back from Atlanta last week, a classic rock station south of the city was playing one '80s hit after another when this song came on. And all of the hopes and dreams, weights and burdens of a 9-year-old boy came flooding back.

After a few lines of the song, a tear rolled down my cheek . . . not because my parents never heard the song, nor because they came back from Hawaii even more dysfunctional than when they left . . . but because I know what love is . . .

"Love is patient, love is kind. It does not envy, it does not boast, it is not proud. It does not dishonor others, it is not self-seeking, it is not easily angered, it keeps no record of wrongs." 1 Corinthians 13:4-5, NIV.

And I am so thankful that my Father loves me.

I regularly shave my head for Cancer Freeze, a local non-profit that raises money for cancer patients around our area. I ask contributors and supporters to donate, and, if we meet our goal, I shave my head. Folks are so good to give, and the money raised goes to the cancer patients' uninsured expenses like travel and lodging.

Hannah and I visited Florence, Alabama . . . arguably the music capital of Alabama . . . and had dinner in the revolving restaurant high atop the needle on the banks of the Tennessee River. It had not been long since I had shaved my head for Cancer Freeze, and it was particularly cold in Florence that night. Hannah threw me her grandfather's old beret and said, "Here, wear this. It will keep you warm, and you'll be sexy, too."

I wear that beret now even if its 90 degrees outside . . . as long as she asks me to!

—THE CROSS BETWEEN— THE LAKES

Part One

We lived in the Lake Forest subdivision in what most people would now call Spanish Fort, Alabama. Our house, a wood-sided, two-story house, was at the bottom of a massive hill . . . in my mind's eye, it had to be a quarter of a mile long and as steep as any double black diamond ski slope . . . but, then again, I was five. The road in front of our house was split . . . that is, one lane of traffic was separated from the other lane by a median, and though we were at the bottom of the hill as far as the road was concerned, our yard sloped off in a different direction.

Our backyard melted down into a creek bed. That creek was *the* creek that fed *the* lake that was the namesake of the subdivision. Regrettably, I don't have a reservoir of memories filled from that creek bed. I should . . . every boy with a creek bed in his back yard ought to have memories of snakes and snails, tadpoles and polliwogs. I remember going into that creek bed once . . . vaguely.

I think I never went into the creek bed because my dad was swarmed by yellowjackets somewhere near its banks. I can't remember many of the details . . . I just remember he was running a chainsaw. Other than that, I simply remember that if ever someone mentioned the creek, the subject of "the yellowjackets" was a common response. Being so young, I didn't even understand the subject, truth be told. I knew that yellowjackets would sting, but the swarms I always envisioned were much akin to the swarm of bees on any good Saturday morning cartoon. Bazillions of angry little stinging flyboys, mobbed up in a nearly solid blob, and inescapable. That imagery was enough to keep this 5-year-old boy far from the creek.

And in "the cross between the lakes," like my dad, I have been swarmed by yellowjackets, and it is certainly such a memorable event that I am always leery to go near them again. So leery, in fact, that for a full year, I avoided the spot where the angry little flyboys emerged from the ground like flying lava . . .

It was only a few years after we had moved to the lake house. Our residency there had come in stages . . . we moved the house from another location, and there it sat for some four years, unattended. We worked on it for another year before it was complete enough that we could move in, but there was still plenty of work to be done. Then, for two more years, we continued to work on the yard and the driveway, and we undertook to build a shop. So, the stages took time, and time was something precious. We had three small children, Banks being a toddler, and life was happening all around us. We worked in spurts, and if that meant that we spent an hour or two on a random Saturday in the yard, that was still progress in our eyes . . .

Hannah wanted to remove much of the underbrush around the house . . . the yard still appeared more like in the woods that adjoined our house, as opposed to a manicured piece of property. While we did have a path for a driveway, and we had some semblance of a yard on both the front and back of the house, one particular side of the house looked like a place where Sasquatch might otherwise have taken up residency. If nothing else, it was inviting for snakes, and that was unsettling to us as parents . . .

We spent the first few days pulling up all the underbrush that was manageable by hand. Typically, privet hedge or yaupon holly is no bigger around than your finger, coupled with a root base no wider than the outspread fingers of your hand. These small saplings are easy to grab hold of. Like the top of a carrot, all we had to do was grab the sapling itself and pull up from the ground, root and all. It was particularly important to pull the roots, too . . . these two types of Alabama invaders are very aggressive when they besiege your property. Perhaps only surpassed by the mighty kudzu, these two nuisance plants will take over any open spot that gets enough sunlight to promote the growth, so leaving the roots was not an option. For, if we had, they would soon reinvade.

For days, we pulled saplings by hand, loading the bed of the truck to the brim . . . if not more. We burned every last prisoner . . . there could be no sympathy in this battle, for to show sympathy would surely mean the Amekalites would return to wage war again. We pulled so many tiny invaders from their bases that even our gloves had callouses . . .

By day three of that particular project, the side yard was looking pretty well. The smooth dirt was fresh and clean, and everything we could pull up was gone. We had scoured that yard from one end to the other . . . the fresh turned dirt and smooth-as-a-baby's-butt appearance was something of a victory banner for us . . . but the war was not quite over. There were three larger privets in a clump in the middle of the yard.

"You back the truck up to the closest one . . . all you have to do is get within five feet or so, and I'll hook the chain to it. Just gently ease forward, and the weight of the truck's momentum will pull it out," I told Hannah. She nodded her head and shut the door to the old Chevrolet half-ton. I gestured for her to roll down the window . . . but she didn't understand my instructions. That was a God thing . . .

The privet hedge fanned out about two feet off the ground. Its trunk was as big around as my wrist, and the entire hedge stood some eight feet tall. Its wiry limbs were thick and matted . . . a tangled mess that could barely be pierced by a machete. I swung a few times in vain, thinking I might make a larger opening at the base, so as to avoid

A "dad" is different from a father, I think. At least in my vernacular. A "father" is a thing . . . a definition of kinsman-ship. A "dad" is a relationship explanation. This is my Daddy, though I always pronounced it "Deddy." He died May 18, 2022. I started calling him "Deddy" from an age that precedes my memory . . . and now, all I have are those memories and the stories they tell.

   Those stories, though, will likely come almost exclusively from my childhood, for our adult relationship was rocky . . . to say the least. But no matter how rocky the road may have become, he was still my "dad," and I loved him so.

climbing down on all fours . . . but after the third "thwack" of the machete, I realized my efforts were largely pointless. The spider web of tiny twig-like branches where a shield against invaders, protecting the main arm of the branches from my blade. "All fours it is," I said to myself as I sat the machete down on the ground.

I guess I was in my late 30s then . . . I remember that my knees did not hurt nearly as bad then as they do now. Getting up and down off the ground was not something that intimidated me. Now, I do sometimes worry that, while getting down on the ground is not hard, it's the getting back up that my knees seem to object to. Plopping to my knees, I pulled the chain taut from the back of the truck and wrapped it three times around the trunk of the privet. The wiry limbs poked me in the back of my head and neck, through my shirt, and into my back. They clutched at my shirt and held fast . . . looking back, I'm reminded of that scary looking jack-o'-lantern figure from some '90s horror movie, the name of which I can't recall, with tree-like limb features for arms and legs. It felt as though the hedge had a hold of me. Putting my whole body in reverse, I crawled backward out from under the hedge as it tried to pull my shirt back over my head. Sitting up from my crouched position, I fixed my shirt and made eye contact with Hannah in the side mirror of the truck. I gestured my fingers forward, and she eased the truck down the hill. The chain pulled snugly at the base of the hedge, and the whole thing—roots and all—came out of the ground like a perfectly extracted wisdom tooth.

I waved to Hannah to stop and began to unwrap the chain from the tree. Hannah climbed down out of the cab and came and helped me load the couch-sized hedge into the back of the truck. "Two more to go," she said as she climbed back into the cab. She backed the truck up to the second hedge . . . this one slightly larger than the last . . . and we started the same process over again. I didn't even bother with the machete, instead, opting to go straight down on all fours and shimmy under the lowest branches, nearly to my belly.

This hedge was much wirier and felt like an awkward teenager groping on a first date. Limbs and branches pulled at my hair, my ears, my neck, my shirt, and anywhere else that was not planted squarely in the dirt. My outstretched arms wrapped the chain twice around the calf-sized base of the hedge as a particularly sharp limb poked into my neck. It burned, and I recoiled with pain, but I was essentially trapped under the hedge like Hulk Hogan on the wrong end of one of André the Giant's body slams. Reaching back to pull the limb from my neck, another limb poked my forearm . . . and it was at that moment, I knew I was in trouble. Out of the corner of my eye, I saw the venomous little yellow and black menace clutching to my forearm as his torso throbbed . . . pumping all the venom he had as he went.

And in what was merely an instant, I found myself surrounded by bitterly angry yellow jackets. What was worse, I was essentially on my chest and knees, and my face was only a few inches from the hole that they were now evacuating. Apparently, the war against the privet hedge had now turned into a fight for survival against the yellow jackets. Bombs started going off all over my body . . . "Pow!" "Pop!" "Kerpow!" The yellow jacket counterattack was more than I could stand . . . I had no choice but to retreat.

Emerging from beneath the hedge, I surveyed my first option for evacuation and saw Cape and Banks standing some 25 feet from where the swarm was beginning to tornado. Banks was wearing nothing but a diaper. I made eye contact with Cape and yelled, "Ruuuuunnnnn!" and then I turned in the opposite direction. I knew that the yellow jackets would follow me, and I dared not lead them to the girls. In the opposite direction, I found Hannah in the truck . . . and yelled to her to "Shuuut the door!" . . . and thank God she did, for the God thing I spoke of earlier was that the window was still rolled up. We made eye contact as I flashed by her, and I could see fear in her eyes . . . I'm sure she saw it in mine, too.

For the next twenty seconds, I swatted and slapped and clapped and stomped, running all the way around the house . . . coming to a stop at the back door. Yellow jackets clung to my shirt and pants like they would die trying . . . and they did. Cape and Banks were looking at me through the window of the back door of the house . . . I was grateful they had heeded the warning and ran inside. I later learned that Cape . . . my little hero . . . grabbed Banks when she saw the swarm and ran, making sure she protected her sister first.

A few seconds later, Hannah rounded the corner behind me . . . clear herself of any attackers, she began swatting them off me. Soon, I was down to my boxer shorts and running back into the house. My clothes lay in a pile in the back yard with yellow jackets still swarming them. Looking out the windows to the side yard, the biggest swarm of yellow jackets I had ever seen raged full on . . . just like in those Saturday morning cartoons.

"Thank you, Jesus, that they didn't go after one of the girls."

"Seven, eight, nine . . . nine times," Hannah said, with her index finger still touching my neck. "They got you at least nine times." I recalled in that exact moment that my dad was stung 13 times. My ears were ringing, and my heart was pounding . . . but everyone was safe. Hannah doctored my wounds as best she could, and I spent the rest of the afternoon in a Benadryl-induced coma . . .

That night, the yellow jackets met a gallon of gasoline . . . and the war was over.

Part Two

My mom and dad divorced when I was in the third grade . . . I've written about that, and I don't feel inclined to start today. I did, once, remind the reader that, sometimes, the truth is too painful to tell . . . so a veil must be cast over it and the story told through the eyes of another. Such was the case when I wrote "Indeed, She Was a Grand Ole Dame." But I digress.

They lied to me, though . . . "Your dad is just going to go stay on Dog River for a little while," they told me, as if there was no permanency to the matter. They never even mentioned the word "divorce," nor did they explain that they had been fighting far too much or that their marriage was in trouble. Instead, they left room for hope . . . though I didn't fully understand "why" my dad was moving, there was hope that he would soon be home again . . . because no one said otherwise. That "hope" was for them—not me. You see, it was far easier on them to leave room for hope in my heart than it would have been to tell me the truth . . . that they were getting divorced, and there would be no reconciliation.

Not long before they divorced, we lived in Lake Forest . . . in a wood-sided brown house on Ridgewood Drive. I remember the house well and have vivid memories from those years . . . perhaps, because I was so blissfully ignorant that I thought all was well in the world . . . and my innocence had yet to be shattered. Those were good times with friends like Boone Eiland and his little sister, Emily, Chris Daniels, and more... it's amazing how much ground we could cover on a Mongoose BMX bike.

Ridgewood Drive held fond memories, for sure . . . that is where my mom bought the Steinway grand piano that was the "Grand Old Dame" from an estate sale. Later, she gave her away to a co-worker . . . to live another chapter of her life and play music elsewhere in someone else's life. Perhaps . . . that, too, is why the music died.

Ridgewood is where my dad brought home the Millennium Falcon and surprised me with the gift. Han Solo's "bucket of bolts" star cruiser spaceship from the Star Wars movies was a must for every young boy of the age, but few were fortunate enough to have one to play with. Daddy surprised me with the present for no particular reason . . . just handing it to me with a brimming smile as he came in the door from work on a random weekday. It was the "best gift ever" . . . but then again, in those days, Daddy was good at surprise gifts. It was part of his love language.

In those days, Daddy was good at the "gift of time," too.

Time makes memories . . . and of all the gifts Daddy ever gave to me, his time was the most valuable of all. And now there is no more . . .

. . . but I digress.

"Walt, look in the grey toolbox and bring me the biggest wrench you can find," he hollered from underneath the old Chevrolet Luv pick-up truck. I shifted tools in the bottom of the box from one side to the other, trying to find "the biggest." Satisfied that "this" surely was . . . I laid down on the ground next to his knees . . . they were sticking out from under the truck . . . and handed the big crescent wrench to him. He took it from my straining hand . . . the wrench dangling from the ends of my fingers was nearly too much for my outstretched fingers to keep extended. But then again, I was only about five.

"Now, get in the truck, and do exactly what I tell you." His voice was stern, yet assuring . . . as if to say, "You can do this, but make sure you do it right." I obliged . . .

The front end of the truck was sitting up on jack stands. The front wheels dangled like big earrings hanging off a blue-haired woman's lobes . . . the truck was old and blue and a bit haggard, too. The back tires on the truck were bigger than the front tires. As if it were some sort of drag racing truck, the big back tires suggested that Little Boy Blue was fast and mean . . . and cool. And the last part rang true with me. It was a cool little truck, at least in my 5-year-old eyes. What was cooler, though, was that my dad and I were turning wrenches together . . . a rite of passage . . . men, working on the truck together . . . fixin' stuff . . . "Aarrrgh, Aarrrgh, Aarrrgh," as Tim Taylor might grunt.

"Now, push down the clutch pedal," Daddy shouted from underneath the truck. There were three pedals . . . and I had no idea which one was which, so I hesitated. "The clutch is the one on the left. Toward the door . . . " his voice was muffled as it came from underneath the truck and around the doors. "Push it all the way to the floor."

My little legs could barely reach the pedal, much less allow me to push it to the floor. I clutched the steering wheel with my mightiest grip and extended my leg as far as it would extend. I even pointed my toes, trying my best to get the pedal "all the way to the floor," but my effort was in vain. I simply wasn't long enough to get the job done that way.

"Hang on, Daddy. I can't reach far enough down," I explained.

Studying the situation, I decided to let go of the steering wheel and slide my back and shoulders down into the butt of the seat. Now, with my shoulders wedged against the backrest of the seat, my back lying flat in the seat itself, and my tiny tail hanging off the edge of the seat, I had gained a good ten inches of reach. My feet fumbled against the pedals until I was certain I had blindly found the one closest to the door, and I pressed with all my might. My leg craned outward as if it were a mile long as my back arched, and I pressed my shoulders against the backrest of the seatback.

"Clack, clack, clack, clack, clack," the pedal chattered as I pushed.

"That was the emergency brake." Daddy laughed from underneath the truck. "But that's okay. I should have already had it set anyway. Push the pedal next to that one." And I did . . . and a chorus of praise came from underneath the truck as Daddy made it known I had done a good job . . . and though I only had to hold the pedal for a few seconds and then press it down a couple of more times, we fixed that truck. We did . . . he and I . . . me and my daddy.

I climbed out of the cab of the truck and helped him pick up tools and clean up the mess. We clanked tools as we tossed them back into the toolbox. Then, we collected the trash and the worn-out parts he had just replaced and threw them all in the garbage. Wiping the grease from his hands with a rag, he handed it to me and nodded. I wiped my hands, too . . . the rite of passage was complete.

"Come on . . . let's go for a ride and make sure you did a good job!"

"Can I drive?" I asked with some measure of seriousness. "I know how to drive now, Daddy."

Best friends are hard to come by. Boone Eiland and I were the fastest of friends as children. We fought many an invading army together in the imaginary battlefields of our backyards, and even started a golf ball business on the golf course that was near our houses. I haven't seen Boone in a few years . . . but, through the marvels of technology, we keep up with one another. Time washes away some things . . . but not true friendship, and I know that, to this day, we are still fast friends . . . even though time may have washed a few more wrinkles into our eyes.

Daddy had this abrupt, chattered laugh . . . like a woodpecker pecks, Daddy would laugh just slightly more elongated . . . "Ha-ha-ha-ha-ha," he laughed at my suggestion, and then made some indication that I did know how to drive, but "Maybe we should wait until you get a bit older."

No matter, I was still as proud as an Osprey carrying his freshly caught fish back to the nest . . . "Look what I did," was my mantra as I strutted to the truck and climbed back up into the seat. I rolled down the passenger window and popped open the vent window, too . . . and we cruised those hills around Lake Forest for the next twenty minutes or so.

I stood tall in the seat . . . that was before seat belts became a must . . . and my head nearly hit the top of the cab. Daddy kept his arm up on the seat behind me and occasionally, as we rounded a curved or slowed for a stop sign, he'd grab the back of my shirt or cup his hand around my arm. I didn't need a seatbelt back then . . . I had my daddy. I found all the comfort and security I ever needed in knowing that his arm was there to catch me if ever I fell.

That Millennium Falcon that Daddy gave me . . . I played with it for a year or two . . . and then, like a mothballed Navy battleship, it sat in the bottom of my closet for another year or two. My mother eventually sold it in a yard sale without much fanfare or protest on my account. I had grown out of playing with Star Wars action figures by that age . . . the gift was short-lived in the grand scheme of things.

But, I'd go back today and work on that old truck with my daddy . . . just to turn one more wrench or have one more ride . . . because that gift of his time was something that never aged. Memories only get riper with time, and the sweetest memory of all is that of a father in a child's eyes. Remember that, gentlemen . . . toys and games come and go, but memories with Dad will last forever. Here I am, 48 years old, and waxing eloquent through a few shed tears over the memory of working on a truck with my Daddy . . . that is a true gift.

That is "why" I go shepherding outdoors. I hope to make memories that my children will one day look back on and wax eloquent themselves . . . as they laugh and cry about all that we shared together. Better that they recall fond recollections with their parents than yearn for what could have been . . . for that pain is too great to write about.

Part Three

Not far from our house on Ridgewood Drive . . . still, in the Lake Forest subdivision near Spanish Fort, Alabama . . . lived Wayne and Sheila Strickland. Uncle Wayne and Aunt Sheila, as I referred to them from birth, were my mom and dad's best friends. Many a Saturday afternoon was spent at their two-story house watching Alabama football games . . . many a hamburger cooked on the charcoal grill . . .

and many a story told around the dinner table, too. Uncle Wayne built his house on a steeply sloped lot just across the tee box from some particular hole on the course . . . on Bayview Drive, as I recall. Bayview, like Ridgewood, was split, with one paved lane traveling each direction. The lanes were separated by a grassed median. Wayne's house perched over the top of the road . . . his driveway had a steep incline before it leveled off into his garage. Spilling out of the driveway, one lane sat higher than the other, and on the other side of the road lay a ravine, of sorts, were the tee box sat above a murky pond.

Wayne was a tall man in the memories of my youth. He must have stood 6'2" or 6'3" . . . slender and sleek, he had a sophisticated look about him. He had a baritone voice that commanded the room, but he was gentle, still, and it was easy to be in his company, for he made everyone feel welcome. Aunt Sheila was smaller in stature . . . standing not much over 5'3", she was a strawberry blonde in those years, and she always had a smile as big as a country moon. Quick with a hug and generous with her laugh, Sheila was one of those Southern ladies you always wanted to be around.

Back in those days . . . people weren't scared to socialize. Families didn't worry about COVID or the business of life, and the worst boogeyman imaginable was "the man in the white van" . . . and no one had ever actually seen him . . . so kids usually roamed at will along the streets of the neighborhood. Families routinely gathered for backyard barbeques and football games while kids traversed the backyards of this American landscape, with little regard to the fear that captivates so much of American culture today.

I couldn't count the miles we put on our bicycles in Lake Forest. We were like a little bicycle gang, rounding the curve from down the street . . . we'd be stacked ten or twelve deep, with no regard to traffic—mainly because there wasn't any—and we'd ride for hours on the blacktop, trails in the woods, and, when we thought we could get away with it, on the golf course, too. My little red and yellow Murray bike served me well in those years, and the card clackers in the spokes of the wheels always let folks know I was coming . . . me and my gang.

The golf course always provided a source of entertainment, too. We never played golf . . . we were too young in those days, and, frankly, probably not really interested either. We preferred GI Joe or Cowboys and Indians in the woods. Golf was probably too mature for our liking. Once, though, while playing army in the woods near the course, I found an old golf ball that had been long ago lost to a wicked slice . . .

As I recall, I was taking heavy imaginary gunfire from the advancing enemy, and I had few options. My retreat was closed off by a flanking pair of brothers who lived up the street. My best buddy, Boone, was trapped and pinned down by two other kids . . . and it seemed we would soon be taken prisoner. Squatting down behind some heavy hedge and a pine tree, I noticed the golf ball wedged in the dirt . . . musty and grey, the ball had long ago lost its luster.

I plucked it from the dirt clutch that held it, grasped it firmly in my right hand, and with my left hand, pulled the pin and yelled, "Grenade!" I heaved that grey ball up over the hedge, and it landed right between the two brothers . . . blowing them to smithereens! "Boone! Come on!" I yelled as he crawled toward me, and we soon escaped into the woods . . . despite the brothers' protests that we couldn't use a golf ball as a grenade . . . only pinecones.

It wasn't long after, a day or two maybe, that Boone and I realized there was money to be made in "them there woods." We went back the next Saturday and found seven golf balls in various conditions and states . . .

"Hey, mister, we found these balls in the woods. Would any of y'all like to buy them?" The men in the golf cart studied over the balls, and soon enough, one of them reached into his pocket and offered two dollars for all of them. "Heck yeah!" Boone said. We were rich at a dollar a piece, and we soon spent an hour or two most Saturdays foraging in the woods, and then another half hour on the golf course selling our wares.

But I digress . . .

Boone was with us on one particular trip to Uncle Wayne and Aunt Sheila's. I can't recall the occasion, and I can't recall whether Boone's parents were with us. Bo and Debbie were great people. Boone looked just like his daddy, who was a man's man. A hunter and fisherman, always good to get outside with us boys and promote "boys being boys," we all loved Bo. Debbie, too. Likewise, she was the perfect yen to Bo's yang . . . she was sweet and kind-spirited . . . a certain softness to complement Bo's manly gruff.

"Come on, Boone. Let me show you something cool," I said as we left Wayne and Sheila and my parents in the living room of Uncle Wayne's house. We ventured outside, and there sat my dad's Chevrolet Luv pickup truck . . . clinging to the steep slope of the driveway like an Osprey clutching a limb in a stiff breeze. "Climb in the back," I said. "We're going for a ride!"

"Really?" Boone asked with expectation.

"Yep," I said, matter-of-factly . . . "My Daddy taught me how to drive it." Innocently enough, Boone climbed into the bed of the truck and leaned around to talk to me through the driver's side door.

I rolled the window down after I shut the door, and Boone . . . probably a bit smarter than I was . . . asked, "Are you sure about this?"

I reassured him, explaining that "Me and Daddy just worked on this truck, and while he was doing the fixin', I was doin' the drivin'."

Seemingly satisfied, Boone shrugged his shoulders and said, "Okay." With that, I grabbed hold of the steering wheel and pushed down firmly on the same pedal Daddy had me to push down on several times just a few days before. Now . . . if Boone and I were Bo and Luke Duke, and this were an episode of the *Dukes of Hazzard*, right about now, that ole narrator would come into our heads and say, "Now folks, if you don't know, ole Walt just pushed down on the clutch. And that transmission was the only thing keeping that little Luv truck in one place. So, hold on to your hats, boys, cuz this ain't gonna be purty."

And that narrator would have been right.

As soon as I pressed the clutch down, the truck jerked into motion . . . instinctively, I pressed harder, somehow thinking subconsciously that by pressing harder, the truck would surely stop. My leg strained with anxiety against the floorboard as my body slinked down into the seat, trying to, once again, gain leverage from the seat back. I pressed with all my might, never having expected the truck to actually move. I was panicked, and I began to scream.

Boone did, too . . . for he could see everything that I could not. I could barely see over the dashboard . . . much less could I see the terrain that sloped off into the pond behind us. Boone did, though . . . later telling me with every ounce of 5-year-old bravado he could muster, "I was going to jump . . . just like the A-TEAM."

After the truck rolled a few feet and didn't stop, I desperately searched for a solution and grabbed the stick shift . . . pulling down, because Daddy had me to do that, too. I unknowingly pulled the truck out of first gear and into neutral, and the truck rolled faster still. My fear was overrun by panic, and my panic was swept away by chaos as the truck continued to pick up speed in the descent.

Hitting the junction between the steep slope at the end of Wayne's driveway and the relatively flat asphalt of the first lane of Bayview Drive, the truck jolted as it transitioned from the 45-degree angle to the flat asphalt. Coins and wrenches and sunglasses and little boys went flying through the air as the truck's suspension did little to absorb the flux that came. I found myself lying in the bench seat with my face nearly to the passenger's door, and I was desperately trying to get up so I could see anything besides the vinyl that stuck to my cheek. The truck, though, had too much momentum, and the flat asphalt of the first lane did little to slow our descent toward the pond. And while I was grappling with the vinyl seat, the thought of the pond first blew up in my mind's eye . . .

I was crying in fear at this point, and honestly, I had given up all hope that I could stop the truck. I remember thinking that Boone would surely drown when the truck submerged into the pond . . . and I had more or less resigned myself to accept whatever fate the catastrophe had in store for us. My eyes squinted nearly closed as I ugly cried in those few seconds . . . as the truck continued to pick up speed rolling backward down that rough and tumble hill. I never saw Boone or his face, but I imagined he was in more shock than I was, and my heart hurt for what I had "done" to my best friend.

It felt like we had traveled a mile or more, though in hindsight it was hardly more than a hundred feet. One hundred feet . . . in a perfectly straight line, down one of the steepest driveways I have ever seen, and across one lane of traffic . . . and "KERRRRPLOWWWW!!!"

My head whipped back, and my entire body slammed into the seat back of the bench seat. I hit so hard that I bit my tongue and could taste the slight hint of blood in my mouth. Bewildered and disoriented, I had no idea what happened, except that I had the

When Bay graduated from high school, all Banks wanted, more than anything, was to be "Cape's little sister." Of course, she always had been, but it's been a blessing to watch these two little girls mature together into young women . . . and a special blessing to watch their bond grow stronger as time marches forward.

keen awareness that we were not in the pond. "Did we hit a car?" I wondered silently as I scurried to get back to the driver's side door to get out of the truck. In my dazed and confused state, it had not occurred to me to get out of the passenger door that my forehead now pressed against . . . I only knew to go back from whence I had come.

Isn't that what we teach our children? Go back from whence you came? I hope so . . . for that is, after all, what we do. "Start children off in the way he should go, and even when they are old, they will not turn from it." Proverbs 22:6 is a good lesson and reminder to us parents that there is one thing that can calm any storm . . . and in the midst of the wreckage and carnage of the storm that was my daddy's Luv truck, the only thing I knew for sure was to go back to what I already knew . . . the way I should go. The same lesson has proven invaluable to me time and again, even much later in life.

I pushed the door open, now heavy from the gravity of the slope, and emerged to find Boone rubbing his head. He was lying flat against the tailgate of the truck, and it appeared he took a pretty good "whack" somewhere from the bucking bull ride he had just endured. I immediately felt guilty for the oddest of things . . . "I had cushioned seats, and he didn't," I said to myself as I hurried to comfort him and help him out of the truck.

By the time we got through checking each other over, we were both in shock. Neither of us could fully comprehend what had happened, but we were both thankful that neither of us was anything more than a little bumped and a little bruised. "Are you okay, boys?" came the call of an unfamiliar voice. A motorist coming up the road had stopped . . . checking us over like she was an over-attentive granny, the nice lady poked and prodded, pulled at our collars to look at our necks, and checked behind our hairlines, too. "Heavens to Betsy!" she exclaimed. "Where are your parents?!?" Her tone suggested that she was soon to demand an explanation from our less-than-attentive parents about how two 5-year-old boys wrecked a truck . . . and perhaps, she was right in her expectation . . . but my mind turned to the dread of my parents demanding the same expectation from me!

Looking back, I honestly don't remember much about what followed. I think adrenaline probably coursed through my veins, and I lost focus of those events. I don't even remember if I got a spanking . . . though I feel certain I did. I do distinctly remember Uncle Wayne, though, turning to my dad and saying, "If it hadn't been for that one telephone pole, those boys would have ended up rolling down that ravine, and God only knows what would have happened."

My dad nodded his head in agreement and said, "There's not a tree or a knob in sight for fifty yards in every direction but for that one telephone pole. It's a wonder . . . "

No, Pops . . . it wasn't a wonder. It was the good Lord looking after me and Boone that day. Sometimes, He saves us by wrecking us. He's done it to me more than once in my Duke Boy life.

"Yeeeee-haaaaaw! And Amen!"

God bless, and have a wonderful day!

Chapter
THREE

CREEKS, STREAMS, AND RIVERS

NEIGHBORS

Our youngest daughter, Banks, is 13. Blonde-haired and blue-eyed, she is the epitome of the all-American girl. Her smile is infectious and rivals the morning sun in its radiance. Of course, I am a little biased. She has a twinkle, though . . . one that is inescapable. Her twinkle can turn your worst mood into something, well, at least mildly tolerable. But most times, her twinkle reminds you to smile. And that is enough.

So, it's not surprising that she finds joy in spreading joy. Joy, that is . . . of the floral sort.

Farmers' markets are a time-honored tradition and a staple in many Southern towns. Andalusia is no different. Every Wednesday afternoon and Saturday morning in the summer, farmers, hobbyists, crafters, and gardeners from all over the county would spread their wares out across tables and blankets that covered the Court Square. Our favorite vendor, the McKathan boys—probably no older than Banks—could grow the best sweet corn. Huge golden kernels that popped with fresh, sweet juicy flavor . . . it was like no other. "Must be something in the dirt," I remarked to Banks on one occasion. She just rolled her eyes at my explanation as to why their corn was so much better than my own. Their dad is an old friend, and their mom was usually with them at the market. She'd sit off to the side and let the boys handle their business. And, like a good neighbor, we'd buy their wares.

Hannah usually took the girls to the market. They'd buy sweet treats from Mrs. Henderson, who always made some of the best homemade desserts you could find. Occasionally, Hannah would come home with a weeping hibiscus, or some knockout ginger lily that she bought from Ms. Marie Williams . . . or some other green thing that she probably made up a name for . . . like I would know the difference. They always came back with big red tomatoes from the Reycrafts and a bag of fresh produce from the other vendors. But more than anything else, they always came back talking about our neighbors, their troubles and their triumphs, and the joys of life.

And it never failed that I'd be somewhere in town, and someone would remark, "I saw Banks and Hannah at the farmers' market this week. She sure is sweet!" I'd grin, not knowing which "she" they were referring to . . . and certainly not wanting to acknowledge that, perhaps, one of them was not sweet! But usually, they meant Banks . . . and "she" is. She learned it from her momma. And her neighbors.

As crops go, the year this particular picture was taken was a bumper. Two years later, a ravenous morning glory vine invaded our garden, and picking flowers that year was something like wading through the swamp to find lily pads. It was quite unnerving to say the least, for no one knew what trouble lurked beneath the sea of vines and leaves. I let the soil sit dormant this past year and kept it mowed and clean shaven. My hope is that the morning glory will go dormant again . . .we shall see next spring!

"Daddy, I want to plant flowers to sell at the farmers' market," she declared, at the ripe old age of ten.

"Well, I think that sounds pretty good, but we will have to talk to Momma about that first," I responded, careful not to discourage her, but surely not with any commitment . . . for fear that Hannah would not approve. But, she approved, and so it was . . . that Banks' budding enterprise began. Soon enough, it was time to plant.

Hannah's father, George Gantt, had planted wildflowers for years. I'll never forget the time he caught two folks from Wisconsin in the flowerbed at The Cottle House Bed & Breakfast picking all his wildflowers. The expression "madder than a wet settin' hen" comes to mind. He might have been more frustrated with me than he was those flower pickers . . . I'm afraid I wasn't always the best garden hand. Still, though, he always found the patience and the time through the years to teach me as he went. "You mix the seed in with grits," he said. "Gives the spreader something bigger to fling than just those tiny zinnia seeds." He was always neighborly about it . . . quick to overlook my almost non-existent understanding of anything "green."

And Hannah and I taught Banks those same lessons . . . passing the lessons down and preserving them for the future.

The seed was dark black against the creamy contrast of the dry grits. Banks twirled the handle of the hand spreader and grinned. The blades whirred at her belly as the grit grains blew in the wind. She squinted her eyes to protect them, but she never hinted at stopping. Her pace quickened as she glanced down at the hopper. "I'm not gonna have enough," she called out, coughing up a few dry grits as she finished. And she was right.

"That last row will just look funny," Hannah commented. "But it will be fine."
And it was.

A few weeks went by, and neighbors from around the Straughn community would stop and inquire.

"What are you gonna do with all those flowers?"

"Make sure you put them straight into water when you cut them!"

"You gotta get in there and pull those weeds."

All good, neighborly concerns . . . and a few pieces of good advice, too. And Banks listened . . . and worked . . . and kept her garden up.

After six weeks or so, her efforts had really shown themselves worthy. Zinnia stalks stood 14- or 16-inches tall, and they danced in the late spring breezes like sea oats blowing in a Gulf Shores' sea breeze. Banks waded through the waist-high green leaves holding the buds between her fingertips . . . inspecting them and giving them her approval. Hannah supervised the inspection process . . . I was simply there for moral support . . . They'd prune the "deadwood" and pull weeds as they went. The wind flicked Banks' ponytail, and her blue eyes bounced across the waving sea of green as she slung bushels of weeds to the outside edge of the bed. "There are some more, Daddy!" she'd holler through the wind. I'd mosey over and scoop up the dead invaders, banishing them to the bed of the truck and, soon enough, the burn pile.

A few weeks passed, and the days grew longer. School was out, but work never stops. I left an hour or so early that Friday . . . the next day would be the first day of the summer season for the farmers' market, and it would be Banks' first day selling her wares. Hannah had already helped her gather a money box and some tablecloths to cover our old rickety fold-up table. A few camping chairs would be nice to rest tired legs through the heat of the day, and the vases and jars they had assembled looked like soldiers lined up to charge the western front. From mason to peanut butter, there was nearly one of every type. Some blue, some clear, some huge, and others more normal in size.

"How many flowers should we cut?" Banks asked Hannah. I was thankful she didn't ask me.

Hannah said, "I'd cut ten dozen on your first day and just see how things go." So, we did . . . carefully selecting only those flowers that were in full bloom, to avoid overripening if you will. Anna and Heidi (The Martin Homestead on FB) passed by, and seeing us in the patch, they turned and came back.

"I'll buy a dozen from you right now, Banks!" Her eyes grew wider and brighter as Heidi handed her eight dollars. "And don't worry . . . we will buy some from you every week!" And they did . . . because they, too, are neighborly.

Banks' first few years at the farmers' market went great . . . Hannah and I alternated assistant duties, and Banks sold out every weekend. In fact, she usually sold all of her flowers within just a few hours. She made great friends and grew fond of her regulars, too. She became a staple, and she was only 10.

This past year was her third year at them. On opening day, Banks and I arrived on the Court Square around 6:45 that morning. A few vendors were already setting up, and our sweet friend and neighbor, Allison Gordon—the manager over the farmers' market—was eager to welcome Banks as a new vendor. We set up her table and carefully placed her hand-painted signs and bouquets, and she was all set.

"I love you, sugar." I offered, holding her hand.

"I love you too, Daddy," came her quick response.

"Mrs. Allison is here. There is Mrs. McKathan, too. If you need anything, you just ask them, and they will take care of you." Banks confidently nodded in affirmation, and with that . . . I turned and left my daughter on the Square . . . with our neighbors. An hour and a half later, my Bible study concluded, and I returned to find her sold out and perusing the other vendors' booths. Banks was always good to patronize the other booths . . . it was her way of being neighborly . . . of saying, "Thank you."

Some folks ask from time to time, "Do you think it's a good idea to leave her by herself?" And granted, as the district attorney, I know better than most what a twisted world we live in. But Hannah and I pledged long ago to "train them up in the way they should go," and the path to maturity and adulthood can't be paved with fear and lack of responsibility. On the contrary, Banks was surrounded by good neighbors. We knew

Hannah is a much better "mom" than I am a "dad." Truthfully, she should be writing the books and telling the stories . . . although, she is not quite as adventurous as I am . . . so her stories might be limited to the backyard! She goes with us on day trips but regularly confesses that sleeping on the ground is not something she longs to do. The older I get, the more I agree with her! And, truth be told, she is the zinnia expert. Banks and I are just the manual labor. She directs, and we work! Just as it should be . . . right?

they would tend to her every need, and she would learn much about the way she should go . . .

That is the way we all should go, isn't it? To love our neighbor? Maybe the world would be a little bit better if we'd all love a little more and fret a little less.

And, as Hannah says, "A little love makes for a good garden, too."

OLD JEEPS, PRETTY SMILES, AND A GOOD, GOOD FATHER

Banks grinned as she climbed into the old Jeep. I knew she had not yet decided if she was embarrassed to ride in it or if she thought it was cool, and I realized the grin she wore was a sheepish expression of some combination of the two. The door creaked as she pulled it shut with a slam of finality. The other kids in the parking lot turned at the clamor . . . I noticed several of the boys nodding and pointing with approval, while the girls seemed disinterested in our 1979 Cherokee Chief.

This old truck is best described as rugged. Built at a time when trucks were, in fact, trucks, and not some sort of hybrid crossover that can't decide if it is a truck or a car . . . the Cherokee Chief was the original Sport Utility Vehicle. The motor growled as we pulled out of the parking lot, and the frame rattled over every bump. Banks loves this old Jeep because of what it means to "us" . . . we go ride the logging roads in the woods around our house together . . . Lincoln occasionally sticks his head up between the seats and surveys each of us . . . we've had some good times in this old Jeep. And with only 69,000 total miles . . . it is barely broken in.

And Banks knows the Jeep is dependable, too . . . more than once, we've been in a tight spot and thought, surely, we'd have to call for rescue, but the old Cherokee Chief dug deep and pulled us through. It never gives up, and it never breaks down . . . "Fifty years old, and good as new," Banks once remarked.

Now, my other truck is quite the opposite. It is a 2012 Dodge Ram 2500 with over a quarter of a million miles . . . and lately, it seems it's in the shop more than on the road. Newer and "prettier" . . . if that's ever an appropriate way to describe a truck . . . the Dodge certainly has become temperamental and troublesome, to say the least. We love that truck, too . . . we've driven all over the South in the old Dodge, and we've had some grand adventures . . . so we have a sentimental attachment to it, too.

But the Jeep is my preferred vehicle in the fall and spring. The only air conditioning comes on when you roll the windows down . . . so driving it during the heat of the summer is not always pleasant. And this particular Wednesday evening, there was just a hint of fall in the September air . . . so I decided to drive the Jeep to pick up Banks. I noticed what appeared to be a look of surprise on her face as I turned the corner at the bottom of the parking lot. She and a gaggle of other kids stood huddled in small circles of community around the parking lot. Five girls here and seven boys there and three more girls near with five more boys further over there, the kids had obviously migrated to their peer groups as they left the building.

I could see Banks saying her "goodbyes" as I rolled to a stop not too far from where she stood. The old Jeep's motor gurgled and growled at idle as Banks made her way to me. Pulling off, I sized her mood up and asked, "What are you grinning about?"

"Well, I was just surprised to see you pull up in the Jeep. Where is your truck?" Before I could even answer, she answered for me . . . "In the shop again?"

I nodded my head in affirmation and asked, "How was church?"

"It was really good," she responded. "We are studying about the Israelites and how they struggled to stay obedient and faithful to God, but how He was always faithful to them no matter what." She added a few minutes' worth of commentary and explanation as the old Jeep roared down the road . . . all the while, I grinned with appreciation, considering that her faith is so much stronger and more mature than mine ever was at her age.

"Dad, it's funny. I love going to church when you don't make me go. But if you tell me I have to go . . . I sure don't want to go! But if you don't say anything about it . . . like right now . . . I can't wait to get back to church! I love being there and going!"

I chuckled a little and said, "I think that's just human nature." She cocked her head a little bit, like the RCA dog, and her expression suggested she didn't understand. "Well," I went on, "if I make you clean your room, that's one thing. You do it begrudgingly, and it's like pulling teeth to get you to do it. But sometimes, I walk into your room, and it's spotless . . . and I never said a thing to you about cleaning it up. You decided to do it for yourself, and you never complained or resisted, and you cleaned it better on your own that when I tell you to."

She nodded her head in understanding, as it was clear she was beginning to understand my point. "It's kind of like Lincoln," she offered. "If you put a leash on him and try to make him go somewhere, he fights you the whole time. It doesn't matter where you are trying to take him, he will fight you. But if you leave him be, he will likely go without you even telling him what to do."

"That's exactly right, sugar. That's a very good example of what I am talking about."

"Well, I'm just telling you I can't wait to get to church . . . but I gotta tell you, Dad, I sure do wish you had been coming, too."

All at once, my heart sank, and my countenance dropped. I had not been to Wednesday night church in about a month, and I knew exactly what she was talking about and where she was going . . . so I started tugging back at the leash. "Well, sugar . . . I had work . . . and a crime scene . . . and . . . " My own words melted in my ears into the wah-wah of Charlie Brown's teacher. Though my tongue pulled back on the leash . . . my heart knew she was right.

So, I stopped talking. Turning into the driveway, I stopped the Jeep and turned to her. She had a confused look on her face . . . a look that said, "I hear what you are saying, but I know you are just resisting me because you think I am telling you to do something." I nearly melted in the seat, for I knew that, in this moment, my 12-year-old daughter was shepherding me.

"You're right, baby girl . . . I don't have any good excuse at all, and next Wednesday, I will be in church. Because I love being in church, too!" She smiled a big ole' Southern Belle grin and batted her eyes at me as I brushed the hair from her face and kissed her on the forehead.

And driving the rest of the way up the driveway, I realized how Romans 8:28 is always "right on time." God does work for the good of those who love Him . . . in all things. This old Jeep has been around for what likely seems like a thousand years to some folks. It doesn't have the luster and shine of a new truck. It doesn't have fancy bells and whistles, and it sure isn't very comfortable on a hot day or on a real cold day . . . but it's always faithful to come through when we need it the most. This old Jeep has never left us stranded. Neither has God.

And though, like the Israelites, we sometimes fall for the lure of something "shiny and pretty," the reality is that the false gods of life will always break down on us. And they do. But God is always there . . . ever faithful to rescue us.

He rescued me that night, once again. He used an old Jeep, a 12-year-old girl, and a Bible study about the Israelites, all working together by His hand and for my good, to remind me where my focus needed to be. I wanted to resist . . . it was simply my sin nature speaking out . . . but my daughter shepherded me to where I needed to be.

You see . . . the Shepherd never pulls His flock. He always walks behind them, gently encouraging and coaxing as He goes. God doesn't use a leash, my friends . . . He simply uses love and a special smile, working together for our own good. And I'm so thankful He does.

It's Wednesday . . . and I've been waiting a whole week to write this story and share it with you . . . because I can't wait to go to church tonight!

God bless, and have an awesome day!

Nostalgia is a strong sentiment. A mixture of emotion, love, and memory, all wrapped into one; an old truck or a Coke sign or an old gun can all invoke strong reflections from one's past.

I still have fond remembrances of my grandfather every time I see an antique El Camino on the highway. I hope one day, the girls read stories like this one . . . or perhaps see an old Jeep Cherokee driving down the road . . . and do the same.

— S O M E T I M E S   Y O U   J U S T —
H A V E   T O   B E   S T I L L

Johnnie moved to south Florida about five years ago . . . she was pursuing something.

She lives in Crystal River, a small intercoastal town a few miles from the blue water of the Gulf but flanked by the clear freshwater springs of Kings Bay. "Five hundred springs in a 600-acre Bay," she advised. Our captain guided the small boat through a maze of channels and anchored boats as Johnnie explained her love for the manatee.

She grew up in Virginia. Once, during a long weekend, she drove solo to Crystal River to swim with the manatees. It was an idle curiosity for her, but she immediately fell in love with the first manatee she encountered . . . and then the next . . . and the next. She drove back to Virginia and couldn't stop thinking about her up-close experience with the 1,000-pound-plus gentle giants. She went back to Crystal River the following month, "And at least once a month . . . but sometimes, two or three times in a month . . . for the next year and a half," she added. "It seems like all I did was drive back and forth. The guides all new me on a first name basis." So . . . she moved . . . searching for something.

Now, locals suggest she is a manatee whisperer . . . and I admit, she certainly has a knack for talking to them. Her full-body-length tattoo starts on the top of her shoulder and rolls down her side . . . creeping around on her back . . . and hides behind the waistline of her shorts. It's an aquatic scene . . . underwater, fish, urchins, porpoise and yes . . . a manatee. She tells of her bedroom where she has manatee art on the wall, and of her personalized license plate . . . M-A-N-A-T-E-E. She talks of the custom window decal of the silhouette of a manatee that she had made for the back window of her car, and how every article of clothing she owns has a manatee on it.

It's fair to say that Johnnie is fanatical about manatees . . . and I don't suggest that in a disparaging way . . . but I still couldn't help but wonder what she was looking for.

The landscape on either side of the canal was littered . . . yes, littered . . . with houses. We made our way up the spring-fed canal through a residential neighborhood. To one side, apartments blot out the horizon. To the other side, massive houses fit for kings line the waterfront. Piers and boat houses dot the water's edge. Basketball goals and privacy fences protrude upwards . . . piercing the sky. I've seen this same story re-tell itself over and over again . . . here, Fairhope, Alabama; Apalachicola, Florida; the Florida Keys; and so many other places . . . men come searching for something . . . and when they find it, they plant deep roots in their little piece of heaven. Soon enough, everyone else does the same thing . . . and that heaven is trampled underfoot by condos and stucco.

Imagine if we found the Garden of Eden . . . and we subdivided it. Don't laugh too hard—we've done it before.

The water was crystal clear . . . like the most transparent glass observatory. Even in six or seven feet of water, I could almost count the grains of sand on the canal floor. Small fish navigated in and out of the safety of the aquatic vegetation that clung fast to the sandy bottom. It was such a beautiful seascape, I had to remind myself that, "this is freshwater." Oftentimes, the only place you see sand this white and water this clear is in the passes of the Gulf of Mexico . . . but these underground aquifers pump millions of gallons per hour of some of the purest fresh water in the country . . . and thus, the saltwater effect. Crystal white sandy bottoms and visibility under water for as far as the eye can see.

Johnnie was the first one in the water. The rest of us followed soon after. We were the first boat into the canal . . . the sun had crested the horizon not long before. Johnnie had given us keen instructions about interacting with the manatees . . . not to touch them, not to chase them, not to harass them . . . the girls listened attentively. Each nodded her head in understanding when the time came. "There is one manatee in here right now," Johnnie said. "He is sleeping, so let's not disturb him."

We wore wet suits . . . the water was a chilly 70 degrees as it bubbled up out of the ground. That's what draws the manatees to these springs . . . they come every winter and congregate in these springs, in search of the warm, flowing waters. A manatee is a mammal, and, contrary to what their appearance suggests, they have very little insulating body fat. So, the thermal energy of a 70-degree aquifer is vital to their survival during the cold winter months. Without these springs, the manatees would simply freeze to death.

We each had on a diver's mask and a snorkel . . . the ominous sound of Darth Vader's deep breaths echoed through my ears each time I drew in a breath of my own. I swam up to Bay and looked her in the eyes . . . craning my head back so we would be face to face, looking through the masks underwater. I drew in a deep breath and, in my deepest voice, announced, "I am your father, Bay." Granted, I didn't sound much like James Earl Jones, but she got the Star Wars reference . . . rolled her eyes . . . and swam off.

Dad jokes.

"Hey buddy . . . yeaaahhhh, how are you doing?" I could hear Johnnie talking through her snorkel. She was talking to the sleeping giant on the floor of the canal. He was a brute . . . probably ten feet long and easily weighing 1,000 pounds. His little arms were folded underneath, and he lay motionless, suspended in the water column, just a

The beauty of the manatee is something I am not sure words, or even pictures, can describe. So big in size, they fear virtually nothing. As such . . . they are warm and kind and docile creatures. They are curious, too . . . and maybe even affectionate. They certainly are not shy for human interaction, though naturalists and rangers alike, warn that desensitizing manatees to humans is dangerous. But what a tribute to conservation! Growing up as a boy on Mobile Bay, manatees were as rare as mermaids and sea serpents. Now, every year, a returning pod comes and shelters in the Mobile Delta during the winter. A true testament to our conservation efforts.

few inches off the bottom. His eyes were closed, and he seemed at peace. "Hey buddy . . . are you awake?" Johnnie asked as she swam closer. The manatee opened his eyes . . . and turned slightly away from the encroaching visitor.

I could see two more manatees approaching from up the canal . . . a momma and her calf. Even the calf was large, perhaps five feet in length, and the calf probably weighed 350 pounds. They swam at the surface, sticking their noses up to take a deep breath on occasion.

Johnnie was still talking to the big male.

The girls and I stayed motionless and waited . . . the momma and her calf had taken notice of us and were slowly approaching us. I talked through the snorkel . . . "Let's just sit here and wait." Everyone nodded in agreement.

A minute later, the calf made its way to where we were floating . . . Bay lay still as a stone . . . her arms stretched out wide and her legs cast behind her, as if she were skydiving. The calf swam up to her . . . face to face . . . and felt Bay's face and body. Manatees have hundreds of thick, course hairs on their heads. These hairs are as much appendages as they are hairs . . . and they have some element of antenna incorporated into them as well, for the manatees use these hairs to see and to feel. Yes, they have eyes, but their eyesight is very poor, so these hairs help their eyes fill in the gaps. The manatee searched Bay's face and then worked its way down her torso, backing up again to be eye to eye with her. And then it sat there . . . hovering . . . with her.

Bay was quiet . . . I could see the corners of her mouth stretching outward from the snorkel . . . she grinned wide and bright. Bay found what she was looking for . . . and it appeared the manatee did, too.

Sometimes, you just have to be still.

Had Bay flailed her arms or kicked towards the manatee . . . I have little doubt that it would have retreated, and she would have missed this very intimate encounter. Had she forced the issue and been too demanding, I know the manatee would have resisted. Had she been too loud and made too much noise, I am certain she would have driven the manatee away.

I don't know what that manatee was searching for. I don't know what Johnnie was searching for. I just know that in the midst of all of their restlessness, Bay was still . . . and because of that, something beautiful happened.

"Be still . . ." It really is just that simple sometimes. People often search for something in vain, never realizing where it is . . . or even what it is they are searching for, because they will never "be still" or quiet.

"Be still and know that I am God." Psalm 46:10, NIV.

— T H E   T H U N D E R   R O L L S —

Part One

Martin Hall is at least ten stories tall. I say "at least" because that's the floor Bay lived on. Perhaps there were more . . . but ten was enough for me.

Driving up the highway towards Oxford, I recollected "Move in Day" . . . hundreds of freshmen girls carrying way too much stuff to their first college dorm experience, and an equal number of dads and moms lugging the overloaded décor up the stairs . . . save a lucky few who managed to catch one of only three elevators in the building . . . like pack mules hiking the rim of the Grand Canyon, most of us took it one step at a time.

Floor numbers were like badges of honor for the dads. We all compared notes as we labored up the stairs . . . "Three? You've got it easy brother. I'm on 6," the big burly red-headed man carrying three boxes told the tall, skinny pale man with two arm loads of hang-up clothes, one over each shoulder. "Six? Shoot! I'm going to 9, my friend," came the call from one flight down . . . from the barrel-chested Black man carrying two duffel bags in each hand. And I could always lay down the Ace of Spades . . . "Well, gentlemen, I am going to 10." A chorus of moans would follow as they all knew . . . I was wearing the crown as King Nothing of the 10th Floor. Hannah and Bay were apparently Queen and Princess as we hiked up and down those ten floors more times than I care to recall. But, within a few hours, we had made our last trip . . . the truck and the U-Haul trailer were completely unloaded, and our legs were as tone and shapely as they had been since we were teenagers. I collapsed on the bed and quickly resigned from the decorating committee . . . "I'll go get extension cords from Lowes," I volunteered. Hannah put her hands on her hips and then said, "You are in the way, anyway!" She winked at me as I scurried out the door . . . with little interest at all in what girly thing ought to be hung here or there.

"Matt said to take a patience pill before you get here." Bay's text was ominous. Matt, one of her two best college friends, reminds me of Hannah. Not scared to take on any task, Matt is a "get to it" kind of girl, and she is always eager to help. Tall and slender, she physically resembles Cape, but her grit and determination are Hannah made over. "I know why Bay is so drawn to her," I thought to myself as I drove past an Oxford City Limit sign. "A patience pill . . . that doesn't sound good. Must be the same horde of pack mules all huddled up waiting for their turn on the trail."

I didn't have a patience pill . . . literal or figurative . . . but I did know what to do. "Dear Lord, I don't care if there are 100 people there in line, and I don't care if they all are ill tempered. Please let me control who I am . . . Please give me the strength to let my patience reign supreme, so that this day is a good one for Bay and for Matt. Amen."

Patience is a virtue . . . and it would be needed more today than I could imagine . . . and I would hardly need it at all to load the truck. For, you see, God is good, and when I pulled into the parking lot at Martin Hall, there just happened to be a truck loaded to the gills, pulling out from a nearly "front door" parking spot. George Jefferson himself couldn't have found a better spot on the East Side! Bay and Matt came scrambling out of the lobby, and Bay leapt into a hug . . . It took me back.

I remembered when she was four or five . . . we called her "Thunderfoot" because, in our old house, one had to tread lightly on the old hardwood floors, elsewise you would sound like a thundering herd of bison storming down the hall. Bay never minded the bass drum effect she left in her wake every time she traversed the house. You could actually hear her from outside . . . it was quite humorous, but it was also one of my favorite sounds . . . for, every day when I got home from work, I'd park my truck near the back door of the house and, as I made my way up the porch stairs and onto the stoop, I could hear "Thunderfoot" coming . . . "Thump, thump, thump!" Her feet pitter-pattered across that hardwood floor, and as I'd open the back door, she would leap into my arms for a hug.

This day, though, she was too big to leap . . . still, tears welled into my eyes as I squeezed her tight . . . and they do as I type this, too . . . for I had no idea how valuable that "Thunderfoot" hug was way back then. Only now, as a father to a grown woman who may never get a running-jump-hug again, do I understand that it was more precious than gold . . . and far more precious than the false gold of career and success that kept me away for far too long when she was a toddler. Reminiscent of days gone by, I squeezed her tight and picked her feet up off the ground, anxious to soak up every bit of the moment. She squeezed me tight around my neck and kissed my cheek . . . "I'm so happy to see you, Daddy." My voice cracked as I quivered, "Me too, Butterbean."

And then that fleeting moment was gone . . . like the hugs of yesterday . . . now just a memory of "Move in Day" . . . for Bay was now extremely excited to report that on this day . . . "Move Out Day" . . . within the last hour, many of the "Move Out Day" marauders had left, and we should be able to ride the elevators. "That is great news because it is late," I said, looking at my watch. "4 o'clock on the nose. What time is the rain supposed to be here?"

"Around 6 o'clock," Matt said, as I gave her a hug, too. "So, we have two hours."

"Daddy, you're going to be so proud . . . " Bay interjected. "We have already packed up all of the little stuff in my car, and we only have a few things left to get. Just the mattress pad, the cubby over my desk, and that big chair. Two hours is plenty of time because that's really all it is . . . but we have to be careful with that chair because Momma doesn't want us to ruin it."

And I was proud . . . whether she had packed her car or not . . . she finished her first year at Ole Miss with all A's, save one struggle in Spanish 203 that resulted in a C, and she was an Honors college student. She made great friends in Matt, Sarah, and others; pledged Chi Omega, just like her mother; experienced The Grove and all that Ole Miss life has to offer; and so much more. Yes, I was proud . . . and I didn't care if she had packed one single thing.

We spent the next hour riding the joyride called the elevator . . . and getting the truck loaded. True enough, Bay and Matt had packed all of the little stuff in her car. And, though her little Acura looked more like Lamont's truck from *Sanford and Son* . . . she was, in fact, packed up and ready to go. We took extra care to wrap the "big chair" in plastic wrap in case the rain did catch us, and by 5:30 p.m. . . . half an hour ahead of the rain . . . we were ready to go.

As I made the finishing ties on the tie-down straps around the bed of the truck, Bay and Matt began to say their goodbyes . . . "I don't want to leave, Daddy," came the cry. She was teared up and hugging Matt. It warmed my heart to see such a friendship flourish . . . I had prayed for this very thing . . . "Lord give her a few close friends who will love her in our absence . . . " and He was faithful. And as eager to provide for her as He is, I started contemplating "just how long we could stay" and still beat the rain.

A huge line of thunderstorms was advancing across northern Mississippi . . . forming nearer central Mississippi and rolling northeast into our line of travel through Alabama, these were massive storms sparking Severe Thunderstorm Warnings and a Tornado Watch for all of the northern parts of both states. Checking the radar app on my phone, the ominous markings of red and orange and yellow mushrooms were billowing far closer to Oxford than I expected. Like plumes of smoke rising from a fire pit of pine logs and tar paper, the thunderstorms were blowing up all around us . . .

Studying the radar, I recalled that ominous scene from *The Perfect Storm*, where six sailors aboard the Andrea Gail, a commercial fishing boat out of Gloucester, Massachusetts, made a last-ditch effort to survive a terrible Nor'easter by turning to make a dash for Greenland. But tragically, their decision could not save them. Realizing the storm had engulfed them, the captain looked at the crew and said, "She just ain't going to let us out, boys." And she didn't. Those men all lost their lives, God rest their souls . . . for the sea is a wicked mistress.

Still surveying the route home through the radar returns on my phone, plumes of red, orange, and yellow billowed all over the screen . . . "She just ain't gonna let us out, Bay," I remarked as I showed her the phone. Her eyes widened momentarily, but with her ever the-glass-is-half-full spirit, she quickly reasoned, "Well, if we are going to get wet anyway, we can take Matt out for supper!"

And even though my Spidey-senses were saying, "Go home, go home, go home," my heartstrings were pulling me back to let my daughter have a few more minutes with her dear friend. Matt's sheepish grin let me know she, too, didn't want us to leave. She had another final the next day and was staying one more night in the dorm. I could tell she didn't want to be alone in the storms . . . so we stayed.

Proud Larry's, a local eatery, is staffed by truly hospitable Southern folks and serves a fantastic homemade pizza selection and some great homemade Italian dishes, among other things. Bay and Matt clamored back and forth about all things "Ole Miss," and I ordered a meatball sandwich. As the girls talked, I stared out the window into one of the darkest and angriest skies I had seen since staring down the gaze of Hurricane Ivan. Lightning raged in the distance as the thunder chased it away . . . this was no "Little Drummer Boy" storm . . . this was the whole dang percussion section of the University of Alabama's Million Dollar Band . . . all banging and clanging to the symphonic rhythm of the lightning flashing across the sky . . . I could hardly enjoy the meal for the dread of driving on through the night in what looked to be *The Perfect Storm.*

Part Two

An hour passed . . . we ate pizza and meatballs and drank too much Dr. Pepper as a prelude to a nearly six-hour drive. The girls laughed and shared memories and talked of plans for the summer. And everyone avoided the topic of "leaving" . . . as if we didn't discuss it, it would never happen. But alas . . . we had to go.

We parked two blocks from the square. Oxford is like many Southern towns . . . the courthouse was built in the center of the square. That is, a block of roadwork was situated in a square around the courthouse, and the town expanded out from there. Many rural Southern towns have been bypassed . . . In the interest of speeding up travel, major highways were built that bypass the downtown areas . . . and thus, over time, those downtowns wither and die. I've seen it happen too often. A bypass is nearly certain death for most towns.

But not Oxford. In fact, the downtown area is vibrant and booming. Bars, restaurants, men's stores, and one of the most famous bookstores in the South, all wrap around the courthouse like a frat boy's necktie on his way to Game Day. Condos and townhomes sit just off the square, and commerce flows in every direction, like arteries to and from the very healthy heart . . . the epicenter of this quaint and spirited Southern college town.

Bypass the heart? Only if you want to see your town on life support . . .

We ran . . . or should I say, the girls ran . . . and I intermittently walked really fast, jogged, and then walked some more . . . through the rain the two blocks back to our vehicles. The girls soon said their tearful goodbyes, and I withdrew to my truck. I knew I didn't want to see them say goodbye . . . I'm not one to watch my daughter cry

*Bay went to Ole Miss alone. Driving off and leaving her
on the steps of Martin, her freshman dorm, was one of the
hardest things I had ever done. But I must admit in hindsight
that the distance between us brought us so much closer together.
Along the way, there were a few thunderstorms. They are common
in this life. But Bay was fortunate to make the acquaintance
of another freshman girl from similar a background. A country
girl at heart, Mattie and Bay became the best of friends and
still are today. It seems that sometimes, the storm that rumbles
the most also compels the quietest of seas.*

and remain unmoved myself. In fact, Bay and I have this unspoken agreement when it comes to goodbyes. At the moment one of us—mainly her—senses tears might begin to flow, we retreat, and that is that . . . "Goodbye" is over, and hopefully, we don't reduce each other to tears. The plan doesn't always work, and there have been plenty of "goodbyes" from college visits that ended far too abruptly, where still, I cried. Yesterday, I was visiting with a friend over lunch. We were discussing relationships between fathers and sons, and both reflecting on our own.

"My wife asked me if I had ever cried in front of my dad," he explained. "I thought, without thinking, 'men don't cry.' But then I realized one of the difficulties we've had in our marriage is my emotional stonewall." He was starting to figure a few things out . . . and I couldn't help but consider that plenty of men do cry as both an expression of joy and of sorrow. After all, "Jesus wept," and I know of no more perfect example of masculinity than Him.

I don't cry often. I understand my friend's point. But great loss and great love should move any man to stirred emotions . . . otherwise, he is nothing more than a stone, unable to shed a tear nor absorb love. For, a man completely unstirred by loss or love never truly experienced the love that leads to great loss, or the solitude that is only vacated by great love.

Soon enough, Bay and Matt's goodbyes were over, too . . . Bay abruptly darted to her car, and through the splatted water dripping down the side window of my truck, I knew that she was crying. At least she could "Blame it On the Rain" . . . the tears on her cheeks, that is . . . but that, too, would have been false.

I followed her out of town, for, no matter how smart Siri thinks she is, she will never be able to navigate like a college kid trying to get from one side of town to the other. We turned left and darted right . . . I was certain we were running a Formula One circuit, and that, soon enough, Al Unser, Sr. would appear in the rearview mirror of my Dodge truck trying to gain position. Bay wasn't necessarily driving fast . . . in fact, she was conscientious of the speed limit. However, we cut through two parking lots, drove down three alleys, and, at one point, I thought we were going to deliver pizza to someone as we cut through a neighborhood. But true to form, in seven minutes, we crossed town and avoided the 25-minute trip around the—you guessed it—bypass.

The rain came in waves on the windshield of my truck, sometimes, pelting the windshield like buzzard droppings in the middle of the Mobile River Delta. Other times, the tiny drops simply tickled the window like those red and yellow and blue sprinkles being dropped onto creamy cupcake icing. Either way, drops reminded me of tears, and I began reflecting on things . . . events in my life . . . that made me cry.

One such occasion was Bay's birth.

"Do you think you will cry when you see her for the first time?" Hannah quizzed me a few weeks before she delivered. "No!" I responded emphatically. I recall thinking her absurd for even asking such a question . . . "Men don't cry." And I rarely had.

God made each man unique when it comes to labor and deliver. Some compete for floor space with the labor and delivery doctor. Others, like myself, do not want a front row seat . . . we just want to be in the cheap seats. Still others don't want to be at the show at all, content to wait in the waiting room until the show is over.

Midway through the delivery, the doctor asked me to come do something . . . I don't remember what . . . and I politely declined. I held Hannah's hands tight in my own as she pushed through the contractions. Our eyes stayed fixed on each other through most of the process . . . the gaze occasionally broken by her winces. I wiped her forehead from time to time and tried to coach her through her breathing exercises. "Sorry, Doc, my job is up here." And it was.

"Here she comes!" a nurse exclaimed. Hannah and I stayed transfixed on each other, and I could see the tension release in her facial expression once Bay had truly been "born." Nurses cooed and ooed over how pretty she was . . . you know that's a lie—not because she isn't beautiful, but because no baby is ever pretty when they come out of the birth canal. First, they look like they were mauled by Slimer from Ghost Busters. Some of them have coneheads. Others are all red and puffy. Let's be honest . . . they ain't pretty.

"Here you go, Dad . . . come look," they beckoned. Reluctantly . . . hesitantly . . . I turned to see Bay for the first time. I didn't know what to expect or how I would even react. When my eyes found her on the little bed where the nurses finished up their duties, I saw the most beautiful and angelic baby I have ever seen in my life. Sure, her face was squished up like a Pug, her skin was as red as an Irishman's hair, and she was already crying . . . but she was absolutely the most beautiful thing I had ever laid my eyes upon. As they handed her to Hannah, I began to cry . . . uncontrollably, at just how beautiful she was. "Thank you, Jesus," was all I could think . . . over and over . . . for, that was MY daughter.

"I thought you weren't going to cry," Hannah teased through tears of her own. I couldn't even respond. I lay my head on Hannah's chest, nose to nose with my first-born daughter . . . and perhaps, for the first time, I realized that real men do cry.

Part Three

The windshield wipers of my ten-year-old Dodge truck stick every once in a while . . . a slight pause mid-stroke, as if they are going to quit . . . but then, just as soon as the pause comes, it is gone, and the rhythmic dance across the windshield resumes. The pause woke me from my trance of daydreams about the day Bay was born. We were between Oxford and Tupelo. Bay drove ahead of me . . . she had called 15 minutes prior and said my truck threw up too much spray from the road, and she wanted to be in front.

The concrete slabs of the old road had held strong over time. The road was in good shape, and it did a fair job of shedding the water from the rainfall. Every hundred feet or so, one slab of the road ended and the next one began . . . there was a demarcation line . . . a divider, if you will, at about that interval. The truck tires thumped every time they crossed the divider . . . first the front tires, and then the back. Ba-dump . . . Ba-dump . . . Ba-dump. The percussion of the tires matched the pace of the whistle of the windshield wipers. Ba-dump . . . swish . . . Ba-dump . . . swish . . . Ba-dump . . . swish. The rain pelted the window, too, as if the snare drum rolled almost without pause, and the deep groan of the old diesel was the perfect deep bass complement to the high pitches of the rain pelts and the wind. This was the Dodge Ram Tough symphony . . . and I found the rhythm relaxing. I could feel the stress of life drifting away.

I rolled down the window and let the rain splatter on the door frame. Tiny droplets from rain drops bursting on the door frame sprayed my face and my left arm. They were cold and refreshing, a welcome relief from the heat . . . for, this old Dodge only has one air conditioner, and when the windows are rolled up, the air conditioner is "OFF." The spray from the invading rain wet my face . . . I squinted my left eye slightly, trying to avoid further invasion, and then I chastised myself for not getting my real air conditioner fixed.

"But it's a ten-year-old truck," I said to myself. I often wonder if it's time to cut the cord, so to speak. "I love this old truck," I remind myself, as a compelling reason not to sell it. "There are a lot of memories in this truck, and she has been good to me," I further contemplated. "But even good trucks die eventually . . . as we all do," I surmised.

I sometimes wonder what Noah did with the Ark after they offloaded all of the animals. Tear it down and use the wood for something else? It's reasonable to conclude that raw materials would have been scarce, so I'm sure he salvaged some part of it. Maybe he lived in it for a while? Maybe he left it to rot . . . who knows? But I know this . . . it served him and his family well. Now, my Dodge truck is no Noah's Ark, but it has served me and my family well, too . . . and, though we haven't spent days on end sleeping and eating in this truck, we have logged 246,782 miles thus far, and she'll go a few more. "I don't care so much about the truck . . . I care about the memories that we might make tomorrow."

Rain began pelting the windshield even harder. I clicked the windshield wipers up to high and rolled my window back up. I checked the radar on my phone. Huge mushrooms of orange and red bloomed all over the screen, with a few exceptionally large plumes between us and Birmingham, Alabama . . . two hours east of us. "That storm there," I studied the screen, "will roll off to the northeast before we get to it. But this one here, it will power down on top of us somewhere near Jasper, Alabama." And the interstate between Birmingham and Montgomery looked to soon be littered with the deluge of heavy thunderstorms.

I checked the warning boxes on the weather app . . . as the weatherman always say, "You must respect the polygon." There were four Severe Thunderstorm Warning polygons on the screen, and the entire states of Mississippi and Alabama were under a Tornado Watch.

"Bay?" I called her phone.

"Hey, Daddy."

"I think we are going to have to drive around these storms. There are some wicked thunderstorms blowing up, and it looks like these are supercells. We are going to have to watch for tornado activity, too."

"You are such a weather nerd," she said through a grin. "But I'll follow you, Dad. Whatever you think."

"We are going to stay straight towards Jasper for now, but at some point, we are going to have to turn onto back roads and duck behind this huge storm rolling up from the southwest."

"Okay, nerd," came the reply.

And she'd be correct . . . I am a bit of a weather nerd. I probably know too many types of clouds, and I probably understand barometric pressure a little too much. I laughed at myself as I hung up the phone and pulled the weather app back up.

The sky was dark. We'd been on the road for an hour, and the sun had long departed the evening hazes of grey and white cloud cover. All that illuminated my windshield now was the rain-streaked glare of oncoming headlights . . . and electric flashes of lightning that lit the night's sky like a spotlight from a cargo ship.

A few years back, I found myself with a boatload of "new" alligator hunters. All first timers, I was trying to teach them enough that we might actually catch a nice gator. One of the guys had drawn an alligator lottery tag, and they sought me out to guide them hunting in the Mobile River Delta. We made our way from the boat launch, past the USS Alabama, and around the container cranes and the McDuffie Coal Terminal, heading up the Mobile River and through the heart of the Alabama State Docks. Massive container ships and freighters, oil tankers and Navy Littoral Combat Ships lined each side of the river as we passed. Coming towards us from upriver was a towboat . . . judging by the paint scheme, I reasoned it to be a Cooper boat. One of the greenhorns on our boat "lit up" the wheelhouse of the tugboat with our biggest spotlight. "Hey man," I beckoned. He turned his head to me but kept the spotlight fixed on the 90-plus-foot towboat. "Take that light off that guy's wheelhoooo . . . " I stopped talking when the light completely enveloped me. All I could see was bright white . . . everywhere . . . and for about three seconds, I was "Blinded by the Light." A collective moan and shuffle erupted from our boat as the four guests turned and struggled to get away from the light that bathed every shade of grey and black that we once enjoyed. I could even feel my skin warming under the intensity of the light . . . and then it was gone. "Hey man, maybe you shouldn't "Flic your Bic" at the guy who has a flame thrower!" I tried to laugh it off, but I was a bit perturbed. A common courtesy of navigation is that you never shine your spotlight onto the helmsman of another vessel. Not only had my greenhorn broke the courtesy . . . but he got us all rewarded with a million-candle-watt bath for about five seconds. It took another two or three minutes for my eyes to fully recover . . . by that time, we had met and passed the oncoming towboat that we had so annoyingly spotlighted. He didn't wave back when I threw my hand up as we passed.

Lightning lit the sky up again . . . so bright that I could have read by its light. My eyes clinched involuntarily from the over-stimulation, but in the split second before they clinched, I saw the outline of the gigantic mushroom-clouded-anvil of the supercell thunderstorm that loomed ten or so miles ahead. My study of the radar returned. "This is the path of the storm. This is our path. We are both heading to the same place . . . and I don't want to be there when it gets there."

For the next few miles, I studied the storm intently every time the lightning lit up the night's sky. In two miles, we would pass our last exit, then drive south of the storm. That deviation would add another 45 minutes to our already midnight ride. I debated back and forth . . . studied the radar and the sky intently . . . and weighed the risk of driving into one of the more ferocious storms I had seen in some time versus driving even longer into the night on weary eyes.

I was beginning to think we should have stayed in Oxford for the night, but regret is oftentimes the rearview mirror of life that prevents us from ever moving forward. Lighting lit up the sky again as thunder rattled the windows of my truck. The thunderous boom was so deep and so close that the change in the cubby hole rattled . . . "We have to get away from this storm," I said to myself as I turned on my blinker and pulled off the interstate onto a two-lane, back country road. My hope was to drive straight toward the storm's exact location, knowing that when I go to where it was . . . it would be gone. One last check of the weather app to get a good bearing of where to go revealed my worst fear . . . a Tornado Warning polygon, and we were already in it.

Bay followed without question . . .

And such is parenting. We make tough decisions, and our children follow us, and we pray that, with God's leadership, we are right.

"God be with us," I prayed.

Part Four

I pulled onto the shoulder of the two-lane state highway. The ramp sat above the interstate, and, from this higher elevation, the entire silhouette of the anvil-shaped thunderstorm loomed large overhead. Leaning forward and straining my neck to look upward through the front windshield, then sideways through the driver's side window, I could see the entire shape of the storm . . . illuminated by every strike of

Thor's Hammer . . . and it lingered over us like an angry ogre refusing to let us proceed . . . "You shall not pass!" I imagined the storm's thunderous voice to say.

The truck shimmied slightly as the wind gust over the hood and shook the big diesel from side to side. I looked in the rearview mirror . . . Bay had nosed her car up right behind the truck. Waiting patiently for me to lead, I wondered what thoughts might be traversing her mind. I punched "Tuscaloosa" into my phone's navigation and then called Bay. "Hey, sugar!" I offered with an upbeat tone, hoping to disguise any concern I might have about this storm. "Daddy, I'm scared," she immediately responded.

"I know, baby. It is a bad storm, and we seem to be right on the edge of it. But look . . . we are going to cut through these backroads and go behind the storm down to Tuscaloosa. It's going to take a lot longer to go this way, but this will keep us behind the storm and away from the danger."

"Whatever you say, Dad. I will follow you."

What a compelling sentiment . . . "Whatever you say, Dad. I will follow you." I repeated her statement to myself several times as I put the truck into drive and eased toward the belly of the beast. Just as she said she would, Bay followed.

The GPS navigation took us a few miles down a well-maintained, two-lane state highway. "Turn left in one-half mile onto County Road 42," she commanded . . . and I obliged. The storm loomed large to the northeast, our left, and it seemed the GPS navigation wanted to route us closer to the beast. I was content to stay farther away, but a quick check of the radar confirmed the storm was moving north and east at 45 miles per hour . . . "I doubt we will catch up," I muttered out loud as I turned left on the county road.

Rain pelted the windshield . . . but not a deluge . . . just those big, egg-sized drops of rain that are semi-sporadic. Large and imposing, the drops made quite the noise on impact . . . but they were so infrequent that I was hardly certain whether or not to turn on the windshield wipers. Some smaller debris littered the old county road. Broken branches from oak trees, pine straw needles, and fluffy Catawba leaves painted the grey gravel roadbed. I drove slower . . . potholes and dips were a mainstay on this old, tired road, and under these already tense conditions, I didn't want to complicate things by driving any faster. Bay faithfully followed, zigging when I zigged around potholes and zagging when I zagged around tree limbs . . . she mimicked my every move.

"Whatever you say, Dad. I will follow you." Her words from before resonated in my mind.

"Turn left in a quarter mile on Turner Road." The GPS navigation continued to guide our path. Shortly, I slowed to a stop in the middle of the road . . . the green and white sign illuminated by my headlights said "Turner Road," but it looked anything but . . . a road, that is. Two large, soupy brown mudholes flanked either side of the road at the intersection. The first was as big as a queen-sized mattress, and the other was nearly as big. I turned the truck slightly at an angle so my headlights would illuminate further down this muddy dirt road. "I don't know about this," I thought to myself. Worried that

Bay lived on the 10th floor of Martin. "Move In Day" reminded me that I am not a spring chicken anymore! Though . . . my machismo did muster up enough gumption to climb those ten flights of stairs at least a dozen times . . . once while carrying a minifridge. Yes, there were three elevators in the building, but long lines and my impatience meant I was walking! Sometimes, though, the hardest struggles in life bring the grandest rewards. One of Bay's hardest struggles was being separated from her friends and family during her first year of college. But here she stands, with Martin behind her . . . almost like the building itself is her trophy.

Bay's car might get stuck . . . or worse, my truck . . . I hesitated to make the turn. The mud was thick and soupy, but it appeared as though the road might harden into some sort of white limestone base a few hundred yards in. The rain had resumed by this point, and visibility was diminishing rapidly . . . "Trust the GPS," I said to myself, as I said a quick prayer, "Lord be with us and protect us," and I put the truck back into drive.

Making the turn, I stopped at the edge of the mud and rolled down my window. Motioning for Bay, she cracked her window . . . we had no cell service . . . "You keep your tires in my tire tracks, okay?" She nodded her head as she squinted her eyes . . . rainwater was, no doubt, splashing in her eyes as it hit the edge of her window. She gave a thumbs up and rolled up her window.

"Whatever you say, Dad. I will follow you." Her words rang in my ears again . . . and as we eased onto the sloshy, muddy dirt road, I felt the enormity of the pressure to lead my daughter, be it a tornadic thunderstorm, the quicksand of life, or any number of other obstacles . . . she was my child, and she would follow me, for better or worse. I kept a slow but consistent pace in the mud, and I could feel the back tires of my truck spin in the slop. True to my instructions, Bay kept her front tires, as best she could, in the tracks that my truck tires left. As the rain poured even harder, we finally made our way out of the slop and onto a hard-packed base of crushed stone . . . it seemed the worst was over.

An hour later, and we were driving under the streetlights of downtown Tuscaloosa. It was nearly 11 o'clock, but we were safe from the storm. It raced off away from us, and the plan worked perfectly . . . our path had taken us around the backside of the storm as it moved on up through Jasper, Alabama. Hail damage reports were prevalent, though no tornado was ever reported.

From Tuscaloosa, we made our way through Centreville, Alabama, where Hannah and I lived when we were first married, and on into Selma, Alabama . . . home of the civil rights movement. My friend, Michael Jackson, is the district attorney in Selma, Alabama . . . he once suggested to a group of politicians that they "Ought to be careful when trying to con Walt. He isn't a politician. He will walk up into the room and drop a hand grenade of truth on you, and he doesn't care if you are a good ole boy or not." Michael Jackson understands me well . . . and that was one of the highest compliments he ever could have paid me. He will always be my friend because he understands how the law and justice ought to work . . . and has little regard, himself, for politics. The people of Selma are fortunate to have him in their service.

We pulled into a gas station around 12:30 a.m. . . . . "I need some coffee," I told Bay. "I want a snack," she retorted. Seemed that both of us needed a respite . . .

"Daddy, isn't this the way Big Daddy used to drive from Andalusia to see Me-Mama and Papa in Tuscaloosa?"

"It is, sugar. The exact same way. He taught me this route many years ago. It cuts through the back woods and is a lot shorter than going on the interstate."

"It's kind of scary, though," she said. "It was really dark and desolate way out there in the woods." I nodded my head in agreement, "And it's going to be even worse in between here and Greenville because there are only a few houses on the whole road. But we will be fine . . . nothing bad is going to happen. That's why I am here."

I remembered having those same feelings of uncertainty the first time I drove this route after dark. George let out a belly laugh when I told him, "I sure don't want to break down on that road after dark!"

"Hey, Lawd," he said, assuring me that those are salt of the earth people in that part of the world . . . "Somebody will help you out if you ever do break down."

Bay and I pulled out of that Selma parking lot and made our way down what is surely the least lit section of highway in all of Alabama . . . and, despite her fear . . . she followed me. We didn't see a house for at least a dozen miles . . . maybe more. And we didn't see another car at all. Not one . . . for 50 miles. Driving into the abyss, and still . . . she followed me.

Such is life, isn't it?

Dads, your kids are following you. Long before they can ever drive or read or even talk . . . they begin to follow you. Lead them well . . . for they will follow you straight to hell if you lead them there. Bay and I made it home safe that night . . . on through the night we drove, pulling into the driveway at about two o'clock in the morning. As I climbed out of the truck . . . my old bones ached from the long drive, and I stretched them loose . . . Bay came up and gave me a big neck hug. She held me tight, like when she was an infant and she would clamp hold of my index finger . . . she didn't let go. I wrapped my arms around her and squeezed her tight, so that she'd know she was safe. "Thank you, Daddy, for coming to get me and bringing me home . . . " her tired voice slowed . . . "I love you."

"I love you, too, sugar."

And with that, we were home and safe from the storm.

Lead them, men . . . but be careful what path you choose. The Father goes before us and makes our path straight . . . but His efforts are for naught if we won't follow the path He lays out for us. Much like GPS and George's old napkin-drawn road map of instructions, He knows how to keep us safe in the storm. And He did that night, for sure. "Thank you, Lord," I said as I walked into the door of the house. "Thank you for making the path straight and getting us home safe."

And I climbed into bed . . .

The thunder rolls in life far more often than the summertime thunderstorms of the South. Sometimes, we are the shelter our kids seek . . . let us be a strong one.

God Bless.

G O O D   D I R T

At the beginning of April, Banks and I planted red potatoes and Vidalia onions. I confess, I should remember the particular type of red potato . . . but they had no marquee value . . . I just know they are red. Vidalia, on the other hand . . . is the Corvette of onions. Sweet and saucy, the Vidalia, a geographic cousin to the Georgia peach, is the marquee name of onions . . . so, I remember it.

Nonetheless, I digress . . . we planted potatoes and onions.

The day before, I turned rows in the garden spot . . . every country home place has a garden spot. Maybe it doesn't get used every year . . . most, but not every . . . perhaps. But on a country homestead, the garden is always . . . in the same place.

Because there is always fertile ground there.

It was a cooler spring morning—maybe 50 degrees—and as the sun chased the moon out of the morning sky, it brought the warmth of a spring sun-shower with it. Banks and I both wore long sleeves to ward off the chill in earlier morning air . . . but now, each of us contemplated shedding a layer.

The rows in the garden were long and straight. I'd guesstimate they were 100 feet long . . . plenty of room for more potatoes and onions than we could ever eat by ourselves. "Banks, take your two long fingers and stick them straight down in the dirt . . . as far as they will go. Then, take this piece of potato and shove it down in the hole, and then cover it with dirt." She listened intently, and then followed my directions precisely . . . "Daddy, the hole is too small for the potato to fit in." I studied the situation momentarily . . . "Indeed, it is, baby girl. Can you make your fingers fatter and longer?" She grinned in response as I surveyed the wood line for a good stick. "A good stick will fix almost any problem, little princess."

"How about that one?" she asked, pointing a few feet away.

"Looks perfect to me," I offered, picking it up and handing it to her.

"Hmm," she said provokingly.

"What?" I asked.

"I can't get this stick to fix your bad jokes."

Her smile spanned from ear to ear. I laughed and gently pushed her shoulder just enough to roll her off her kneed perch and into the soft dirt. She laughed, "Heeeeyyyyy!"

I pounced and tickled her ribcage relentlessly! "I bet it will fix your sassy jokes!" I retorted.

A minute or two later, she declared "I'm France!" . . . code in our house for, "I surrender!" I pulled her up out of the fresh dirt and helped dust her off. She grinned and giggled as she told me how "mean" I was. She plunged the stick into the ground two fingers deep. I didn't have to explain why the stick was the proper tool . . . she understood it implicitly. It was twice the diameter of her two longest fingers . . . "Works perfect," she offered. I nodded my head and moved back to my row.

Side by side, we planted potato pieces until we reached the end of the row. The dirt was fresh and earthy. Its smell was strong and intoxicating . . . "There is nothing like the smell of fresh dirt, Banks." She nodded, semi-approvingly. I clasped a handful in my hands, letting it sprinkle between my fingers back to the ground. It was cold, even under the warming sun . . . and soft, like talcum powder. "Isn't it interesting to you that God uses this . . . dirt . . . to make things grow?" I drew her attention. "Of all things? It's not pretty. It's not appealing. It's hardly noticeable . . . but without it, nothing grows."

She studied the dirt falling from my hands . . . "I guess He can do whatever He wants," she declared.

"Yes, He can. But why dirt?"

"I don't know," she responded.

"Could it be that everything has a purpose?" I asked. She nodded her head again, sticking a potato deep into the hole and pulling the dark brown soil back over the top. "Can trees grow plants like this? Can concrete? Can sand, even?" She nodded opposingly each time I asked. "What about you? What is it that He wants you to do, that only you can do?"

Not letting me get too caught up in the profoundness of my thoughts, she looked at me snarkily and said, "Plant potatoes." I couldn't help but laugh . . . she did, too.

We finished the potatoes . . . two and a half rows . . . and moved on to the onions.

The onions were given to me by a friend. They were bundles of very small green onions . . . they appeared to be not much more than a piece of pine straw. We gently pulled them apart, careful so as to avoid tearing the stem in two. "This is one finger, right, Dad?" I nodded my head as she plunged her index finger deep into the soil.

She dropped the first onion seedling down into the hole . . . "White end down," I reminded her. The green shaft stuck up out of the hole a few inches. She pulled the dirt back into the hole and covered the white remnants. Soon enough . . . the rest of our half-of-a-potato row was now dotted with the smallest shafts of green, two by two, on either side of the crest of the row.

Over the course of the next two months, Banks and I went a few times to spread fertilizer.

"Why, Daddy? If God made the dirt so good . . . why do we put fertilizer on it?" Occasionally, my kids make me nervous with their questions . . . and for a few seconds, I had to consider her question carefully. She was intuitive, and her question was valid and needed to be answered.

"The fertilizer is not for the soil, baby girl. It's for the plants. The soil is doing its job . . . the plants just need a little help. Kind of like for us, we have the Bible. That is

". . . we planted potatoes and onions.

The day before, I turned rows in the garden
spot . . . every country home place has a garden
spot. Maybe it doesn't get used every year . . .
most, but not every . . . perhaps.

But on a country homestead, the garden is
always . . . in the same place.

Because there is always fertile ground there."

our 'good dirt.' We study the Bible, but we still go to church to listen to the preacher talk about the Bible. That's not because the Bible needs help . . . but because we do."

She nodded her head . . . "So, prayers are like rain?" she asked. I pondered her suggestion for a moment, and, impressed with the thoughtfulness of her analogy, I agreed . . . and then expounded . . . "Answered prayers are like rain."

This past weekend, we began digging the potatoes. My mother, a novice to gardening, happened to be in town for Bay's graduation. "Potatoes grow underground, don't they?"

"Yes, ma'am," I responded . . . "You have to dig them up out of the dirt."

I was reminded of a funny story that Hannah's Uncle Pickens loved to tell. I shared it with Banks as we dug potatoes.

Pickens rented his "big field" to a gentleman farmer who moved down from somewhere up north. The fellow talked of farming for wheat and corn. Pickens cautioned him that wheat would not grow well here, and while corn did well, "We mostly grow peanuts and cotton." Pickens said that a few days later, the fellow was out in the field tilling . . . preparing to set off his rows and plant.

A few months went by, Pickens said, and "Those were some of the finest peanut plants I had ever seen. They were big, dark green plants. He was sure to have a bumper crop." But Pickens went on to explain that the Yankee showed up at his door one day complaining that he was "going to sue the seed broker." Puzzled, Pickens said they strolled across the street and into the field, as the fellow complained about how those plants had not made one single peanut. Pickens chuckled and grabbed the nearest stalk with both hands and pulled vigorously . . . the plant held fast for a moment, and then, with a lurch, it let go. Pickens shook the dirt from the roots and peanuts dangled from the base of the plant like ornaments on a Christmas tree. The Yankee farmer was amazed and ecstatic, all at the same time . . . and Pickens just let out a belly laugh.

"Daddy, are you sure that is a true story?"

All I could tell her was what I knew . . . "It's always been told to me to be a true story," I said with assurance . . . though I was always a bit suspicious myself.

"I guess the man just didn't know what was under all that good dirt," she said, as she picked up a couple of red potatoes and put them into the bucket.

"I guess not, baby girl. I guess not. And you know . . . that dirt is just across the road, and it is not much different than this dirt right here."

She picked up a handful and let it fall between her fingers and float into the gentle breeze . . . "It's good dirt, isn't it?" she asked.

"Yes, it is, baby girl. Yes . . . it . . . is . . . " And the soil is pretty good, too, I thought to myself.

I hope you see the value in this good dirt.

Chapter
FOUR

A FATHER'S OUTDOOR JOURNAL

B U S T E D   P L A N S

anks and I had a full day. Three stops and activities in North Carolina, with the fourth being to summit Mount Sassafras, the highest peak in South Carolina. It was a busy . . . and tight . . . schedule, because we also needed enough daylight time to leave Sassafras and then drive another thirty minutes to our camping location . . . and still have enough time to set up camp and get a fire going before dark.

Now, I've set up plenty of camps after dark, mind you. But it is never preferred. Stuff gets lost, hooked up wrong, overlooked, and broken. I much prefer to have light in my life . . . it always seems to work out better. But oftentimes, light or no light, the ambitions and expectations of life far outweigh the ability and means of men. This day was to be a fine example of such a dilemma. For, you see, Mount Mitchell, Grandfather Mountain, Chimney Rock, and Mount Sassafras were never meant to be conquered all in one day . . . and they would not be on this day either.

And the first three of those locations will be stories for other days . . . for this is truly a story about God working the details out for us, just when we need it most.

Sitting atop Mount Sassafras, I knew the schedule was busted. It was near 7:00 p.m. when we arrived. The sun would set at 7:42 p.m.. I juggled my time between taking in all of the panoramic views and vistas, playing "photoshoot" with Banks, and searching my phone's maps and resources for a hotel . . . something that had never been a part of the plan. It wasn't necessarily that we couldn't still stay at our campsite, but my estimation that it would take thirty minutes to get there was grossly underestimated. "Fifty-one minutes, according to Siri," I told Banks. She furled the corners of her mouth. "Even if we leave now, it will be dark and late." And we were tired.

Mount Sassafras is not the highest of peaks. At only 3,554 feet above sea level, the summit would be the lowest we'd encountered on the trip. Mount Rogers in Virginia was a towering 5,730 feet. Mount Mitchell in North Carolina was a monstrous 6,684 feet. Fact of the matter was . . . Sassafras was simply the little brother to these behemoths we'd already conquered. But we didn't come simply for the climb . . . "Isn't it beautiful, Daddy?" Banks' gaze was affixed on a far-off mountain ridge in those blue-ridged mountains.

"It sure is, baby girl." I, too, was almost hypnotized by the views.

Situated immediately on the North Carolina/South Carolina state line, Sassafras is not easy to get to. But without a doubt, it is worth the effort. In what was nearly a

When I was writing a story called "The Grand Old Dame," . . . though I sometimes refer to it as "Indeed, She is a Grand Old Dame," I had an epiphany about sunsets and sunrises.

But first, you should know that I've always been drawn to that moment in time where day and night mix like Neapolitan ice cream in the microwave. The swirls of the resulting merger create the most glorious of paintings on God's tapestry. This sunset across the Smokey Mountains from high atop Mount Sassafras in South Carolina is no different.

My epiphany . . . that every instant when someone says, "The sun is setting," is also the very instant that someone else proclaims, "The sun is rising." The two occur at the same time . . . from the same event. More than that, though, I realized that the sunset is a reminder that the Son rose. And so, oftentimes when I refer to a setting sun . . . I always resolve the matter with the declaration that the Son also rose.

360-degree panoramic view, we could see huge freshwater lakes and rivers to the south, towering mountains to the north, and a blazing orb on a crash course with one of those famous blue ridges to our west. "Are we going to stay for the sunset, Daddy?" And who could say no to that?

I sure couldn't . . . "We sure are," I responded. And, so, we did.

And in that moment, when the sun slid behind those far off mountains, I said a silent prayer . . . thanking God for all He had provided to us in this natural state. Certainly, technology and advancements can be considered gifts from our Creator, but I think, too often, we fancy ourselves improving upon His perfection when we invent new technologies. Creation, in and of itself, was perfect. I've always struggled with the concept of man improving on what God did. Now, I recognize that God is in the improvements as well. Certainly, He inspired Gutenberg to print the first mass produced Bible . . . and so I understand that advancement and the perfection of Creation need to coexist. But . . . in this moment, there was nothing more perfect than standing on top of this stubby little mountain with my 12-year-old daughter, watching the sun set upon a landscape of pure beauty that could never be captured or replicated by even the best artists.

The jagged, blue-ridged peaks danced in layers across the skyline. A thin grey haze lay in the valley floors between them, and as the eye unpeeled each layer of the ridges, the hues of blue and grey changed . . . some blues turned purple, and some grays turned white. What was left was the forest green of the spruce and fir trees that blanketed both mountain and valley. This pristine landscape was mostly untouched by man. A few houses dotted the shoreline of a far-away lake, and if one was particularly intentional, they could detect a cut through the forest where surely a road or a powerline must be hidden. And all of this tapestry was covered by a veil of red and orange and purple, laid in place by the setting sun . . . above it, its fire giving way to the blue of the sky.

"This is why I find peace in the great outdoors, Banks." She nodded her head in affirmation. I needed not explain my remarks . . . she understood completely. Anyone incapsulated in this particular moment would understand. I'm not sure I have ever experienced another sunset like it.

"Just think, Daddy, if we had been on time, we would've left here two hours ago," Banks astutely observed. Not having considered the point myself, I grinned and nodded my head, for she was absolutely correct.

"Maybe a busted plan is a good plan after all," I retorted. She laughed. I did, too. Then we drifted back into the silence of the moment and soaked up the remaining few seconds of the sun's desperate attempt to remain visible. Alas, it finally surrendered to the far ridges of the mountains . . . and disappeared into tomorrow.

"I think God knew what He was doing."

"What do you mean?" I asked.

"When He made us late. When our day ran long, and we got here late. I think all that happened just so we could watch the sunset," Banks responded.

Again, the depths of her pontifications caught me off guard . . . she had twice pondered thoughts I had not considered. But given the beauty of all we had just encountered; I couldn't disagree with her conclusion. "I think you are right, baby girl. I think He knew exactly what He was doing."

In the waning twilight, we sat on a huge boulder at the edge of a cliff, holding hands and listening to the sounds around us. An occasional puff of a breeze through the trees; the last chirps of the songbirds saying goodnight to each other, as if they, too, knew the Waltons and John Boy; and, not to be outdone, the howl of a hound dog somewhere far off down in the valley floor . . . it was a serenade like no other . . . and we simply sat and listened. No words . . . just an experience.

Light faded into darkness, and it was well past time to go. The first few stars of night were starting to introduce themselves, and while there was still a crest of sunlight on the horizon, it would soon abandon us completely. And still, with no hotel room secured . . . we had a mission ahead of us. "On the road again . . . " Banks started singing as we climbed back into the big diesel truck.

I joined in with her . . . "Like a band of gypsies, we go down the highway." We both laughed as the engine roared to life and we began our slow, gradual, curvy, winding descent out of the Timmerman Natural Resource Area at Jocassee Gorges, all part of a vast Management Area maintained by the state of South Carolina. Soon, though, deep in the canyons of the mountain roads, we found ourselves with no cellular service and no plan.

We stopped at the first hotel we came to. It was fifty minutes down the road. A trout fishing lodge set in the River's Bend . . . hence the same name . . . and there was no answer at the door. Banks managed to get a call through, and the voice on the other end seemed less than helpful. "No rooms," she said after she hung up. From the parking lot of the River's Bend, we called the Hampton Inn . . . the only mainstream hotel that was anywhere near us . . . "No rooms," she said after thanking the desk clerk for his time.

"Let's just keep driving," I said. And, so, we did. All the while, Banks was steadily calling one place after another. Most had "no rooms available," but it was because most were seasonal locations dedicated to trout fishing and tourists . . . and we were just a few weeks ahead of the season's opening. Almost resigned to driving an hour or more to the next "big" town, I told her to try "that one . . . " Reluctantly, she did . . . it was called the Brook Trout Inn, and no other trout lodges were receiving guests. She had little reason to think this call would end any differently.

"Yes, ma'am. Ummm . . . do you have any rooms available tonight?"

"Well, ordinarily, we would not take guests this late at night. But it just so happens that my parents are staying at the Inn tonight, and my dad is down in the lobby right now." A nice lady on the other end of the phone talked Banks through where to go and what to do . . . and we breathed a sigh of relief that, at least, we had found a place to slumber.

"She was really nice, Daddy." That was encouraging . . . because we both feared we were about to walk into a musty and outdated trout fisherman's hotel.

The Brook Trout Inn's proprietor was a delightful Christian woman. She received us with warmth and gratitude, and I knew that these "busted plans" had a purpose. Banks fried eggs that morning in the common kitchen while this "nice lady" (as Jackie Gleason always said in Smokey and the Bandit) conversed with her . . . as two adults might do over breakfast. I simply watched and listened as Banks was growing up before my very eyes.

"Maybe that means it will be a nice place, too."

She nodded, and said, "As long as it is clean and has a bed, I'll be okay."

Twenty minutes later, a kind, compassionate, and friendly gentlemen checked us into our room at the Brook Trout Inn. Far from a fishing lodge, this small, quaint, family-run motel was a delight to find for us weary travelers. The room was posh compared to our meager camping accommodations, for sure, but more than that . . . it was a really well-appointed room. A big, fluffy, king-sized bed, a good heater, a television—which we never turned on—and, best of all . . . a hot shower. "Heaven . . . " Banks giggled as she fell into the bed. I had to agree.

We both slept like logs . . . treehouses and campsites are not the best place to find deep slumber. So, this soft bed and warm room made for the perfect environment. "You snored like a bear last night," Banks said as we walked to the Inn's kitchen area for breakfast.

I knew I couldn't argue with her, but I did feel obliged to tell her, "You did, too!" We both chuckled and celebrated a good night's sleep as we met our hostess and the Innkeeper, Julie. She held a tray of Belgian waffles in one hand and a tray of biscuits in the other.

"Good morning, y'all! I made some extra breakfast for everyone this morning," she offered as she met us coming through the door.

And now that we'd had a good night's sleep, Banks and I were both ready to eat some "real" food . . . Banks turned and looked at me and said, "See, I told you this was Heaven!" I laughed again, and within just a few minutes, we were chowing down on a breakfast fit for a king. Banks scrambled some eggs in the full kitchen, and we chatted about our adventures. Julie and her husband bought the Inn in 2015, and with the help of their three girls and a boy as the caboose, they opened in 2017. They are great Christian folks, and our time with them was as encouraging and uplifting as it was relaxing and belly-filling!

Loading up in the truck for the next leg of the journey, I turned to Banks and said, "You were right." She looked at me with a puzzled expression . . . "I think He knew exactly what He was doing when He busted our schedule yesterday." She smiled and nodded her head . . .

Sometimes the best plans are the ones He controls . . . not the ones we make.

Hope y'all have a wonderful day . . . even if nothing you planned works out.

——ALIENS, ASTRONAUTS,—— AND THE PERFECT PICTURE

I intended to post Chapter Six of *The Current River Chronicles* today, but life happens, and sometimes, it's spectacular. Other times, it's just funny. Sometimes, it is both . . . so I'll wait to continue *The Current River Chronicles* and tell this fantastical tale of astronauts, Clark Griswold, and two of my girls.

"Girls, the SpaceX capsule is making re-entry tonight. Spinks Megginson from RedZone Weather posted on his Facebook page that we should be able to see it from here. It's going to splash down in the northern Gulf of Mexico somewhere south of us."

Banks looked at me curiously . . . "Is Spinks Megginson an astronaut? Cause his name sounds like an alien name!" I chuckled a little bit at her suggestion, and before I could answer, she added, "I bet he is one of those nasty-looking aliens hiding in a human body!"

We both laughed. "Spinks is a meteorologist. He covers all of south Alabama," I retorted.

She knew what the word meant, but to be funny, she said, "If he covers meteors, why is he talking about spaceships?"

"This will be a historic event, girls." Hannah turned and seemed interested. She and I once stood under the midnight sky on Mobile Bay, basking under the glow of Haley's Comet . . . perhaps she was harkening back to younger days. Banks listened pretty intently, and Cape, the Middle Princess, all but rolled her eyes at me. "I already asked Cousin Lynn if we could go over to the big field behind her house," I said. "She said it would be fine. I think we will get a good shot at seeing the re-entry from that field because it is so open to the south."

"What is it going to look like? How can you even see it at night?" Banks' curiosity was peaking.

"A giant fireball with a long comet's tail," Hannah responded.

"Yes," I chimed in. "When any spaceship comes through the atmosphere, the friction between the spaceship and the atmosphere itself causes the ship to heat up so much that it almost catches on fire."

Banks listened intently. By now, Cape even seemed halfway interested. "I've always wanted to go to Cape Canaveral and watch the Space Shuttle launch," I offered with some measure of dreaminess in my voice. "This might be as close as we ever get to seeing a spaceship. This is the real thing, and this kind of thing has never happened near Alabama."

We discussed it for a few more minutes, and I assured Banks that Spinks was not an alien, reminding her that I had lunch with him not too long ago . . . "You're just lucky he didn't eat you," she quipped.

"Alright, we leave at 9 o'clock! Make sure you are bundled up . . . it's cold outside!" I instructed.

Thirty minutes later, we pulled into the big field a half of a mile from our house. The night sky was majestic enough by itself. The crescent moon that I had admired a few hours ago was gone. Venus, which I had observed nearly holding hands with the moon, was also gone. Orien and his belt marked the eastern sky, and Banks, the astrologist that she is, shouted, "There's the Little Dipper," when she found it. A bright planet loomed to the northwest, but I confess . . . I don't know which one it was.

The air was perfectly crisp. Not so cold that it burned your cheeks, but cold enough that it was refreshing . . . a jacket was in order to keep the cold at bay, but the crispness lifted your spirits and made you stand a little taller . . . as opposed to it being so cold that you recoiled at first exposure.

I stood, admiring all of God's creation and grinning from ear to ear—like Clark Griswold just before he plugged in his Christmas lights—and said, "Isn't it beautiful, kids? Look! You can even see the Milky Way with your naked eye!"

"Where?" Hannah asked. All three of them turned to look where I gestured. I traced the Milky Way with my hands as it passed directly overhead and reached from the east to the west. I missed a great opportunity to teach a valuable lesson then . . . I'll remind you of it now. For me, it is nearly impossible to stand under the vastness of the night's sky and not feel a sense of awe and wonder about what an awesome God we serve. And as I traced the arch of the Milky Way overhead, I should have reminded the girls that, "As far as the east is from the west, so far He has removed our transgressions from us." Psalm 103:12, NIV. Not only has He made all that there is from the east to the west . . . He has also forgiven us of as much.

Perhaps, I'll remember to remind the girls of that lesson at another nighttime adventure. "Girls, that way is south." I pointed toward a clump of trees at the southern end of the field. "The fireball should come from there," gesturing with my arm, "to here. When it comes, I want to take a selfie with all of us and the fireball in the background."

"You and your pictures," Cape grumbled.

"It should be any minute now." I pulled an orange from my pocket and started to peel it.

"What is it with you and your oranges?" Cape asked. She knows how much I love them. I think she was aggravated to find herself standing in the middle of a field at 9:30 p.m. at night in 40-something-degree air.

"Want a piece?" I asked. She shook her head no, with her hands shoved deep into her jacket pockets. "Is that your boyfriend's jacket?" I asked. She nodded her head. "Well, from now on, you can only wear my jackets. I'm your daddy. I'm the one that should be keeping you warm." She rolled her eyes again . . . but she knew I was teasing . . .

sort of. I do tell her frequently that no man will ever love her as much as I do . . . and she knows it.

"What if they crash?" Banks asked.

"Well, let's pray for them," I responded. So, we did. We prayed that they would come home safely and return to their families. Hannah then shared her recollections with the girls of the Challenger explosion. It was somber for the next few minutes . . . but healthy, nonetheless.

Just as I put the last piece of orange into my mouth, a fireball erupted on the horizon. It was distant and less than the spectacular fireworks that I had expected . . . but a fireball, nonetheless. "Theree iiiddd iizzzz," I exclaimed with a mouthful of orange. I pointed southwesterly. Everyone turned to embrace it . . . and, for a moment . . . it was a beautiful thing. All of my girls, save Bay, stood in awe of SpaceX.

Silence for five seconds.

"Let's take a picture! Y'all line up!"

We stacked up in a line with the fireball behind us. Hannah, then me. Banks, then Cape. I held out my arm and pushed the little white circle on my iPhone screen. A flash erupted like lightning in the sky. Not only did I have the phone turned the wrong way, but I also left the flash on! As I had the camera right next to Cape's head . . . I'm pretty sure I did permanent retinal damage to her . . . she recoiled, fussing and groaning about being blinded. Like a goofus, I laughed a little bit as I tried to get the flash turned off and the phone turned around.

"Okay. Okay, I got it. Sorry!" I felt a sense of urgency to get the picture, so we all lined up again . . . little white button . . . press . . . and again, FLASH! This time, we were all blinded... a collective groan came from my audience. Embarrassed, I sheepishly gave up my effort to take a picture . . . "Okay. Never mind. I give up." As it was . . . I took the perfect picture of our vehicle... nothing more.

Turning back to the southern sky, we watched for another ten seconds as SpaceX's descent slowed and lowered out of the upper atmosphere. Almost as quickly as it had come . . . it was gone.

We ambled our way back to the truck and loaded up. There was an air of excitement about us, for we all knew we had just witnessed history. "Girls, that's the first time I've ever seen anything like that. It was pretty awesome." Hopeful for a round of ovation and accolade from the back seat . . . I got nothing. And then it hit me . . . "I'm like Clark Griswold," I said out loud.

"You sure are," Hannah said without even a hint of hesitation, and then she started laughing.

"Who?" Banks asked.

"You know, *Christmas Vacation*. The dad who has all the corny dad jokes, and he always wants everything to be perfect, and nothing he ever does is. It's always a disaster. And it is so bad that it is funny, and all you can do is laugh."

"Okay. Okay, I got it. Sorry!" I felt a sense of urgency to get the picture, so we all lined up again . . . little white button . . . press . . . and again, FLASH!

This time, we were all blinded... a collective groan came from my audience. Embarrassed, I sheepishly gave up my effort to take a picture . . . "Okay. Never mind. I give up." As it was . . . I took the perfect picture of our vehicle... nothing more.

Banks laughed and said, "Oh yeah . . . that's you, Dad." I couldn't see Cape, but I knew she agreed, too.

And they were right. Rarely does anything I plan for the girls go as I hope it will. But it always seems to work out disastrously perfect.

God is good, even in my imperfections.

IT WILL ALL COME TOGETHER IN THE END

"Brrrrrt. Brrrrrt. Brrrrrt."

I opened my eyes, startled by the vibration of my phone buzzing. Looking around to find my phone, I saw "Travis" flashing on the screen. Glancing out the bedroom window, I realized, "It's really early," and I grabbed the phone.

"Hey, good morning," I greeted him, halfway trying to conceal that he woke me up.

"Good morning. You still asleep?" he asked cordially.

"Busted," I thought to myself. "Yeah, but I needed to get up. I was supposed to get up and go hunting with Banks, but the bed sure was feeling good when the alarm went off."

"Well, let me just try to call someone else," he responded.

Immediately, I knew he needed some help. "No, no, no," I insisted. "It's all good. What's up?"

"Anna just killed her first buck this morning," he offered, with a hint of proud father in his voice.

"That's awesome!" I quickly responded.

"But yesterday afternoon, we were hunting and shot a big hog. The hog ran off in the woods, and we searched until dark. This morning, tracking her buck, we found the hog not five feet from the buck. It's the craziest thing. This is a big hog. He's at least 200 pounds, but probably 250 or more. I need help loading him into the truck. I just can't get him by myself."

"No problem, man. Give me about twenty minutes, and I'll be on my way."

I was laying in Banks' bed. I had accidentally fallen asleep there last night. Hanging up the phone, I turned to find Banks propped up on one elbow, listening intently. "Can I go?" she asked before I could even fill her in on the details.

"You know it, girl," I affirmed. "Come on, let's get dressed."

Cranking the truck, the dash thermometer read 26 degrees. Pulling down the driveway, Banks shivered a bit . . . "Jack Frost is everywhere!" she exclaimed. And, true enough, the ground was frosty white everywhere you looked. The morning sun's rays shimmered off the frosty crystals, and it seemed the entire forest had been privy to a disco party. White fields rolled up and down the powerlines and on the edges of the road . . . occasionally, we spied a set of tracks crossing out across one of the

Life is learned before it is ever experienced. Travis Martin taught his daughters, Anna and Kaitlyn, in much the same way as Hannah and I taught our girls. And I know those common threads of parenting are some of the strongest ties that bind.

And this two-for day that they enjoyed . . .well, it was special for us to be there just to help.

frost-covered meadows . . . and the sky was as clear blue as we'd ever seen. The moon hung proudly above . . . refusing to give way to the sun . . . and its marble-like presence only added to the majesty of the morning.

Even in the truck, our breath froze. Banks deliberately blew out long dragon's breath . . . watching the "smoke" roll from her lips and out into the truck. Ice clung desperately to the lower part of the windshield. A swipe of the windshield wipers only made matters worse, and I knew that the frigid wind that resulted from the truck barreling down the highway would only serve to freeze the ice harder. I turned the defrost on full blast . . . but I knew it was virtually pointless . . . "The heater doesn't work," Banks reminded me.

"I know. I guess I just thought a little air moving might help."

It didn't.

Five minutes later, we turned down a long and winding driveway . . . a nice, widowed lady lives here... Travis had always helped her, and in return, she let him hunt her land. A set of dually tracks turned out through the Jack Frost-y field. I knew that to be his truck, so I followed. Rolling over a few terraces and snaking around by a woodland pond . . . the warm water condensed and lifted as steam through the cold air . . . we followed the tracks into a back field. This field, surrounded by heavy hardwoods and tall Southern pines, was almost completely shaded. Consequently, the ice lay thick on the green winter grasses. The emerald elegance was shaded white . . . and was even more impressively beautiful.

Travis and Anna sat in their truck at the opposite end of the field. Soon enough, we met with handshakes and hugs . . . and then it was story time.

Anna's face beamed with pride as she began to tell us the story. Yesterday afternoon, they came to this same spot to hunt for Anna's first buck, but with darkness setting in, they decided to head home. Packing up their gear, Anna noticed movement in the edge of the woods. Frozen in time, they sat motionless to await whatever creature was about to make its grand entrance. A few tense seconds passed, and a behemoth south Alabama boar hog barreled out into the field. (Now, for the unfamiliar, wild hogs are a nuisance. They destroy cropland by the millions of dollars every year, and they reproduce at a fantastic rate. And, while boar meat is usually not very good, it is still best to take him out of the circle of life, to avoid the reproduction and destruction that he might otherwise create.) With one shot, Anna pierced the giant, through and through. He fell, but then stood back up and darted for the tree line. Travis added, "I looked for him until it was dark, but we never found him."

A word of caution here . . . wild boars are dangerous. Just like in the Disney movies, these Alabama boars have razor sharp tusks . . . so sharp that, with growth and maturity, they cut themselves through the boar's top snout and protrude out like elephant tusks. So, tracking a wounded boar in the deep woods, and in the dark, is not necessarily safe. "I wouldn't have looked for him after dark, either," I offered to Travis as consolation.

Anna continued her once-in-a-lifetime tale. "This morning, Dad was my alarm clock. He came in and said, 'It's time to get up.' I sure didn't want to, but now I am glad I did."

They came to the same field and sat in the same ground blind . . . "He came out and started walking down the edge of the tree line," Anna continued. "At first, I thought it was a doe, because his antlers were so dark brown that they blended in perfectly with the trees. But as he got closer, I realized he was a buck."

And with one shot, Anna claimed her first buck . . . a fine one, too . . . a nice, south Alabama 9-point... I know grown men who've hunted their entire lives and never killed one as big.

"It was kind of funny," Travis offered. "There was a lot of blood, so he was easy to track. He didn't run far . . . just a short piece into the woods. We walked up on him and were standing there looking at him and celebrating, when . . . bam! There was the hog . . . lying dead not five feet from the buck. We were both excited to find them both!"

They already had the buck loaded up in the bed of the truck when Banks and I got there. He was a true, main frame 8-point, with one little kicker. "They say if you can slip a ring onto the point, then you can count it. I'd say that little kicker will hold a ring, so I think that is definitely a 9-point," I suggested. Travis agreed, and Anna's smile grew just a bit wider.

A few minutes later, we had that big hog loaded into the back of the truck . . . it took all four of us . . . and then we took a few pictures. We said our goodbyes, hugged necks, and loaded back into our heater-less truck! Travis and Anna were off to clean their smorgasbord . . . if they had a few fish to add to the basket, they would have a true south Alabama cornucopia . . . and Banks and I headed to the house.

My alarm clock had gone off at 5:15 on this morning. Without much hesitation, I turned it off. It was frightfully dark outside and bitter cold. My body craved that warm bed, and Banks was sleeping as snug as a bug in a rug . . . no reason to wake her. Within a minute or two, I was back into my deep sleep . . . all snuggled up and content. I recollect, though, as I drifted into oblivion . . . a feeling of regret. Regret that, perhaps, Banks and I might miss an opportunity together. "Maybe I should get up," I wrestled with my subconsciousness. But alas, sleep prevailed. Driving to meet Travis, that same tinge of regret reappeared. "If we had gotten up, Banks might have taken her first buck, too," I considered silently. So, I resolved that we would hunt mid-morning, as soon as we returned.

And that is where we sit . . . now . . . as I type this. In the shooting house, with two does grazing just a few yards away. "Maybe today will be her day, too."

But regret is not something I live with. I hope you don't, either . . . for, you see, Banks didn't get to kill a big buck early this morning, but still, it all came together in the end.

Travis regretted not finding the hog last night. I could hear it in his voice as he told

I try to find ways to isolate the girls from technology, even if but for a few minutes. Whenever Banks and I are hunting together, she has no distractions, except for whatever might be in the field. Sometimes, we sit silently. Sometimes, we whisper. Other times, we get tickled and laugh out loud . . . but it only happens because neither of us are distracted by the world.

me the story. I could tell he wanted Anna to have the accomplishment of taking that big hog. But the good Lord worked it out for the two of them . . . for, unbeknownst to them, the buck she shot would lead them straight to the hog. It all came together in the end.

This morning, I regretted not getting up and taking Banks hunting. But what if I had?... and at nearly 7:00 a.m., Travis had called? Sitting in the shooting house, I wouldn't have answered. I would have sent him a text that said, "Hunting with Banks. Is it an emergency?" He would have said, "No," and then, hours later, I would have called him. We would have missed a great opportunity to visit and celebrate with friends over their success. Instead, though, Banks and I slept a little longer and had the excitement of seeing a great deer and a massive hog . . . and spent some time with great friends. It all came together in the end.

And that's what *Shepherding Outdoors* is all about. To us . . . we like meat, and we like trophies . . . but the best trophies of all are in the stories and the memories.

OLE BETSY

"Brrrreeeerrrrr" . . . the big six-cylinder Perkins diesel engine roared to life. The entire red frame of the Massey Ferguson shook under my rear end, and the floor plates vibrated to a numbing pace under my feet as the tractor transformed from a sedentary red rock—quiet and still—to a fire-breathing amber dragon billowing smoke as she roared . . . all with the simple twist of a key.

Affectionately, I refer to her as Betsy. Well, truth be told, I affectionately refer to every truck, boat, tractor, canoe, kayak, lawnmower, or other device which I can ride on or in as Betsy. My Old Towne canoe is Betsy. My black Dodge truck is Betsy. And, yes, my Massey Ferguson 4263 is Betsy. I don't exactly know why I have such an affinity for Betsy . . . it is what it is. This Betsy, though . . . she was a shiny, red, 1999, 100-horsepower tractor. No cab or fancy air conditioner . . . this Betsy was a working man's tractor. An open cockpit so you could smell the dirt, feel the summer blaze, and get stung by yellowjackets. And she was my first tractor.

Now, my daddy owned several tractors on his small horse and cattle operation in Baldwin County. He harvested pecans, too, but he mostly used his tractors for hay and such. A Kubota and a Ford 5000 sat side by side for several years in the barn. I remember how much my 13-year-old self felt like a man when I climbed up on top of that big Ford. I used to volunteer to bushhog, especially out by the road.

"All the cute girls always wave to a boy on a tractor," I'd tell myself. And they did. I'd smile as big as the moon and wave like a dog's tail as they passed by. Occasionally, I'd get a horn honk, and every once in a while, some group of teenaged girls might holler as they passed. On those days, I could barely get my puffed-out chest and big head through the barn doors to put the tractor up. "Pretty girls and driving the tractor," I once thought to myself. "This has to be the best day ever."

Years later, I shared some of those recollections with my daddy. He laughed and remarked that he already knew of my predilection for waving at girls from the tractor. "So I got some of the girls from up the road to drive by and wave and honk, 'cause I knew you'd keep bushhogging 'til sundown on the hope they might come back by," he said, letting out a belly laugh that nearly sent him into a coughing fit. At the time, I thought he was joking. Surely that old man wasn't smart enough to outwit the likes of a "man" like me . . . and what girl wouldn't want to honk and wave simply out of sheer admiration? Now, though, I am not so sure . . .

"Affectionately, I refer to her as Betsy. Well, truth be told,
I affectionately refer to every truck, boat, tractor, canoe,
kayak, lawnmower, or other device which I can ride on or
in as Betsy. My Old Towne canoe is Betsy. My black Dodge
truck is Betsy. And, yes, my Massey Ferguson 4263 is Betsy.
I don't exactly know why I have such an affinity for Betsy . . .
it is what it is. This Betsy, though . . . she was a shiny, red, 1999,
100-horsepower tractor. No cab or fancy air conditioner . . .
this Betsy was a working man's tractor. An open cockpit so
you could smell the dirt, feel the summer blaze, and get
stung by yellowjackets. And she was my first tractor."

That old Kubota of his . . . well, let's just say my daddy liked orange tractors before most anyone else had ever heard of Kubota. It was small . . . maybe a 30-horsepower tractor . . . with big fat turf tires on the back. I honestly don't ever remember "working" with it, but I lost count of how many laps I made around the imaginary dirt tract in the pasture . . . especially when the grass was still wet and the dirt was still muddy from fresh rain. Of all the things my daddy did get mad at me about, he never fussed about me driving the Kubota like I was Tony Stewart at Watkins Glen International.

I couldn't drive Betsy like that, though. She was too big, and though she was fast . . . faster than the Kubota . . . one sharp turn, and her big agricultural tires would cut deep and flip her right into a rollover. Betsy was more of a log truck than she was a racecar. Plus . . . I'm way too old to drive my tractor like an idiot.

I plowed my first "real" garden with Betsy. Not one ear of corn came out, and the stalks looked like the variety of clowns you'd expect to find at the circus. This one tall, that one short; this one with long leaves, this one with none. I sort of enjoyed bushhogging those sterile cornstalks in the fall, gave me some satisfaction knowing the tractor did manage to do something productive. But the next year, corn grew plentiful, and, for years since, so have the potatoes and onions, sunflowers and zinnias. Ole Betsy has turned many a row in her life.

And so has my father-in-law's old John Deere. The green tractor isn't nearly as big as Betsy, but plenty strong still. He taught me how to turn rows on that tractor. He also taught me how to log. And we've pulled more logs than I can count out of the woods to the Wood-Mizer sawmill.

Yes, sir . . . I've spent many an hour on an orange tractor, a blue tractor, and a green tractor. But Betsy . . . she was *my* first tractor. Not my daddy's . . . not my father-in-law's . . . but mine. And it wasn't until I had *my* tractor that I came to appreciate what they mean for a family . . .

"Don't you drop her!" Hannah yelled over the growl of the motor. Banks screamed like my hands were ice cold and tried to lurch away from me. She was maybe six months old, and she was madder than a hornet. I swaddled her up in the blanket and coddled her in my left arm. I pulled her close to my chest, and she tried to worm her legs back and forth against the pull of the blanket.

"Come on, girl . . . we are going to make laps like Watkins Glen," I whispered in her ear. She had been crying for an hour. She was going through a phase where it made her mad to fall asleep. Hannah was nearing her wits' end that afternoon. When she came out on the back porch of our tiny farm house, I knew she was spent. I throttled the tractor down to idle and shifted it out of gear. Hopping down, I walked over to the porch and said, "Come on, I have a plan." She was bewildered—and probably mad that I didn't take the baby from her immediately. I said, "Follow me," and led her back to the still growling tractor. I climbed back up to my seat and held my hands out . . . "Hand her to me." And she did, with the admonition about not dropping the baby.

I shifted Betsy into a lower gear and eased off the clutch. We crawled forward at no more than a dog's trot. Banks settled down a little as the world started passing her by. I steered out into the pasture, and we made our first turn. The tractor bumped and burped along, never absorbing any of the divots or holes her wheels found. And with each jolt, Banks' head rested heavier and heavier on my chest. By turn three of our four-mile-an-hour racetrack, Banks' eyes were closed, and by the time I did the second figure eight, she was sound asleep and limp as a wet noodle.

I drove around the pasture for another thirty minutes as Hannah watched from the swing on the back porch. My arm was cramping, but I fought through the discomfort, knowing that Hannah was enjoying the peace and the scenery. I laughed at myself as we passed near the house and she waved and blew me a kiss . . . "Still got it," I chuckled. I grinned from ear to ear and said out loud, "Cute girls like boys on tractors."

Betsy has been a good tractor. She still is. We still plant with her and do our food plots. Once, Bay got my truck axle stuck deep in the mud, and Ole Betsy pulled it right on out. Cape still likes to drive Betsy around sometimes, and Banks has a time or two as well. That old John Deere is still around, too. We use her pretty regularly . . . but not for the big jobs. And we added a little orange to the mix, too, with a Kubota mini-excavator. Cape can run it better than most operators I know.

Those tractors have a lot of miles on them. A lot of hours, too, turning rows and plowing fields . . . all so we can feed our stomachs. But they are so much more than machines . . . best of all, we've made a lot of memories on those tractors . . . and that feeds the soul.

I love this picture. George was such a great man, and he loved his grandchildren . . . even when they had their bottom lip pooched out, pouting because they didn't want to take a picture! Cape always has been the one who marches to the beat of her own drum . . . started at an early age, too!

SHIMMER IN THE CURRENT

The steam rolls off the brim of my coffee cup, like a dragon whispering in the cool of the morning. The heat from the fresh, warm brew feels good on my lips and my cheeks as I hold the cup to the edge of my mouth. The nostalgic aroma of "Folgers in my cup" wafts my nose, and the warmth from within radiates through the cup and into the palms of my hands.

"Good morning, world," I offer, as I watch the opposing sky grow from pink to orange. The layers of color in the horizon look like swirls of cotton candy . . . some blue, some orange, some pink. Directly overhead, the stars fight desperately for survival, as the encroaching sunlight fast ravages what glimmer they have left.

The darkness retreats.

A bump in the twilight draws my attention elsewhere, as my eyes strain into the groggy morning light to see what might be nearby. And what to my wondering eyes do appear? But a slender black creature with a bright white stripe! Alarmed at the sight, I run away! Run away! Fright as I might!

Ah, but yes, my little furry friend has no more interest in visiting with me than I do with him . . . and thankful I am that he does not leave me with his aromatic gift, I sit back down on the hillside to gaze back into the wide wonder of it all. As I do, the gentle nudge of the honeysuckle finds its way around, first my feet . . . its vines wrapping around my bare ankles and toes . . . and then my nose, as her sweet and sultry invitation beckons me to pluck a few of her stamen. Resting the tips on my tongue, I draw the sweet honey from their lines, and I delight in the natural sugar that is the perfect complement to my morning coffee.

The river gently rolls below. An occasionally drift of a cool breeze makes its way up the hillside to my perch . . . the coolness of the waters infects the air . . . and lays around me like a blanket of chill. The spring-fed blue waters are never much more than 60 degrees . . . and on this 70-degree morning, the chill of the water could run even the strongest of polar bears back for cover.

The blue and green of the water dances and rolls . . . with each passing turn, the blue fades to green, and the green turns to blue. In her shallowest depths, she is crystal clear . . . such that, were she still, one would think her to be glass. And as the light rises towards the sky . . . her darkest depths give way to shades of grey, then blue.

Her song is one of elegance and beauty. Always twisting and turning, she dances on from the night and greets the day with the same energy as she left it with. With each trickle and lap and drip of her dance, she moves and twists and turns in the most elegant ballet.

And then the songbirds join in her chorus. The grey and white mockingbird beckons, and the red-headed woodpecker whistles. The yellow-bellied wrens join in with the blue jays' squawks.

Best of all, though . . . the whip-poor-wills.

It's certainly an overwhelming symphony of so many of the wide wonders . . . colors indescribable, sounds unimaginable, touches unrepeatable, and smells so intoxicating.

God is good this Sunday morning . . . as all His creation says good morning . . . and just when everything seems to be in perfect unison . . . the band plays, and the lady dances . . . the grand prince makes his entrance. Announcing to all the world that the Light will always prevail . . . that warmth will always evaporate the cold . . . like the champion that is his Creator, the sun climbs over the rim of these mountains where the red ferns grow . . .

And, for the first time this morning . . . the waters of this Current River shimmer at the coming day.

God bless you all.

With a twinkle in her eye that could light up the world . . .

THE WILD LIFE

As is often the case when any dad talks to any of his children, matters of fact espoused by me are often challenged by my girls.

"There is no way that is right, Dad." Bay, my oldest daughter, who was maybe 10 at the time, was confident in her defiance. "There is no way we have more animals and bugs in Alabama than any other state."

"I'm not sure exactly how it works, Bay, but I promise we are considered the most biodiverse state in the country." My retort was not very convincing.

Of course, had our friend, neighbor, and UPS driver, Mr. Pete, stuck his head in the door and declared, "Alabama is the most biodiverse state in the country!" Well, then . . . Bay would have declared him a genius and awarded him a Nobel Prize!

But for me . . . I am just "dumb ole Dad." So, I turned to Hannah to be my backup. "Don't look at me," she said as she quickly distanced herself from the debate. "I don't have the foggiest clue if you're right."

"Thanks, riblet," I muttered under my breath. Hannah resents any remark I ever jokingly make that points toward the fact that the Good Lord made man first. She usually retorts with some equally sarcastic remark about how if man had been "up to snuff, God wouldn't have had to make woman . . . but y'all couldn't cut it by yourselves." Luckily this time, she didn't hear my gruff, but I admit, I did think to myself a few other disparaging thoughts likening her to the villainous member of the tag team "wrastlin' match" that betrays his partner to help the bad guys win the match.

"You ever heard of the Iron Sheik?" She looked at me like the RCA dog . . . "Huh?"

Back then, we had television, but only basic channels. We picked up WEAR out of Pensacola, WSFA and WAKA out of Montgomery, and WTVY out of Dothan. That was it. No cable, and no internet. That was . . . by choice. We long subscribed to the notion that Worsdworth was right . . . "The world is too much with us," and internet and cable only add to the chaos. Best of all, though, we had public television out of Dozier, Alabama. And with public television came that fellow in the canoe (whose name I don't have permission to use) and the show, *Discovering Alabama*. It's still on air and has won at least one Emmy . . . maybe more. Truly he and the show are Alabama treasures. We watched that show pretty faithfully as the girls grew up. We felt that second to actually being out in nature, the show taught them the importance of being good stewards to what God entrusted us with . . . His majestical creation that we call earth.

And lo and behold, about two weeks after Bay and I went round and round on the subject, that fellow in the canoe declared that Alabama has the most freshwater river miles of any state in the country . . . "Even Alaska," he added. "And that makes Alabama the most biodiverse state in the country."

My head spun around like that little girl on the *Exorcist* movie, and I made a dead cold stare at little miss sassy britches sitting at the far end of the couch. "What?" She had a tone of righteous indignation in her voice.

"You know what," I proclaimed.

"No, I don't." She paused. "What? That thing about the most animals and bugs? That's not what he said." She crossed her arms and turned back to the television.

Well . . . the more things change, the more they stay the same, I suppose. Here I am now, with Bay as my 20-year-old daughter, home for summer break from her studies at Ole Miss. She called a few weeks back to talk of things to come for the summer.

"Could we go kayaking on the Sepulga a few times before the summer heat kicks in?" She referenced the Sepulga River . . . a small river that flows through portions of the Wiregrass and empties into the Conecuh River. We kayaked both rivers more times than I could count as she grew up.

"And maybe we could even go spend some time on the Cahaba, too? And maybe we could go fishing or just ride in the Delta?" She whined just a little as she asked . . . she inadvertently changed her voice slightly, too . . . sounding a bit more like her younger self.

"Baby girl . . . we can do all of those things this summer." And we will.

Because to our family, it was far more important that Bay and her two sisters learn for themselves about the biodiversity of our state. You see, from a scientific standpoint, Alabama is the mother-of-all-states when it comes to biodiversity. With 132,000 freshwater river miles and over 6,000 different species, Alabama is second to none. But more importantly, from a creationist standpoint, Alabama is likened to the Garden of Eden. Everything is right outside our very own back door. And, almost as the Lord offered to Adam and Eve . . . it's all here for our wonder, awe, and enjoyment.

But rather than tell my girls about the Cahaba Lily and show them pictures . . . we paddled the river and saw them firsthand. In fact, on one particular trip, my air mattress deflated, and I stared with insomnia at Cape and Bay, snug as two bugs in a rug, on their air mattress. Finally, near dawn, I crawled out of the tent and stoked the fire. They slept until nearly 8 o'clock and came out bragging about how well-rested they were.

"You ever heard of the Iron Sheik?" I asked. They both shook their head "no" and moved closer to the fire. I prayed for a soothing spirit and a positive attitude. Within a few minutes, we were watching a bald eagle fly straight up the river. Sometimes, the Lord answers prays in unique ways, for this eagle was the first time the girls had ever seen a bald eagle at all, and the first I had ever seen in Alabama, outside of the Raptors at Auburn University. His presence captivated us all and became an easy distraction from my lack of sleep.

Our trip on the Buffalo River was a first in so many ways . . . first long-distance paddle; first multi-night kayak camping trip; first multi-day food pack . . . and on and on. So many things where a disaster, too. Too much of this and not enough of that. It was about 1000 degrees that June. A thunderstorm, the likes of which I've rarely seen. And from it came the grandest of memories and biggest of smiles. We may have failed at individual things . . . like keeping the kayak from flipping . . . but the laughs and smiles we had along the way will last until the grave.

Cape often hunts alone now . . . something few young people will do anymore. Up before dawn, I sometimes hear the door squeak as she ventures out into the darkness of the frigid morning air. She hunts with confidence . . . not fearful of what might befall her, but confident of what she will accomplish. Why take your kids into the woods? Because once they have this sort of earthly confidence, combined with the eternal confidence of salvation . . . nothing can stop them.

"Thank you, Lord," I muttered.

"For what, Daddy?" one of the girls asked, as all of our gazes stayed fixed on the eagle as he glided up the river channel searching for breakfast.

"For . . . this," the other daughter responded with emphasis.

I didn't feel the need to say another thing.

There have been other times when we have been silenced by the beauty and awe that is Alabama. Sunset on Mobile Bay after an afternoon of fishing is about as near to Heaven as one can get, if you ask me. And watching snow fall on the cotton fields of Pickens County is equally beautiful. But neither of those pictures are complete without a boatload of speckled trout or a big whitetail blazing a trail through that new fallen snow.

One of my favorites, though . . . We were alligator hunting in the Delta a few years back. My friend Travis Martin (The Martin Homestead on Facebook); his son, Tyler; and his daughter, Anna, were with us. We've hunted as two families together for many years. Tyler spied a baby alligator sitting on a lily pad fifty feet or so in front of the boat. The girls "oooo'd and aaaa'd" over how cute he was . . . his eyes twinkling in the spotlight. Travis or I, one of us, suggested they enjoy the moment, for he would surely scoot off the pad and hide in the murky depths.

But he did not. In fact, he wouldn't move at all. Drifting ever closer, Tyler leaned down over the front of the boat to get an eagle's eye view. Seeing the problem, Tyler scooped up that baby gator, as he realized he was bound with fishing line. The kids freed him from his restraints, took a few pictures, and sent him back to find his momma . . . unless we did first.

"Funny, isn't it?" Cape pondered. "We came out here to hunt, and we end up setting one free." We all pondered the irony in the darkness of the midnight calm.

"I guess we better take care of them, too . . . if we want to be able to enjoy them," one of the other kids replied.

I sat silent again. Travis did, too. There was nothing we could tell them to add to their understanding. This . . . is a gift. And we shall treasure it.

From the shrimp, oysters, mullet, and redfish, and more of the deltas and bays in the south; to the quail, dove, and black bear of the Wiregrass; to the buck deer, otters, and more of the Black Belt; to the eagles and bobcats of the Cumberland Plateau; to the ducks and fowl of the Highland Lakes . . . we are certainly "blessed and then some."

"The Lord God took the man and put him in the garden of Eden to work it and *keep* it." Genesis 2:15, ESV.

And I pray that we do . . . keep it, that is. That's why we go . . . shepherding outdoors. I pray you do, too.

WILDCATS

As a young dad, I worried as to whether I met with my children's approval. That's not to say that I wanted to be their "friend." No, on the contrary, I always made it clear that I was a parent first, but I still wanted the girls to have a good time when we did things together. I wanted to give good advice. I wanted to give great softball swing instruction. I wanted to always make sure they saw a deer in the green field when we went hunting. I wanted to . . . well, you get the idea.

The fear—if I am being honest—was that if they were bored with the expedition, they would then become bored with me, too. Thankfully, time promoted maturity in my parenting, and now I rarely find myself worrying about whether my children approve of the expedition. In fact, just last night, I told Cape that Travis Martin and I are planning an adventure down the Tombigbee River. We plan to take Cape and Anna, Travis' daughter, with us. They are both the same age and have been friends for most of their lives. Whether Cape has the grandest of times on the Tombigbee is not a concern . . . whether she learns something from the experience . . . well, that is what's important to me.

But, like I said to begin with, that was not always the case.

Cape is our wild child. She once remarked, "The only day I feel normal is on Halloween." Of course, she was four or five at the time, but I'm fairly convinced she was serious. She also had on her Halloween costume . . . she was dressed as a Native American (with a bathmat substituted for a bearskin cloak), and her sister, a cave woman, complete with chicken bones in her hair. "That's my girl . . . that's what normal is in her world," I thought to myself. "Bathmats, feathers, and chicken bones—she gets that from her momma."

I must confess, though, that it was her wild side that helped me understand and learn that meeting my children's expectations shouldn't be a primary objective. In fact, she helped me realize that my fears were inhibiting the girls' growth . . . and it all happened one fateful midday hunt in Pickens County, Alabama.

I had planned to get up early and go sit in what we called "The Bottoms" with the hope of catching a late rut bruiser buck cruising through the hardwood timber. My alarm went off at 5:00 a.m., and the heat in the old farmhouse was working overtime trying to warm the drafty house. I felt the chill on my feet as they met the hardwood floors, and a shiver ran up my legs. Quickly, I slid into my long johns and tip-toed into the kitchen. Hannah shuffled a bit in the bed as I tried not to wake her . . . but the cold got to her, so she grabbed a big armful of the covers from my side of the bed and double wrapped.

Standing in the kitchen, the electric eye on that old stove felt good as the heat rolled up my chest and around my face and ears. My hands cupped over the fiery orange circles of the eye . . . like parachutes catching the hot air. In my groggy state, standing over the hot eye seemed more sensible that actually putting on clothes, so, slowly, I rotated from my left to my right, like a weenie roaster at the truck stop, trying to warm my entire body off the stove. Each time I rotated past the small kitchen window that sat over the aluminum sink, I fixed my gaze out into the darkness of the November morning. The moon was D-shaped and sat low on the horizon—I couldn't remember if it was setting or rising—as it hovered over the pine trees on the other side of the forty-acre field behind the house.

"There's not enough light for me to see," I thought to myself. I stepped away from the stove and peered harder into the darkness. I was "looking" to see how cold it was . . . and I could see Jack Frost glistening in the moonlit grass across the field. "This ought to be a good morning . . ." The red needle on the songbird thermometer hanging outside the kitchen window sat on 27 degrees. Turning the stove off, I muttered to myself, "Let's roll." Then I eased into the girls' bedroom.

Cape and Bay were piled up in a bundle under three generations worth of quilts and old electric blankets. How they slept in such a rat's nest of tangled arms and twisted legs was beyond me.

"Cape." Shake, shake, shake. "Cape." Poke, poke, poke.

"Unnnuh. Leab me lone." Apparently, five-year-olds mix up their v's and b's in the predawn sleepiness of a hunting trip. "Cape, we gotta get up." Shake, shake, shake . . . kiss on the cheek.

She rolled over and turned her back to me. "Unnnuh. Don't wanna go." By now, my feet were chilled through and through, and whatever had remained of the warmth from the stove eye had evaporated. Honestly, I didn't need much discouragement on the crispy cold Pickens County morning . . . so I crawled back into the bed and wrestled a few covers away from Hannah.

Now, I am certain that the biggest buck I would have ever seen in my life strolled through The Bottoms that morning . . . but we weren't there. I was snuggled up cozily to my wife . . . and slept well for another hour and a half. The trade was a good one, too . . . we sat on the back porch on the brisk November morn and sipped our coffee and talked of life. She snuggled up under my arm on the swing as I gently nudged us to and fro with my left foot. The coffee's steam swirled around my face with each sip, and her voice swirled around my ears with each whisper. As a doe and two yearlings crossed the field, Hannah chided me that I was missing out on a good hunt. I simply whispered back in her ear, "I am not missing anything."

I was quite content.

An hour later, the girls woke . . . Hannah and I were on our second pot of coffee, and she had breakfast almost ready. Cape stumbled into the kitchen dragging a quilt over her shoulder. "Why didn't you wake me up?" she asked with righteous indignation. I didn't even bother to explain, instead opting to scoop her up and give her a good morning hug. "Don't worry, booger. We'll go in a little while."

"When, Daddy?" came her immediate reply.

"After breakfast. After breakfast, we will get dressed and walk down and sit for a while." She nodded with pouty lips and buried her head into the crease between my neck and shoulder. I sat her down at the kitchen table and wrapped her in the quilt. She laid her head down on the table . . . "Good thing," I thought to myself, "I would have carried her out of the woods, sleeping like a log."

Breakfast came and went, and then the girls worked on a puzzle for an hour or so. I tended to a few things around the farmhouse, and Hannah cleaned the kitchen. I wasn't in any particular rush, as I had little hope that a midday hunt would lead to anything productive. I secretly hoped I might manage to stall until middle of the afternoon, when we could go sit for the rest of the day. But 'twas not to be . . . as around 10 o'clock, the Middle Princess marched out on the porch in full camo regalia and declared, "I'm ready!" I chuckled and declared, "Alrighty then! Let me get dressed!"

It was a half-mile walk to the best shooting house in The Bottoms. "Let's drive the golf cart to the top of the hill since its midday," I suggested. Looking down at her own legs, she glanced back up at me and nodded in affirmation. We had walked it before, but even she knew that driving the golf cart was a good offer. But we were careful. "Don't bang anything against the cart," I whispered. "Just be careful as you get off." She did, and did a good job of it, and then we hiked down the hill and through The Bottoms the last 200 yards.

And, at about 10:45 a.m., we sat quietly in the shooting house . . . with not even a squirrel in sight. Twenty minutes later, and the five-year-old was fidgety. I was anxious we wouldn't even see one deer . . . this is where the "meeting with expectations" pressure began to mount . . . I "grunted" a few times and tried the "bleat," too, hoping to attract a rutting buck with the animations that might sound familiar to him. I had already sprayed a little doe pee around the base of the shooting house, but I squirted a little more out of the window for good measure. Ten more minutes passed, and nothing.

"Daddy, can I blow on this?" she asked . . . holding up a predator call she had retrieved from my backpack. I tried to discourage her because I knew her wailing away on a wounded rabbit call would likely scare everything out of the woods but the ticks and mosquitoes. She was persistent. "Well, nothing you've done has worked," she reasoned. "So we should try this." I tried again to explain the difference between the predator call and a buck grunt, but she would have none of it.

"Fine, then," I finally relented in exhaustion. "Blow on it, and let's see what happens."

Notice the sequence of the pictures I've included with this story. The first . . . a page or two back . . . was the most recent, and she was 16. This picture, taken several years ago, is from when she was about 13 years old. And on the next page, you'll find her as a wee little girl hunting at the earliest of ages. She is now a woman . . . and the woods helped her grow.

This picture still hangs on the wall in my study. Not because of the result of the hunt, but because the victory was won when she never gave up on trying.

She hesitantly blew one little "eeaaakk." "Like that?" she asked, with a hint of jubilation in her voice.

Sensing her joy, I suggested, "You gotta blow harder and more . . . like a crying baby." She drew a deep breath and then blew on that predator call like it was a bugle, and this was Reveille. Her "eeaaakkks" and "wreeeeeenttsss" echoed down the holler . . . and any buck with a half a lick of sense wasn't about to walk anywhere within earshot . . . but, she was having fun. So, contented again, I just sat and enjoyed the view and the company as Cape serenaded everything within a half mile of Coal Fire Creek. I leaned back and just listened and took it all in.

"Daddy! Daddy!" She stopped blowing and started tapping my leg.

"What is it, sugar?" I asked.

"What is that?" Her arm extended straight out with her index finger pointing out toward one of the biggest bobcats I had ever seen in all my years.

"That, baby, is what you just called up!" He trotted towards us at a pretty good clip . . . he was coming to eat, and we didn't have much time. "Do you want to?" Her head was already shaking . . . "No, you shoot him, Daddy."

And so . . . I did. But that was Cape's kill. It was her first . . . because she called him up. That was what mattered . . . not the shot, but the call. And you know what else mattered to her? How much she enjoyed calling with the call. And she cared less that we didn't see a buck . . . and she still recalls this busted deer hunt as one of the best hunts she ever had.

She learned how to call a bobcat that day, but I learned a lot more about raising little girls.

Sometimes, they shepherd me.

ZEBCO 33s

Fishing has long been a pastime in our family. From farm ponds to freshwater lakes to coastal waters, fishing is part of our past and our future. And, while we don't go fishing every weekend, it is part of who we are . . . it is part of how we go Shepherding Outdoors.

My oldest daughter, Bay, was five . . . maybe six . . . when I bought her first "real" fishing pole—a pink and white Zebco 33. It was the perfect beginner setup because it's nearly impossible to mess up a cast with a Zebco 33. They are as tough as battleships and as smooth as melted butter. And, because I am not a master fisherman . . . as we say in our family, there is a reason why we go "fishing" and not "catching" . . . we needed the perfect combination of "bullet proof" and "easy to use" that the 33 offered. For, you see, that's what would be necessary to match my skills in teaching her how to fish.

I am a "hometown" guy, so I try to shop with hometown folks when I can. Bay, Cape, and I loaded up one morning and headed off to Clem's Bait and Tackle between Opp and Andalusia. My old friend, Coleman Mosely, and his wife, Sylvia, have run that shop for as long as I can remember. It truly is authentic bait and tackle . . . a cricket bin greeted us on the front porch. Ten thousand crickets crawled all over cardboard rolls down inside the bin. Bay squirmed a little and scooted over, away from the crickets, as she made her way past. Three jingle bells rang as we opened the door, and the smell of "old school" met us as we breached the doorway. I held the door for the girls, and they shuffled on in . . . stopping at the counter where Mr. Mosely sat.

He was working a repair on a good-looking Penn International. "How is the Merrell family today?" Mr. Mosely asked. He looked down over the top of his glasses . . . his grey-white hair tufted out around his ears from underneath a Ranger® boats ball cap. Bay and Cape both stopped dead in their tracks. My feet stutter stepped because of the kiddo traffic jam in front of me. The door swung back shut and hit me in the derriere.

"Move forward, girls . . . he ain't gonna bite." Mr. Mosely laughed at the suggestion, and the girls inched forward just enough for me to squeeze around them. They had never been here before. Bay's eyes were fixed on the hundreds of fishing poles lining racks throughout the store. Cape's head danced back and forth between the grey-headed old man behind the counter and all of the cluttered wares in the shop. They were both mesmerized . . .

Though the shop is small, there is a smorgasbord of fishing tackle inside. It is everything a fisherman could ever want. Lures of all shapes and sizes hung by the hundreds from pegboard walls. Plastic worms of red, chartreuse, black, purple, and every other color imaginable, packaged in rows by the dozens, created a rainbow of color across the wall. Opposite the lures and worms, Mr. Mosely sat behind the waist-high counter window, framed with pictures of himself and other local celebrities, showing off their best catches. Pictures of big mouth bass and hand-sized bream covered the window of the counter like old postcards on a granny's refrigerator. To our immediate left, all sorts of hooks and weights and swivels; scales and scalers; pliers and filet knives; and every other tool one could ever hope to use to somehow apprehend a fish . . . by the tens of dozens, if not more.

And in the middle of the room . . . rack after rack of fishing poles. "This place is like fishing pole heaven," Bay uttered, almost with an air of disbelief in her tone.

Mr. Mosely and I both laughed as we watched Bay and Cape slowly ease into the comfort of being someplace new. They bounced from one spot to the next . . . one lure to another, remarking about the "pretty colors" and the "shiny parts." For years, I've told the girls to "only pick it up if you are going to buy it." But today . . . today was different. As long as they didn't hook themselves, they could touch everything in the store. And touch, they did. Cape picked up a minnow bucket and tried it on as a helmet. Bay put on a bright purple life jacket and a Gilligan hat. They pranced around in their newfound wares like fashion models on the runway. Mr. Mosely smiled large, and in that moment, I felt pure "dad" joy . . . my girls were going to be fisherwomen. As I gave them a few minutes to explore, I entertained fanciful conjectures of Bay winning the Bassmaster Classic and Cape sharing co-hosting duties with Bill Dance.

A few minutes passed, and about the third time one of the girls asked, "Daddy, can I have one of these?" I realized this was going to get expensive quick. I promptly turned my attention away from the girls so we could get down to the business at hand. Mr. Mosely knows I am no expert, so I am quite sure he understood the man code when I said, "What do you reckon' the best rod and reel in this place is . . . that I can get for Bay? It will be her first."

"Oh, her first, is it? Well, I have a few I could suggest." His tone said to Bay that he was impressed with her decision to be a fisherwoman, and that he appreciated her decision. She grinned with approval. She has my dimples . . . and they shone prominently that day. Mr. Mosely picked this one, and then that one, and then another one. Bay entertained each as a suggestion, and it felt as though I were watching a seasoned salesman try to negotiate with a shrewd buyer. Bay was no easy sell, but when Mr. Mosely tipped the end of that bright pink Zebco 33 in her direction, I saw a twinkle in her eyes . . . I knew she was "hooked."

"That's the one, Daddy!" she nearly shouted. She grabbed ahold of it like Zorro and commenced to try to carve a "Z" in everything—and everyone—in the shop. She pretended to cast here, there, and everywhere. Honestly, I didn't know Mr. Mosely could move that fast . . . quick enough to wrestle the six-foot-long "Z" carving pole from her hands before anyone "got an eye put out."

She grinned from ear to ear as I handed it back to her. "You know it's not really my first one, Daddy?" I was puzzled by her remark.

"What do you mean, Butterbean?" That was my pet name for her. "I mean, Big Daddy gave me a pole. A cane pole. And I fish with it sometimes." She studied the silver sided bell on the reel as she talked. "It's not nearly as pretty as this one, though."

Hannah's father, George, was a big man. Hence the name, Big Daddy. I often describe him as having stood six foot, twelve inches when he was in his prime. But even though he was barrel chested and had hands like catcher's mitts, when one of those girls climbed into his lap, he melted like a Hersey's bar on the dashboard of a Ford pickup in an Alabama August.

He was so good to them . . . and to me. He truly was a fisher of men and an outdoor shepherd.

Cape drew my attention back to the present. She and Bay seemed to be contemplating a sword fight . . . Bay with her Zebco 33, and Cape with what was bound to be the most expensive rod in the joint. Thankfully, Mr. Mosely intercepted them before anything was broken. And, he had the perfect, three-foot-long, toy rod-and-reel to trade out with Cape's sword. It was not much different than Bay's first toy fishing pole. Cape held the grip tight in her hand as Mr. Mosely cautioned her that they were not, in fact, swords. She and Bay both giggled, and Cape retorted, "I know, silly!"

The tiny mite rod-and-reel combo was just her speed. Yellow and purple, with a plastic fish tied to the end of the line. "This will help her learn how to cast," Mr. Mosely said. "It really does work. It's just not big enough to catch a minnow with." Holding her new prize, Cape wore a smile that rivaled Bay's, and Mr. Mosely and I both knew that I wasn't leaving Clem's without two fishing poles.

And, so it was . . . I bought the girls their first fishing poles. I still have them. They are in my shop. No doubt, they are covered in sawdust from hundreds of boards run through the table saw and cobwebs from as many spiders living in the dark recesses. But that's okay. For, the value was never in the plastic or the metal, the silver or the pink. The value of those worn-out relics has always been in the memories . . . and that is why I still keep them.

Because every time I look to the corner of the shop and see them leaning there . . . I smile at what the Lord has done for me.

Teaching Bay to fish was a tremendous endeavor. Notice the reel is designed for right-handed people . . . well, Bay is left-handed. And teaching her to fish right-handed was challenging for both her and for me. Eventually, I bought her an Abu Garcia Spinning reel with a left-handed setup, and things went so much smoother. But . . . she is the only person in the family who has caught fight both right-handed and left!

Chapter
FIVE

A GOOD, GOOD FATHER

——— W A R M A N D W A S H E D ———

I take long showers . . . or at least I do if I am not the last one in the house to take a shower. It drives Hannah nuts. I'll stand under the pounding hot water for what could be hours . . . or at least as long as the hot water lasts . . . which is never hours, but it sometimes feels like it as time passes. Lost in thought, my mind usually rambles from one subject to another, all the while soaking up the comfort that comes from being warm. Many a short story has found its genesis in the moments under that hot bead. Many a tale has been formulated there, too.

It's especially tempting to linger under the flow when it's cold in the house . . . such as it was yesterday morning. It is a comfort to find warmth in the chill.

I've never really considered why I linger in the shower . . . until yesterday. Banks stepped out of her thirty-minute-long shower yesterday morning saying, "Cold, cold, cold!" like a rapid-fire machine gun, and a flood of childhood memories came back to me.

I grew up in a house that had no central heat and air. We had small electric heaters . . . the kind that always smelled suspiciously when you used them for the first time each year . . . and that was our best source of heat early in the mornings. We had a fireplace, but we were rarely lucky enough to have any hot coals still burning in the mornings, and building a new fire was not something I ever wanted to do that early . . . "I'm not going outside to get wood . . . it's freezing!" So, the heater was the go-to option.

Every morning when my alarm clock sounded, I'd run to the bathroom on my tippy toes, arms wrapped around my chest, and crank up that heater. I'd squat down in front of it just long enough for the hot water to coarse through the pipes of the house, finding its way to the shower head. As soon as I saw the first hint of steam, I'd leap from my crouch at the heater and into the shower . . . seemingly disrobing mid-flight. The water was sometimes too hot . . . arching my back to get away from it, I'd crane around to the knobs . . . adjusting it as quickly as I could. Eventually, I mastered knob location and found the perfect oasis of temperature.

And there I would sit . . . sometimes literally sit in the bottom of the shower . . . soaking up all the heat that flowed forth . . . until I sensed the water was about to turn cold, and then I'd wash my hair and scrub my body in about 23 seconds . . . before the heat completely vanished. By now, the steam from the shower and the little electric heater had raised the temperature in the little bathroom considerably . . . it was probably safe to venture outside of the shower. And, so, I would . . . knowing that, eventually,

Ice forms when water molecules in the air freeze. One frozen molecule draws another to it, and the crystal begins to grow.

Families ought to grow in much the same way. Two become one and bear fruit. That fruit marries, and the crystals ought to draw nearer to each other as the family expands.

Sometimes, though . . . the crystal is shattered. And when that occurs, cold sets in like none have ever felt. The cold of an empty house . . . no heater can warm that heart.

I would have to venture back out into my bedroom . . . into the cold still of the night's morning air.

I rarely wanted to leave the comfort of the shower or that warm, steam-laden bathroom. I always wrote faces or names on the mirror before I wiped all of the steam away. I'd finish brushing my teeth and whatnot and wrap up in a towel . . . knowing I had to leave but knowing I would get to come back.

I wonder where we find such comfort today. I still stand in the shower for far too long. If ever I am late for work, it's probably because I got lost in my thoughts in the shower. But that's not where I find true comfort. Where do you find comfort? I know where mine comes from . . .

I am washed . . . that is where I find true comfort. Washed . . . and though sometimes I leave to the cold darkness of the world, I know I will always come back to the warmth . . . because I am washed . . . and where I sit, it is warm and joyful. For He always keeps me wrapped in His arms. Sure, sometimes I hurt. Sometimes I get cold. But He is never too far away.

I pray your day is warm and washed, too, my friends.

Jesus loves you.

—THIS DAY, I CHOOSE— TO FOLLOW

I am sitting in a tree stand this morning . . . it's bitter cold . . . 31 degrees. I got up with the frost and walked through the dead of night to come here undetected. I sit silently, listening to my own exhale . . . watching it crystallize as soon as it leaves my body . . . and drift ever so slowly in the dark morning's air.

There has rarely been a sound this morning, save my stomach growling on occasion. A snap in the woods here or there, and a dog barking in the distance, nothing more . . . not even the raven.

I can taste the coffee in my mouth . . . the recollection of warmth comforts me, as cold air sneaks its way down the back of my jacket. I shiver, but for a moment, uncontrollably. Not because I am cold . . . but because the cold found its way in. Such is life . . . an ongoing effort to seek warmth and avoid darkness.

Now, though . . . now . . . ahhh, the sun climbs over the horizon in front of me and stretches its arms up toward the sky. With its every effort, it grabs hold of the heavens and pulls itself upward . . . and light falls, and then night falls . . . all around me.

My face is warm under the bright beams. Cascading through the sack cloth netting I made to shield me from the bite of the wind, the sun's warmth is a welcome reminder that the light always prevails.

Birds start to cackle and chirp, both near and far. The sun's warmth energizes them, too. A wren lands on the rail of my stand and flutters at me a time or two . . . not quite sure if I am supposed to be here . . . and then flitters off just as quickly as she came.

My fingers tingle as they come back to life . . . even the wool of my gloves is not enough to ward off the cold Alabama morning air. As the sun began to win the battle against the night, I hold my fingers up . . . sails to the sun rays . . . to warm them.

My face and cheeks are chilled, but my PMC beanie has served its purpose well . . . keeping my head and ears toasty warm.

The north wind raises her voice this morning. No doubt, she is angry that the sun woke her. The rest of us, though . . . we are relieved at the welcome sight. Everyone looks for a lifeboat, even when they don't know they need one. The sun is my lifeboat this morning . . . not that I was near death . . . but that the warmth is simply a welcome relief.

And soon, I must go . . . vacating the tranquility of these cold winter woods for the eruption . . . the disruption . . . the chaos we call life. I'll be at the courthouse in an

In Mark 6:31, Jesus invited the apostles to, "Come with me by yourselves to a quiet place and get some rest." This is my quiet place. This is where my heart can rest. What about you?

hour or so . . . and then I must try to show warmth to someone's cold, chiseled pain. I will try to offer light to conquer the darkness of someone's addiction. I'll need to wrap someone up in the love of a brother.

And I can't do any of these things alone. That's why I sit silently in the woods this morning . . . being still and knowing that I am not in control, but that He is. Right now, He goes before me, making the path straight. I simply choose . . . follow Him or make my own way.

This day, I choose to follow.

What say you?

God bless.

— PADDLING THROUGH — THE PAIN

On this day in 2016, I was on a journey like no other with my friend Travis and his son, Tyler.

For days, the dead still air only encouraged the mosquitoes. So thick, I was fearful to breathe through my mouth, for I had already engulfed a fair amount of bug protein by accident, simply by breathing deep. The drone of the mosquitoes buzzing was deafening . . . in the silence that is the Florida Everglades. Miles from any man-made sound, the mosquito symphony was all that occupied my senses.

I could taste the iron from my own blood each time I inhaled one of the blood suckers. I could almost smell them as I occasionally sucked one up a nostril . . . violently expelling them in instantaneous bellows of air. Of course, I could feel them . . . death by a thousand pin pricks. I could hear them . . . their droning buzz was maddening. And I could see them . . . darting away just as I swatted.

Nothing brought relief until I doused myself with Deet. And not the grocery store brand of Deet . . . but special-order-80%-Deet that comes with a warning: "Do not put this product directly on human skin." We doused our clothes with it . . . and soon, my lap looked like a mosquito cemetery. Once they landed on my clothes . . . death was imminent.

On through the otherwise silent night, we paddled . . . we were lost. And long overdue. Six hours earlier, we should have made camp. We should be fast asleep, building up our rest for what would be a brutal paddle into a coming tide the next day. Instead . . . we searched . . . and collected mosquitoes. The lights of Miami and an occasional jet airliner were the only signs of civilization. No cell service. No gas stations. No boats. We were on our own.

And there is no such thing as dark until you've been lost on a moonless night in the Everglades. My eyes hurt from the strain . . . "Everything looks the same," I muttered to myself. Desperately trying to find an opening in the mangrove swamp . . . a channel that might lead us to freedom . . . peering into the blackness was not dissimilar to staring into the sun.

I could see virtually nothing.

And while I've written parts of this story many times . . . and it deserves to be

Sunset off Mormon Key, at the southern edge of the Everglades in the land of 10,000 Islands.

The Florida Everglades are a vast refuge for the unadulterated imagination of man. Uncorrupted by time or influence, the Everglades give men the opportunity to roam through the recesses of life . . . one paddle stroke at a time. Boys become men here. Fathers become dads here.

told . . . the misery and fear of that night is not what I want to write about today. For, certainly, the good Lord guided our strokes that night, and we eventually made camp six miles past our intended destination. We camped at the Watson Place, an abandoned homesteader's farm that was one of the few spots of dry ground in the Everglades.

The next day, we woke late . . . another crew of campers at Watson Place—who, no doubt, we woke when we made landfall as lost and weary travelers—were gracious in their exit. We never woke as they packed their gear and cooked breakfast. I did dream of bacon that morning . . . but that was all.

That day, my back ached as I paddled into the oncoming tide. We had three miles of head-on tidal confrontation to get out of this river and into open water. As we paddled out . . . the water rushed in. Two full strokes moved my kayak a mere few feet. I dug harder and paddled faster. My arms burned from the lactic acid buildup. My back ached from the tension. My head pounded from the dehydration. I was exhausted . . . and water and bananas were all I had to sustain me. To stop paddling meant chaos . . . the current grabbed hold of the boat like an eagle clutching a mullet in its talons, ripping away any progress I had made in seconds.

Don't stop. Don't ever stop.

I repeated the adage of *The Little Engine that Could* . . . "I think I can, I think I can . . ." and alternated that with prayer . . . "Lord, if you will get me outta here . . ." You know . . . one of those "let's make a deal" prayers.

As always, He was faithful. And three hours later . . . we finally sank our toes into the soft sands of Mormon Key. Tyler, Travis' son, laid flat in his back in the sand. I just sat . . . motionless on a log. My body cried and moaned like the steel hull of a rusting freighter tossed about at sea. Travis was drinking a little water and scouting hammock locations . . . he was much more fit for the occasion.

Energy starved and calorie craved, we ate like ravenous wolves that night. Travis cooked stir fry . . . I think Vienna sausage was the main component. I don't even know if it was good . . . I just know there was none left. We ate until our bellies bulged and our sternums belched . . . and then we fell fast asleep. I could have slept on a cactus that night . . .

But again . . . the hard day ended with success, and we all had grateful hearts that the Lord had seen us through. But the hardship of fighting an incoming tide and a head wind for hours on end is also not why I write today.

The next morning, I woke with the sun. Rested and at peace . . . I had a warm cup of camp coffee and some quiet time. Tyler was fishing around the bend, and Travis was preparing breakfast. "This is why I do this . . . " I thought to myself. "To be in awe of what God has done." I have always been inspired by the great outdoors, but the masterpiece that is the Everglades is unlike any other. For, it is as dangerous as it is beautiful as it is peaceful . . . and that is the majesty of it all.

A few hours later, Travis and I paddled side by side . . . Tyler was ahead of us, and we were making the eight-mile paddle from Mormon Key to Rabbit Key. The sea was calm, like glass. I watched the sea turtles poke their heads up as we passed . . . intruders in this land, they were curious about us. The southerly breeze was perfect for this leg of the journey as it carried us . . . even if only a little. Such is the Lord's aid for us in this journey we call life . . . isn't it? We want a big push . . . but most of the time, He carries us . . . a little. That's because He knows that we need to be able to do some of the work, too . . .

Stroke, stroke, stroke.

"I'm working on a new project," I told Travis.

"What is it?" he asked between strokes.

"I've been trying to get outdoors with my girls more often. And in more meaningful ways. It seems we always bond when we go hunting or camping or kayaking. I just want to make it count."

"You do . . ." he said. And just as in life . . . we paddled on. And perhaps, one day soon, I'll finish telling you about our adventures in the Everglades. But that is not why I write today.

Travis sent me this text this morning: "This time in 2016, we were kayaking between Mormon Key and Rabbit Key, and you talked about the start-up of *Shepherding Outdoors* and connecting with your girls more. You have done that and more. I am excited about your book. I can't wait to read it . . . I know there will be countless lives you will touch with it for years to come."

I sometimes forget how hard the road has been. Struggles to get up and keep paddling against the burdens of the day. Struggles to keep peering into the future . . . even on days when I don't know what the next "word" might be. Reminding myself that I really do "think I can" and continuing to pray . . . not for deals made, but for guidance . . . and then the struggle to follow as I should. Yet, somehow, through it all, the journey that started somewhere near the swamps of the Everglades has brought me here . . . years later, to the day . . . to *Shepherding Outdoors*.

Travis's text this morning came right on time. I needed the encouragement to keep looking forward and the reminder of where I have come from. And his text was a great reminder of the milestone that is my first book. At times, I was lost. At times, I struggled against the current. But in the end . . . the journey was complete.

Keep paddling, friends. I know you can.

— J U S T   O N E   M O R E   M I L E —

Cape and I lumbered through the snow and ice. Snow lay upwards of two feet deep outside of the narrow footpath that we walked. Hikers before us had done a good job of treading the path such that we were not breaking through the crust with each step. Our steps were labored, though . . . for we were without any sort of cleats or spikes, and the down-trodden path was either a slushy mush or icy hard. The ice was treacherous . . . with each ice patch came the tension of knowing one slight imbalance could spell aching disaster. And exhausting . . . every muscle of our legs clinched, trying to hold our feet steady as we shifted weight with our forward momentum. The treachery of the ice patches made the slushy puddled a welcome respite. Though they crunched and swished under the soles of our waterproof boots, the slush provided traction and stability, and the dirty mud bottoms of each puddle was soft and cushioning to the joints, not jolting and sharp like the ice.

The snow-covered evergreen forest was beautiful. Truly, God had painted this landscape with careful strokes . . . but it was bitter cold atop Mount Mitchell that morning. The sun had not long broken dawn, and the forest was eerily quiet. Our steps announced our presence like elephants marching . . . awkwardly . . . in the snow. Our breath froze and appeared like dragon's breath as soon as it left the warm confines of our lungs . . .

"It was 17 degrees when we were at the summit," I said to Cape.

"I think its colder here," she said. "These snow-covered trees are keeping the sun completely out." I was impressed by her logic . . . especially at the age of 14. And I reasoned she was probably right. My breath was freezing to ice around my facemask . . . and occasionally, I pulled shards of ice from around the cloth that surrounded my lips.

"But it will be warmer, soon," I offered as a means of encouragement. We were actually hiking down in elevation and would soon get below the snow lines.

"How much further, you think?" she asked inquisitively.

"Just one more mile."

She laughed. That phrase . . . "Just one more mile," had been uttered countless times on our expeditions. Searching for a wounded deer and curious about how much further we'd walk to find him . . . "Just one more mile." Paddling across the Mobile River Delta, running well behind schedule at near midnight, and wanting to know how long before we make our next predetermined campsite . . . "Just one more mile." Hiking the trails of the remote and uninhabited Little St. George Island and wanting to know how much longer before we stopped for lunch . . . "Just one more mile."

But for every mile we toiled, there was always a reward to be had at journey's end. This day . . . it would be the view from atop a rock face near Missionary Ridge. A remote place a friend had confided to me . . . from this rock outcropping, it is said that you can see across five states . . . all from near the top of the tallest mountain east of the Mississippi River. And, while I didn't know if we would see anything once we got there because I noticed clouds rolling in from the west at dawn that morning . . . it did not matter . . . we still had "just one more mile" before we found rest. And whatever view we found from this scenic perch . . . we would gaze with wide wonder at the spectacle below. But rest would be key . . . for "rest" is what gives us encouragement to keep pushing on.

The Apostle Paul was a journeyman. Like us, he traversed continent and country, to parts and places unknown. He was shipwrecked, marooned, snake bitten, imprisoned, and so much more . . . and even he had miles to go before he found rest.

On the road to Damascus, he encountered Jesus. Consequently, Paul was left blinded by lesions over his eyes . . . but he knew he had encountered Jesus. A few days later, the scabs fell from his eyes, and he surrendered to the awe-inspiring authority of God. Much like Cape and I when we finally found our secluded rock outcropping, Paul could finally see... more than he ever imagined. But even then, Paul didn't stop. There was work to be done . . . and in much the same vein, Cape and I could not have simply sat atop those rocks until we froze or starved to death. Despite the culmination of our mission, there was still work to be done. Paul knew he had work as well . . .

Some might consider a conversion to be the mountaintop experience that they had worked so hard to obtain . . . but not Paul. Paul spent the next few years in tutelage with Ananias and others, forgetting his old ways and learning all that he could about the teachings of Jesus. You see, those old ways never fulfilled Paul. Those old ways, by the way, were filled with an insatiable lust for causing pain and grief to anyone who followed Jesus. But he never found contentment or happiness in the persecution of Jesus' disciples. No matter how many letters he carried, no matter how many accolades he received, no matter how much blood he spilled . . . it was never quenching.

So, after his conversion on the road to Damascus, Paul studied. He committed himself to becoming a new man who reformed himself to the teachings of the One he knew to be true. For years, he studied . . . and then he commenced his missionary journeys all across what we know as the Middle East. From those missionary journeys came most of the books of the New Testament . . . the books we read and study today, so that we, too, might be more sanctified. Most people abandon their New Year's Resolutions by January 12th of the new year. Paul resolved to be a new man in Christ, and he spent years pursuing that resolve. What strengthened him?

Christ.

Do you hear that . . . ? That's the beat of her drum. You'll never hear another drum like it.

What do you resolve? And what does it promote? Wealth, fame, glory? Those things promote the false god of self . . . and they will only lead you to the same feelings of dissatisfaction that Paul suffered during his quest to persecute Christianity. Lost and alone . . . you will suffer in misery. Resolve to pursue Christ, though . . . and you will be rewarded with the most glorious view of the setting sun that you have ever seen . . . the sunset of life with an eternity in fellowship with a loving Father. Like Paul, we all have continuous work to be done . . . our mission never ends.

Have the wrong resolve, and you will quickly find yourself abandoning the quest. Resolve for righteousness . . . and your quest will be fueled for a lifetime.

Cape and I found our perch and speculated as to where one state ended, and another began. We surveyed mountaintops and valley floors, and more than anything else, we were blown away at the absence of any indication of man. For more miles than I could count, we couldn't find one radio tower or road or truck . . . just the beauty of God's green earth. And then we kept hiking to make camp . . . "How much further, Daddy?"

"Just one more mile, Middle Princess."

So be resolved to carry on friends . . . "Just one more mile." Though you may be tired, your feet may hurt, your breath may be labored . . . carry on "just one more mile" . . . for the worker is worth his keep.

God bless.

FRIENDS IN LOW PLACES

Part One

Chris and I pondered the situation. "I asked him if he wanted to go, and he said he did," Chris offered.

"Well, let's go get him," I responded. Chris was always better at forming relationships . . . I was a logistics guy. So, we did.

Scott was a mutual friend, but, admittedly, I barely knew him. More of an acquaintance, we had met a few times but never carried a solid conversation. Chris, on the other hand, well . . . he was my best friend and had started to form a good relationship with Scott, too. Trouble was, Scott didn't want any new friends. He was contentedly miserable in his own life of indulgence. Chris put the truck in "Park" in Scott's driveway. I slipped into the back seat so Scott could sit in the front. Chris went to get him while I shuffled about. "I am afraid he won't come out if he knows you are with me," Chris suggested. I considered having just stayed home for the greater good, but, as I like to say, "We are where we are, and we got what we got." I nodded my head and stayed put. A few minutes later, Scott and Chris emerged from the house.

Taking a seat directly in front of me, Scott later told me he didn't even know I was in the truck until I started talking. "Scared me a little when your voice came from behind me," he said as he craned his neck around.

Scott later told me that, as Chris and I talked, all he could do was reminisce about "our" history, though it was really no history at all. You see, what I didn't know at the time, but he confided in me later, was that he was a big supporter of my opponent in my first election. "They told me all the awful things that they had to say about you, Walt. I didn't know you . . . I barely knew them, but I believed them. When I got arrested for public intoxication, they were quick to tell me how you and all of your buddies were having good laugh at my expense." Of course, I assured Scott that nothing of the sort was true, but that was years after the fact. In the moment, driving down the road with Chris and I, Scott recalled, "All I could think about was, 'Here is this jerk who said all this crap about me.' But the more y'all talked, the less it all made sense. I couldn't understand."

I write this story with Scott's permission . . . because today, he is a dear, dear friend, and we have an uncommon bond.

But all those years ago, such was not the case. "Scott, we reached out to you and invited you to this men's conference because we know you are hurting." He sat motionless in the truck. His gazed was transfixed out the front windshield. Chris continued, "Do you think that alcohol is a god in your life?" Scott shrugged his shoulders a little and furled the corners of his lips, as if to acknowledge that such could be a possibility, but he dared not actually admit it.

"I don't know what you are searching for, Scott, but it isn't in the bottom of a beer can or a bottle," I offered, with some measure of experience speaking from behind my words. Chris nodded in agreement and dovetailed nicely into my comments with his own. Scott remained relatively muted, though he occasionally fought back some emotion.

"We will walk with you through this journey," Chris suggested. "But you have to take the first steps."

Scott's best diversionary tactic is humor. He is one of the funniest men I know . . . quick with a joke, he always has a funny anecdote in his arsenal. Scott is also one of the most charming men I know. He can quickly "own" a room with his big smile, his wide eyes, and his great personality. Behind all of that window dressing, though, was a shattered confidence, desperate to seek refuge away from the pain . . . and that refuge could seemingly be found in his drunkenness. As Chris and I zeroed in on confronting his alcoholism, Scott relied on his humor to divert the conversation. He had done it for years . . . and he was a master. Slowly and methodically, Chris and I brought him back to "center." By the time we arrived at Bethany Baptist Church (we had sat and talked in Scott's driveway for a considerable amount of time), Scott was mildly curious that there might actually be "a way out."

Of course, Chris and I knew that the way out was Jesus and a band of brothers willing to fight the battles with him.

Scott confided later that the more we talked, the more confused he became. "Everything you were saying was contrary to what I believed. I had convinced myself you were a different person than you appeared to be . . . and I was struggling to make sense of it all." Scott teared up as he shared this memory with me. His voice locked as he fought to contain the emotion . . . my eyes filled, too. Ironically, he stared out the windshield as I drove down the road to his house, just as he did all those years ago. "I just didn't know . . . I'm sorry," he offered. Scott knows today that I love him . . . and now he knows me well enough to know that I may not be the demon that "they" painted, but he knows we all have our demons.

Looking back, I am fairly confident that Chris organized this particular men's conference at Bethany. He has always been a strong advocate for men's ministry . . . and it seems only logical that his hand was in this. There was a main session where all the attendees would listen to one speaker, and then the attendees were free to choose from any number of break-out sessions to attend. It seems Johnny Hunt from First Baptist of Woodstock, Georgia, was the main speaker. Scott remembered that . . . not me. Johnny gave a powerful message about being men *of* God and *in* God. We all felt a combination of conviction and motivation, knowing we could all be better men *of* God, but also feeling motivated that we are all mighty warriors *in* God! After a powerful time of prayer and worship through song, we adjourned for the break-out sessions. The menu was diverse. The program given to me when I walked in the sanctuary had big bold title words for the break-out sessions . . . Leadership, Marriage, Responsibility, Pornography, Adultery, Children, Addiction . . . there were so many topics. After each bold heading, a short paragraph described the purpose of the break-out. Seemed simple enough . . . big words for the feeble minded like myself. Given the conversation the three of us had over the previous hour or so, it seemed fitting that Addiction be the first order of business.

"Scott, I think I am going to go to this session on addiction. You want to go with me?" He looked at me somewhat sheepishly and nodded his head. He knew I wasn't asking him to admit he was an alcoholic. I was simply asking him to go . . . with me . . . to a meeting about addiction. By this point, I had revealed enough of my past to Scott for him to appreciate that we had some commonality, and so, he reluctantly agreed.

We walked out of the sanctuary and across the way. The closer we got to the old sanctuary; the slower Scott walked. He was growing reluctant. No doubt, the enemy was in his ear . . . "You don't have a problem. You can stop whenever you want. Beer is good; it's people that are bad." I'm sure the excuses mounted as quickly as the resistance. I could see it in his eyes. So, I stopped and turned, in an effort to reassure him. Men scurried past us as if this were a busy Manhattan street corner. "You see all these men? They are all here because something is broken. We all need a little tune-up, Scott. None of us are strong enough to go it alone. That's why we are going into this class on addiction. That's why I am going with you." He nodded his head again, and his feet shuffled forward. "It's going to be fine. When it's over, you will be glad we went."

I put my hand across his back and onto his shoulder, walking side by side with him to the classroom. Men parted to the side to make way for us . . . not that we were royalty of any sort . . . but they recognized the support mechanism that was employed, and they wanted to be supportive. We nodded our heads as we passed . . . "Hey, brother! . . . How are you doing? . . . Good to see you." Turning into the classroom, I kept my hand on Scott's shoulder as he walked in first. The teacher looked up and greeted us . . . every head in the room turned to say, "Hello." When Scott sat down, I sat down next to him and patted him on the knee . . . "We are good, bro..."

I could tell it made him slightly uncomfortable. He wasn't used to healthy fellowship with men. His relationships mostly consisted of drinking buddies . . . Scott had never been in this environment before. It was understandable that he might be uncomfortable. I just wanted to be supportive and reassuring.

Friends in Low Places: Scott, myself, and our friend, Pastor Gary Miller. Ours is certainly an uncommon bond tied with the strongest of tethers . . . Jesus.

"Hey, my name is Walt," I offered.

In customary recovery meeting fashion, several in the room responded, "Hey, Walt!" Most of the room turned to Scott.

Unfamiliar with the custom, Scott said, "And I'm Scott. I am with him."

Again, the majority of the room responded with, "Hey, Scott." And then the leader spoke up and said,

"Good afternoon. I am so glad you all decided to join us in this healthy conversation about how we can all best deal with our sex addiction." As the leader went on to talk about the various forms of sex addiction, Scott and I realized the quite humorous predicament we found ourselves in. Now, granted . . . sexual addictions are very real and very serious . . . but we were here to talk about alcohol! Scott put his hands on his knees and stared a hole through the wall in front of him. I did much the same, surveying the crowd . . . as the elected district attorney . . . knowing I knew several faces in the room.

And it was then that I replayed the events of the minutes before the meeting . . . the intense conversation in the foyer, the arm-locked-walk down the hall, the pat on the knee . . . every man in this room thought Scott and I were much more than friends. I couldn't help but chuckle to myself, knowing that Scott would never forget his first recovery meeting . . . and I prayed to the Lord a promise . . . "I promise, God, that from now on . . . I will always read the fine print," for I just read the paragraph following "ADDICTION" in the program . . . and it was clear that this was not meant to be a discussion on alcoholism.

Scott and I relived this meeting a few weeks back, and we shared belly laughs until the end. God knew what He was doing . . . He put us there so we could be humbled, humored, and have the memories. And here we are . . . all these years later . . . the best of friends.

And best of all, God used Scott and his recovery to give my youngest daughter, Banks, one of the most beautiful gifts anyone could ever receive.

Part Two

Fast forward ten years . . . we've come a long way from taking a wrong turn into a sex addicts recovery meeting.

In the meantime, Scott progressed from being curious about recovery and flirting with investing in the relationship he had with Jesus, to living sober, giving his testimony at recovery meetings, and working in a recovery program. Funny how God sometimes takes us the long way around to get us where He wants us to be.

And where God wanted Scott to be was at the New Life Christian Mission Center in Enterprise, Alabama. New Life, as we call it, is a residential addiction recovery program where men live in a safe, sober environment and, likewise, study and learn the correlations between life and addiction, addiction and sin, and then learn how best to cope with temptation, so as to avoid relapse. Interestingly, the man who brought the vision for Crossover Ministry, the residential rehabilitation program that he and I and five other men founded 17 years ago . . . well, he graduated from New Life. God used New Life to mold him, and that led to the seed being planted that is now the towering tree of Crossover.

Every Tuesday night, I would drive to Enterprise to eat supper with Scott as he and the men from New Life would go to the First United Methodist Church for a Celebrate Recovery meeting. The church hosts the meeting, complete with a phenomenal praise and worship band and a great meal. Scott and I always enjoyed each other's company, but the meetings and the music were special, too. After some time, I began to feel some measure of conviction about being away from my family every Tuesday . . . so one Tuesday morning, I asked Banks, my youngest daughter, "Do you want to go with me tonight to see Scott?"

"What is it, Daddy?"

"Well, it's a church service where we eat, sing some good songs, and then a speaker gets up and talks about addiction and recovery. The food is always good, and the band is awesome. Plus, we get to talk and goof off on the ride over and back."

Reluctantly, she agreed. That night, we went and had a great time. Scott enjoyed getting to see her, too . . . they are buddies. On the way home, I asked her if she enjoyed the trip. She grinned and nodded her head. She talked about the baked chicken and green beans, the drummer from the band, Scott, and how much she enjoyed the meeting.

We continued going . . . faithfully . . . every Tuesday night. We made new friends. We saw old friends. We always encountered Jesus.

One night, Scott and I sat next to each other at the round table, where he was to my right. Banks was to my left. The band was playing some inspiring music . . . my foot tapped to the beat. Scott tapped his fingers to the same. Banks rocked her head in time with the music. We were all "dialed in" and intently focused as the band covered MercyMe's, "Flawless" . . .

"No matter the bumps,
No matter the bruises,
No matter the scars,
Still the truth is
The cross has made,
The cross has made you flawless.
No matter the hurt,
Or how deep the wound is,
No matter the pain,

Still the truth is,
The cross has made,
The cross has made you flawless..."

With my eyes closed, I prayed for Scott and all the men and women at New Life. They needed to know the cross would make them flawless, too. Addicts are usually shackled in shame, for the depths of their addictions have taken them places no one thinks they would ever crawl down to. Forgiving themselves . . . and realizing that God will forgive them . . . is one of the hardest battles an addict ever fights. Too often, shame compels them back to using. "Getting high" numbs the shame and makes life tolerable. Of course, "getting high" also takes them back down into the depths . . . and the cycle repeats itself. Finding Jesus and accepting that they can be made flawless in His eyes is so important for their healthy recovery.

Opening my eyes from prayer, the chorus rang out through the amplifiers and speakers. The message of the music was inescapable. I looked to my right, and Scott was dialed in. The older Black man to his right was, too. He was chiseled, and his sharp chin was offset by his curly salt-and-pepper hair. His eyes were intently focused. I knew he "got it."

The young man in front of me, directly across the round table, was not. His body had slid down in the chair, his head almost resting on the back stop of the chair. Arms crossed, his eyes searched the ceiling of the room for anything entertaining. He would rather be almost anywhere but here . . . but, such is life in a recovery program. The seed is strewn, but the soil is always diverse . . . sometimes it is fertile, other times it is hard and barren.

Next, my eyes drifted to my left to Banks. She was singing loudly . . . and her body pulsed back and forth in time with the beat of the song.

"Still the truth is,
The cross has made,
The cross has made you flawless..."

Tears rolled down her face. She didn't attempt to contain them. She didn't care to wipe them away. She was not ashamed. Seeing her, I could hardly contain my own.

The band played on . . . "No Longer Slaves" was next on the set list, and the timing was divinely inspired.

"You split the sea so I could walk right through it.
My fears were drowned in perfect love.
You rescued me, and I will stand and sing,
I am a child of God!"

Now, tears rolled down my cheeks, and a lump the size of a lighter knot formed in my throat. I wasn't entirely sure why I was emotional . . . but it was provoked by watching Banks. Turning to Scott, I could see that he, too, was dialed in on Banks. We both knew the Spirit was moving within her.

And, though I wasn't exactly sure what was going on in her heart, I knew it was something powerful. I reached over and took her hand in mine. She looked at me, just for a moment, and smiled, then she turned her attention back to the lights above the stage with a transfixed gaze. It was powerful.

At the end of the service, we made our way back to the truck to come home. Banks was different . . . somber, even. We drove just a mile or so before she started crying again. Before I could ask what was wrong, she shared her thoughts. "Daddy, I am ready to be baptized. I want to be with Jesus."

We had started this conversation twice before...

Proverbs 22:6 tells us we are to "Start children up the way they should go, and even when they are old, they will not turn from it." . . . and neither time did I discern that she was adequately trained. You see, I've seen kids rushed down the aisle at the first hint of Jesus in their heart only to see those same children, as young adults, make genuine professions of faith. I quizzed her . . . if she didn't know what she was saying or why she was saying it . . . there was more training to be done.

This time was different, though.

"Why do you want to get baptized?"

"Because Jesus saved me," she answered.

"How?" I asked.

"When He died on the cross, His blood took away my sin. Sin that I was born with. Sin that I can't get rid of by myself."

I started to tear up as I drove down the road.

"And I know I need Jesus to help me get to Heaven to be with Him and with God." She cried more tears of joy.

"I just love Jesus so much, Daddy. And the service tonight made me realize I need Him."

And from there . . . we had a beautiful conversation about what Jesus has done for me in my life and what He is doing for her in her life.

Hannah was working late that night, so Banks didn't get to share with her, the Good News. The next morning, though, as soon as I woke Banks up, she went straight to Hannah and told her, "Momma, last night, I asked Jesus into my heart!" And then she told Hannah all of the exciting details. From there, she pretty much told everyone she came into contact with . . . we should all be so excited for our salvation . . . and, no doubt, she was *en fuego*!

That Sunday, we went to church just like any other Sunday. But on that Sunday . . . Virginia Banks Merrell walked down to the front of the church during the invitation and declared to all of those who were present, that the shed blood of the cross . . . has made

"That Sunday, we went to church just like any other Sunday. But on that Sunday . . .Virginia Banks Merrell walked down to the front of the church during the invitation and declared to all of those who were present, that the shed blood of the cross . . . has made her flawless . . . and that she is 'no longer a slave to fear, for she is a child of God.'

God is oh so good . . . and He is so proud to call you daughter, Banks Merrell. And your mother and I are, too."

"*Therefore, if anyone is in Christ, he is a new creation. The old passed away; behold the new has come.*"
—2 CORINTHIANS 5:17

her flawless . . . and that she is "no longer a slave to fear, for she is a child of God."

God is oh so good . . . and He is so proud to call you daughter, Banks Merrell. And your mother and I are, too.

We love you more than you shall ever know . . . but not nearly as much as He does.

And that, my friends, is the story of how God used a recovering alcoholic named Scott—now a dear friend to me and our family—and his recovery to give my youngest daughter, Banks, one of the most beautiful gifts anyone could ever receive.

Follow the path that God would have you to go. For, you never know where it leads.

God is good. He can make you flawless, too.

Chapter SIX

BY THE CAMPFIRE

FREEZERS AND NAKEDNESS

"I will be home shortly," I told Hannah as I hung up the phone and walked into the courtroom. "I'm sorry, Judge," I offered an apology for being tardy. He nodded his head, but his eyebrows remained furled . . . he expected some measure of an explanation. "Our freezer went out, and my wife was calling to let me know." He relaxed his expression and then offered a few conciliatory remarks.

We spent the next hour taking testimony and presenting arguments about various pre-trial legal issues on a murder case. When I walked out of the stuffy confines of the south Alabama courtroom, I went straight to my truck. Stepping out into the fresh air of that fall afternoon, I could feel the rejuvenation of the crisp, cool temperature on my skin, and the bright sun bounced off the western horizon as it ran from the eastward moon. I climbed into the cab of my truck and threw my files and my suit coat into the passenger seat. That three-quarter-ton Dodge diesel growled to life, and, almost immediately, I could feel the stress of the job leave me . . . as if the truck itself was fueled by the tensions of the day. Rumbling down the road toward our small Loango, Alabama, farm, I cherished the opportunity to leave work early . . . but dreaded the task that lay before me. Driving home, the roar of the mud tires and the rumble of the needed-to-be-repaved road lulled me into thoughts of yesterday, bathed in anticipation of things to come.

My mind drifted . . .

We lived just an hour-and-a-half or so from the Gulf of Mexico. I grew up in Baldwin County, and as a young buck, I spent a considerable amount of time in a 16-foot, wooden Stauter-Built (pronounced Stow-ter) boat, roaming the grass bed of Mobile Bay. That 35-horsepower Johnson never went anywhere fast, but it was always reliable . . . but as I aged, my childhood sufficiencies gave way to adult-like expectations, and that 35 Johnson wasn't enough. For shame, too . . . that was a great boat, but keeping up with the Joneses took hold in my thirties, and I soon found myself the proud owner of a brand new 22-foot bay boat with a 200-horsepower Yamaha motor. For comparison's sake, imagine the Stauter as a mule and the bay boat as a racehorse.

But don't ever forget . . . life is, oftentimes, a turtle's race.

Within a week or two of buying this new boat, Hannah, Bay, Cape, and myself drove to Mobile and set out to catch redfish and speckled trout. We picked up my mother

Cape went through his hilariously awkward phase where she just didn't know how to smile. I remember being a kid and going through the same phase . . . funny how, as parents, there are some things we simply don't know how to teach our children. Thankfully, though, we can lean on others for guidance. And thankfully, Cape and I both found our smiles!

and her husband in Fairhope and launched at the public ramp across at the end of Pier Street. The motor purred as the boat comfortably slid across the light chop of Mobile Bay. The salt tickled my nose, and the spray of the occasional bow break glistened my face. Middle Bay Lighthouse sat off the starboard bow as we cruised across the bay, eager to fish the rock jetties around Gaillard Island. A bird sanctuary, it is known to locals by another name . . . not fit to print . . . think thousands of birds all standing in the same place day in and day out . . . Slowing to a drift near the northeast corner of the triangular-shaped island, we found refuge on the leeward . . . calmer water that was a result of the island itself blocking the south wind. Just ahead, a school of juvenile mullet huddled close to the rocks, hoping to avoid detection from larger predators trolling just out of sight. In the deeper water, they made the perfect bait, and in the shallows, they made the perfect target. One swing of the cast net landed us 11 healthy bite-sized baits for the bull red and gator trout we hoped to catch.

The small mullet flopped and flipped in the bottom of the live well. Their tail wags sounded like machine gun fire as they "flap, flap, flapped" against the bottom of the live well basin. But slowly, the water filled in, and their gasping gills, thirsty for air from the oxygen-rich waters, calmed. Soon enough, the soon-to-be hook holders settled in comfortably to their new environment. And, though doom would be their fate, they seemed quite content that no larger predator lurked in the outskirts, waiting to gobble them up.

But the south wind grew stiffer, and, within an hour, the boat pitched and rolled uncomfortably. No fish and a lot of wind will shorten most every fishing trip, so we turned east and motored back to the launch. The inaugural fishing trip for my new boat wasn't much of a success . . . seems big motors and fancy rigs don't do much to overcome poor fishing skills and foul weather.

A week passed, and the boat sat idle in the yard. A heavy canvas cover protected it from rain and falling leaves, but that cover was burdensome, to say the least. Hopping out of my truck after a long day at the office, I pulled at the edges of the boat cover as I passed near . . . ensuring that the lines were all still taut. After my second, still-in-stride tug at the cover, my nose caught a distinct odor . . . an odor I knew to be a sign of something ominous . . . that familiar smell of death and rotting decay. I stopped dead in my tracks . . . one hand still clutching the cover. Motionless, I attempted to get a more discerning sniff, and that's when I heard a noticeable buzz . . . a droning sound, if you will, coming from underneath the cover of the boat.

I loosened one strap, and then another . . . the two of them side by side, and just far enough apart for a grown man to slide between. Lifting the cover for an inspection, the putrid smell of rotten fish overwhelmed me. I dry-heaved a few times as I recoiled away from the boat. Saliva filled my mouth as I spat it away, trying desperately to rid my taste buds of the horrific encounter . . . and then it hit me: "I left those mullet in the live well."

I'm fairly confident that the color left my face as I realized the droning buzz I heard was thousands of flies orbiting around under that boat cover. And, soon enough, as I took one deep breath and reached into the live well, the contents of my stomach left as well.

"My Stauter-Built didn't have a live well," I thought to myself as I pulled the last hunk of rotten pudding from the live well. Seems the turtle was winning the race . . .

My recollections were interrupted by the realization that I was nearly home. The big diesel slowed to a near crawl as I waited for passing traffic so I could turn into the driveway . . . fully aware that my memories of rotten mullet brought on my realization that several hundred pounds of deer meat, beef, pork, fish, and all sorts of vegetables, now lay in a rotten lump at the bottom of our freezer.

Earlier that day, Hannah told me enough for me to know that the situation was not good. Given the fact that when she cracked the lid, the smell nearly knocked her off the back porch . . . and that all she clearly saw in that brief moment was larvae . . . I knew enough to know that, based on her description, the mullet from the live well might as well have been in that chest freezer.

"I am going to see if I can pick it up with the tractor," Hannah told me earlier on the phone. "I am just going to haul it out into the middle of the pasture and leave it. We can clean it out and leave the food for the buzzards and the coyotes." It seemed a reasonable enough plan to me, though my court obligations kept me from discussing the details with her any further.

Coming into the driveway, my eyes drifted out into the pasture where I spied that big white chest freezer, semi-cocked at an angle like a ship listing as it sinks. The lid was open. A few items littered the grass around the freezer . . . the likes of which I couldn't entirely discern . . . and there was no immediate sign of Hannah. Pulling past the house to my normal parking spot next to the playhouse, motion caught my eye. Turning to my right, looking through the glass of the passenger door, I saw my beloved bride running straight toward me.

She was running. She was nearly naked. A line of clothes dotted the pasture in a straight line behind her. And . . . she was running straight to me.

Now, Hannah is a free spirit. And, of course, I quickly deduced that freezer duty was going to have to wait. Because . . . there were clearly other, more important details that needed to be tended to.

Flinging her bra to the wind, she never broke stride . . . I quickly shed my tie and put all of my files back on the driver's seat of the truck. "What passion this woman has!" I thought to myself, as I rounded the front of the truck to meet her. Holding up my arms and steadying myself to catch her . . . I knew this would surely be one of those sappy-love-embrace moments like you see in every Julia Roberts' movie. Just as I turned to catch her, she veered slightly and ran right past me. "The Streak" was running so fast that the blow-by curled my hair as she passed.

When I look at this picture now, I see three beautiful girls
and my lovely bride . . . and I reflect upon all of the
things I can't remember. The monogrammed robes were a
Christmas present . . . I think. I see tissue paper and an
empty box on the floor . . . and it's pitch black dark outside.
I wonder . . . did we get up before dawn for Christmas at
our little farm house?

   Could be.

   I do recall, one year, Bay and Cape waking us up about
4:30 in the morning because, "The sun was almost up, and
Santa Claus had already left!" Maybe this was that year!

"Fiiirrreee aaannntttttsssss!!!" She screamed as she went straight to the water hose in the back yard. I was still so caught up in the hopeful romanticism of it all that I simply stood there like an idiot . . . scratching my head, trying to figure out how I so terribly misunderstood the situation.

An hour passed, and she was fully dressed. We sat on the back porch in a swing, staring at the still-full freezer in the pasture. Two deer crossed the field behind that big white box, cocked at one end by the kickstand of the fire ant bed that it was sitting on. I got up and pulled open the screen door to the kitchen.

"Where are you going?" she asked.

"Inside to unplug the refrigerator," I responded. She cocked her head slightly to one side and stuck both her feet to the porch floor. The swing stopped abruptly. I knew the question was "why" even though she never uttered a word.

Before she could ask, I winked at her and said, "'Cause I like it when I come home and find a naked woman running around in the pasture!"

MEMORY LANE

I watched the new Chevrolet holiday commercial this morning.

Both nostalgic and sentimental, the commercial tells the story of a man reminiscing of days gone by, sitting in the dirt-covered, ragged convertible Chevrolet that he bought his wife many years earlier. Putting a Christmas wreath on the barn door where the car had sat for years, the old man is drawn to the car. Sitting in the driver's seat, he smiles emotionally, as he starts reflecting on the flood of memories that, no doubt, infused his recesses as his hand feels the vinyl seat and the steering wheel. He starts to cry as he pulls his wife's picture from the gauge cluster. Like a teenaged boy who always wants to have her picture nearby . . . the car now is his memorial to her.

His daughter, seeing him come out from the barn and shut the doors, secretly has the car restored. After the holidays, the old man returns to the barn to remove the wreath. Opening the door to say "hello" to his girl, he finds his daughter's surprise. She greets him in the yard for a joyful reunion, and they ride off into the distance together.

I cried at the sentiment.

Just because one door closes, that doesn't mean we don't have other doors to open.

I have an old truck. "Old," though, I suppose, is a relative term. It's a 2012 Ram 2500. It's a work truck with some bells and whistles. I've had it for ten years . . . I bought it used. It has 247,000 miles on it, and the driver's seat has a rip in it. The seat cushion is mashed flat as a pancake from years of butt compression. But . . . it has been a good truck.

I use it in the woods, pulling logs; in the fields, pulling tractors; and for our home, hauling little girls. It's still tough and strong . . . no reason to get a new one. This one will do, just fine. We've been all over the country in that truck. Chris Jackson, Blake Turman, Keith Castleberry, and I did 18 hours straight, and then back again, to go help our brother, Jason Livixx, do winter maintenance on his Oscoda, Michigan, church. As a courtesy, we came up with a code word . . . four grown men driving that many hours in a truck together . . . if someone said "banana," you better roll down the window.

Bay and I drove to the Buffalo River in Arkansas on that truck. I'll never forget the look on her face when she saw that little '50s roadside motel in Jasper, Arkansas. "Why does the neon sign say 'color?'" she asked innocently enough. I chuckled, and later explained to her how to turn the knob on the television—and adjust the rabbit ears.

"I have an old truck. "Old," though, I suppose, is a relative term. It's a 2012 Ram 2500. It's a work truck with some bells and whistles. I've had it for ten years . . . I bought it used. It has 247,000 miles on it, and the driver's seat has a rip in it. The seat cushion is mashed flat as a pancake from years of butt compression. But . . . it has been a good truck."

Quail hunting in the south is a gentlemen's sport that produces some of the finest delicacies of God's provision. Sure, the all-white meat is of the finest quality, and that is certainly a delicacy. But the bond formed over the hunt, be it man to man, or father to daughter, is far more nourishing.

Cape and I rode to the Everglades in that truck. Stopping for the night at a truck stop just a few miles from our launching point, Travis Martin took the girls inside to get some food while I fueled up. "Cape, will you get me something for supper?" She nodded her head in affirmation. A few minutes later, they came out of the store grinning like the cat that ate the canary.

"Here is your supper, Dad." Knowing that, at near dawn the next morning, we would put paddles in the water for four days of Everglades isolation . . . she bought me the Macho Man Super Deluxe Truckstop Burrito with extra salsa. They all busted out laughing . . . I ate it anyway.

That truck brought Lincoln home from the vet for the last time. It took us to George's funeral, too. It's been to most every cheerleader camp, 4-H meeting, ballet recital, and everything in between.

Maybe that's why I can't get rid of it.

I have another truck, too. It's a 1979 Jeep Cherokee Chief. It only has two front seats, no air conditioner or heater, and the windshield wipers and headlights work . . . sometimes. The girls hate it, I think. It's loud, the windows are hand-crank, and the radio only works if someone in the Chief decides to sing to the rest of us. Banks told me once, "I'd rather walk to school than have you take me in that thing."

Lincoln loves it, though. He'd ride to Alaska and back with me in that Jeep if I asked him to. The creamy paint is being overrun by a combination of mold and rust. The hood has a butt-sized smash in it. So does the rear quarter panel. The pulleys whine, and the power steering pump gurgles. It stalls on you if you give it gas going up a hill, and it maxes out at about 50 miles per hour . . . I think—the speedometer doesn't work. I've never passed any other car when driving the old Jeep, but I've been passed plenty of times.

One headlight points up toward the sky. It's a great tool when coon hunting . . . puts a light right up in the trees for you. The other headlight points, more or less, forward . . . when it doesn't jiggle. The brakes work . . . if you plan ahead. But don't worry, it has seat belts. But that's about the only piece of interior trim left in it. The headliner is gone. So are the door panels. All of the insulation and carpeting is stripped, too . . . but that's okay with me. I can just take the hose and wash out the floorboard when it gets dirty.

I love driving that old Jeep. I'd drive it every day if I didn't have to keep my suits clean for court. But on the weekends, I love to roll the window down, prop open that vent window, and hit the open road . . . I drive it everywhere I go from Friday night to Monday morning. It occasionally runs hot in the church parking lot . . . I just tell Hannah and the girls (who ride in a different vehicle due to the lack of seats) that's just the Spirit coming out of it. They are rarely amused.

But what I love most about that Jeep . . .

It belonged to the dad of one of my dear friends. Kevin Rodgers traded me the Jeep a year or so ago. It had sat abandoned in a field for twelve years. I worked on it for six months before I got it to where I could drive it up and down the road.

Kevin told me a few months after I started driving it that his momma saw me one day driving around the square in Andalusia. "She smiled," he said, "and told me how good it did her heart to see you driving down the road with your arm hanging out the window. She said, 'It reminded me of your daddy.'" Knowing that moment warmed her heart and brought back fond memories for her did more for me than any windblown road trip ever could.

I get it, old man. I understand why that convertible means so much to you. Cars carry all sorts of memories down the roads of life. And those memories are so very precious . . .

And don't ever forget . . . people aren't much different from my old trucks. You may think you are beat up and dusty. Maybe your motor doesn't run quite right anymore, and maybe you stall sometimes going up a hill . . . but I promise you this . . . somebody out there holds all sorts of sentimental memories about you, too. You might be a little rusty, but that doesn't mean you are all used up. Call your kids and grandkids . . . share a few memories of the road of life during the holiday season . . . and round them up for one more trip down memory lane.

Many a day, Lincoln and I would load up in the old Cherokee Chief and just ride the dirt roads. He was the best listener I have ever known.

NO SMOKE, NO FIRE

My wife, Hannah, grew up in Andalusia, Alabama. It is a small, quiet town that may be most well known for her mother, Brenda Gantt, the sweet little old lady who found internet fame by teaching the world how to make biscuits, and for the fact that, "We pass through it on the way to Destin." Brenda spent her toddler years in Pickens County, but grew up in Northport, Alabama. Her father, Cecil Hicks, was born a sharecropper's son, and they made their livelihood in the sandy loam fields and in the flood plain of Coal Fire Creek, a dozen or so miles outside of Carrolton, Alabama.

Cecil and his wife, Flo, were married in 1944 in Lucedale, Mississippi, by a justice of the peace. Cecil was 23, and Flo was 17. Cecil worked in the shipyards for a year or so while they lived in Fairhope, Alabama, in an apartment. Flo said, "We had the most beautiful views of the sunset that I ever did see." The apartment overlooked Mobile Bay, from near the foot of Fairhope Avenue, just atop the bluff that stands guard over what is now the Fairhope Pier. Soon enough, though, the war efforts started winding down, and they moved back to the Hicks family farm in the Springhill area of Pickens County, Alabama. Flo always remarked that, "It was a long way from Fairhope to Pickens County." Having been to both, I know that her assessment was true in mileage and community.

Cecil grew up in a farming family. They row cropped "about 80-acres back in those days," he once told me. "We also ran cattle and had an old mule to turn the ground and pull wagons. Corn, mostly," he offered. "But we also grew field peas and potatoes, and we had a big turnip patch. We only ate what we could grow or shoot. So, we ate a lot of yard birds, a few deer, and a turkey every now and then, too. We sold the calves."

Times were simpler, I suspect, in the mid-1940s in Pickens County, Alabama. Enviously simple, I'd imagine. Quiet nights filled with the song of the whippoorwill, accompanied by the chorus of a thousand crickets, and clear-blue-sky days clouded only by the dust of the plow and the mist of the morning fog . . . much different from today. Crickets are drowned out by passing semi-trucks, and the clarity that comes from the peace of mind of simple living is clouded by the clutter of the internet. "I've seen a lot of change in my life," Flo once remarked . . . "Oh, yes, Lord. A lot of change," as she shook her head and walked back into the kitchen of her Northport home.

Flo and Cecil Hicks, with their three children, Ken, Brenda and Steve, from left to right.

Cecil quit smoking once. That was years before I did. He would announce to the room that he was taking the trash can to the street, and he would ease out to the carport. A few seconds would pass, and he'd open the kitchen door and holler . . . "Walt, come help me. This can is too heavy!" Quick to answer the call, I'd go outside to find the trash can already at the street. He'd chuckle at my baffled expression, and, in a sheepish voice, he'd say, "Give me a cigarette." Then we'd smoke together and ease back in the house. If anyone ever questioned his smell of smoke," he'd say, "I was just keeping the boy company while he smoked."

And good company he was, too.

Cecil loved to speak of the change he'd seen in his lifetime, too . . . sometimes good, and sometimes bad. He was generally a light-hearted and jovial man . . . shorter than most men, and a bit portlier, too, and his personality fit the stereotype that such statured men usually carry. He most often had a smile, and he took pleasure in seeing other people smile. He loved to tell a story . . .

"I remember one morning, Hannah"—he had shared this story with her several times—"I was out working in the fields. It was spring, and we were turning the ground, getting ready to plant. That ole mule was being stubborn, and I was having to work a lot harder than I wanted to." His smile formed a crescent along the lower half of his face as the wrinkles around his eyes drew tight with fond recollections . . . "We were setting out rows, and the mule must have gotten into the neighbor's mash because he sure didn't want to walk a straight line that day!" We all chuckled as he sat up in his velvety green recliner, so as to have a better ability to deliver the story. The fire crackled in the fireplace behind him as he drew us all in. "I always knew when it was coming on near time for lunch because I could see the smoke from the fire." The fields he plowed surrounded their wood-sided, stick-built country home . . . nothing more than a few rooms heated by wood fires and no indoor plumbing. "When I saw the smoke, that meant I needed to get to a stopping point and go on up to the house and draw water to wash up.

"With the mule being stubborn and all, I had worked up a pretty good appetite. We'd set off a row . . . the whole time I was walking toward the house . . . and I couldn't see any smoke. Then we'd turn the other way, and we'd set off the next row. I just knew that by the time I got to the end and turned around again, there would be smoke coming from the stove pipe. But every time . . . no smoke."

Cecil described the dust caking to his cheeks as the morning wore on and how the perch of the sun in the midday sky said it surely was noon or later. The coolness of the morning air had long faded, and the only thing hotter that his brow was his temper. "I was so mad and hungry, I finally threw those plow handles down, hollered at the mule, and marched across the field to the house. I didn't even bother to wash up . . . just stormed up onto the porch and straight into the house." He chuckled a little as he looked around the room to make sure we were all still listening intently. "When I went through the door, I realized what had happened . . . and thank the good Lord I managed to figure it out before I raised any Cain and put my foot in my mouth!"

Cecil said that coming through the back door, he saw a bowl of piping hot field peas, some cornbread, and a few pieces of country fried deer steak in the center of the tablecloth-covered round table. Flo was finishing up washing a few dishes at the double-basined cast-iron sink that sat below the single-paned window. She stared out the window overlooking the field where he worked. Behind her sat their beautiful, new, white enamel, General Electric stove that had been delivered the day before.

"Yes, Lord . . . a lot of change," Flo said from the other room, as the rest of us laughed at Cecil's forgetful adjustment to the changing times.

But sometimes, the more things change, the more they stay the same.

Through the years, the farm had become less of a farm and more of a retreat. Hunting trips in winter and play-cations during the summer. And through the years, not much changed, except the world around it. Electricity is still about the only modern amenity at the old farmhouse now. No cable. No central heat or air conditioning. No internet, and no telephone . . . and in the kitchen sits the very same General Electric stove . . . it still works today almost as good as it did all those years ago. That's not to say that all of those modern conveniences aren't available in Pickens County. They are. But Cecil and Flo never felt obliged to embrace those changes, instead preferring that the simplicity of life remain intact at their old Pickens County farmhouse.

Some years later, George and Brenda took our girls and their other grandchildren to Pickens County for a week-long summer vacation. Brenda cooked on that old stove while George tended to chores that needed doing around the farm. All of the kids played in the yard . . . they hunted Big Foot; they made supper in a dirt kitchen out under two cedar trees; they caught fireflies at night; they painted their faces . . . and they soaked up all that the good Lord provided under those crystal-clear blue skies . . . unpolluted by the clutter of modern-day conveniences . . . and they had the time of their lives.

And of course, all the family have been back to that old dust-covered farmhouse more times than anyone can remember. It is where Hannah learned to ride a horse. It is where Bay and Cape both killed their first bucks. We chased rabbits and killed water moccasins, trailed deer through the briar patch and saw eagles soar in the air. We shot coyotes and watched bucks fight. Cape even called up her first bobcat in one of those fields. We froze our tails off and hiked out of the midnight woods to the warm glow of the lamplight of the old farmhouse . . . always welcoming us back, no matter how long we'd been away.

That old farmhouse is where we found God in all His glory, uncorrupted by man. A lot has changed since 1944 . . . but thankfully, not everything. For that old Pickens County farm is where we have gone shepherding outdoors . . . more than a few times.

Pickens County, Alabama

Surely Peter and Jesus walked these woods . . . for here is a church built on a rock!

—THERE ARE PLENTY— OF ROCKS ON THIS MOUNTAIN

"**M**a'am, is the chapel open?" I asked the grey-haired woman standing in the driveway. Her hair was "kept," as my grandmother would say . . . meaning she went to the beautician once a week and did her dead level best to not get her hair messed up, wet, wind-blown . . . or anything else until she went back to the beautician the following week. She had on her walking clothes, and she was walking laps around the chapel's driveway. "Well, my husband is in there with the air conditioner repair man, but you go on in."

"Yes, ma'am, we won't get in the way . . . just want to look around for a minute." I took my hat off as I walked into the chapel. I'm sure my hair screamed homicidal maniac, and my clothes probably suggested something sinister as well. Ted Watson and I had been working outside all morning long. Ted's wife's aunt has a house not too far from the chapel . . . we had been doing some maintenance and upkeep. Finishing up around midday, we set out to take in a few sites and grab some lunch. The Sallie Howard Memorial Chapel, nearer Desoto State Park than any town, was the first stop of the day.

Coming through the door, we were met by a jovial fellow. He stood to greet us from the first pew. Another fellow, whose name I never caught, was working on the thermostat on the far side of the room. "Good morning, gentlemen," he offered with an outstretched hand.

"Good morning, sir," I responded. "Do you mind if we look around?"

He was quick to oblige, shaking hands and introducing himself. "I'm Ron Reynolds. Pastor here at Sallie Howard Memorial Chapel. I've been here for 13 years," he offered.

Inside the quaint chapel, the imposing boulder situated at the far end of the room consumed every gaze. The tongue and groove wooden floors blended well with the natural aesthetic of the rock . . . the white walls offered a soothing contrast to the dark grey of the boulder, and the natural brown hue of the floors blended it all nicely. But still . . . it was a massive boulder . . . the aesthetics of the church were consumed by it.

"We are having some air conditioning work done. Trying to get the heat back on. It was cold last Sunday without it . . . but we had a packed house," the pastor offered.

"Oh, you still hold services every Sunday?" I asked. I thought, perhaps, this might be a circuit church or a "special events" church where services were not regularly scheduled.

"Oh, yes, sir. I've been here 13 years, and we haven't missed a Sunday yet. Even when COVID set in, we never missed a Sunday. We just moved outside . . . and that was in the spring. It was cold! But we met out under the pavilion. And we had lots of folks who came, too. Why, lots of times, we get snow up here on top of the mountain . . . that won't stop us either. We are always going to come together to worship the Lord!"

I could hear the enthusiasm in his voice. It was so refreshing and inviting . . . already, I regretted this not being a Sunday, for I was certain this would be a wonderful house to worship in. "So, do you have a regular congregation, or is it more of a tourist congregation?"

"Oh, we have some occasional visitors, but for the most part, our congregation are all mountain folk. They live up here on the mountain top. Their mommas and daddies probably came to church here, too . . .

"Mrs. Virginia Lee rode her horse here for the longest time. Rain, sleet, snow . . . it didn't matter. She rode her horse to every service. Her son . . . as you might have guessed . . . is named Robert Lee. As he got older and had a family of his own, he drove his truck. He was as faithful to attend as she was . . . but he wasn't about to load his family up on horseback!"

He continued . . . "These mountain folk are salt of the earth people. Most of them don't have fancy cars or lots of money. They are hard-working, honest as the day is long, blue-collar folks who enjoy the simpler things of life. They enjoy the creek and the meadow, the sunset from the ridge, and the cool touch of the north wind. And they aren't too distracted by modern technologies that they forgot who Jesus is."

"Amen, brother." I thought to myself. "If ever there was a man who would truly understand what Shepherding Outdoors is, it's this fellow."

"We had an outhouse for a facility until not too long ago. That didn't stop people from coming . . ." he continued with the history of the church.

He wasn't an uneducated man. He wasn't a simpleton. His vocabulary was strong. His thought processes were complex. He was an intelligent man, and I had the distinct impression that to assume his congregants were extras in the movie Deliverance would have been an erroneous assumption. I gather, by his description, that Mrs. Virginia Lee, a widow, was a very intelligent woman, quick with her wit and sharp with her tongue . . . when needed. I gathered that the rest of the congregation was equally mannered . . . intelligent folks who chose their way of life . . . as opposed to being born into it.

"Mrs. Mattie made me a hickory nut pie not too long ago," his stories continued. "Have you ever cracked a hickory nut?"

In fact, I had never actually cracked one myself, but I'd watched George crack many through the years. I think he did it more for the satisfaction of knowing he conquered

Sallie Howard Memorial Chapel, near Fort Payne, Alabama.

Ron Reynolds, Pastor at Sallie Howard Memorial Chapel.

the nut's nearly impenetrable defenses, for I hardly remember him ever eating the nuts. And as I recall, eating one or two myself, they were rather earthy and bitter . . . "I'm not sure 'this' is worth all the trouble," I thought to myself as I swallowed the musky nut. George cracked a few more and offered me another . . . I declined.

"Cracking enough to make a pie would have been quite the undertaking," I responded.

"Yes, it was," he quickly affirmed. "It must have taken her hours with her tiny hands just to crack the nuts, let alone bake the pie. She was the picture of brotherly love. So is this chapel," he continued. "Built in 1937, it has been in continuous service ever since. You might say, it is a rock to this mountain-top community."

I never quite figured out why Colonel Milford Howard decided to build the chapel around that large boulder. I do know he built it as an honorarium to his dearly departed wife, Sallie. Maybe he built it around "the Cornerstone." Maybe it was because Jesus said, "On this rock, I will build my church."

Or maybe . . . just maybe, he knew that rocks like Virginia Lee, Mrs. Mattie, and so many others up here on this mountain . . . all would be drawn together. For, it appears to me that they are all rocks of testimony . . . and what would the world be if we had more of them?

Brother Ron? He is a rock, too. Thirteen years straight . . . driving up on top of this mountain to bring the Word. His wife? She is a rock, too. Spending the day with her husband as he dutiful attends to the needs of the church.

Yes, there are plenty of rocks up here on top of this mountain overlooking Fort Payne, Alabama . . . but it seems to me they all point to the same rock—the Cornerstone. I bet you are a rock, too... and on you, part of the church rests. Go forth . . . bake a pie, fix the air conditioner, do whatever it takes... to spread the Good News.

THE AMERICIAN SPIRIT

Part One

I woke at 7-ish that Monday morning, weary-eyed and tired. Bay's college roommate, Mattie Beth, was visiting from her hometown in the mystical parts of the Mississippi Delta, Banks had friends to spend the night for most of the weekend, and Cape burned up the roads running between cheerleading practice, basketball camp, and her boyfriend's house. With all of that action . . . it was no wonder I was so tired.

This was not your ordinary Monday morning, though . . . I smashed the 5 o'clock alarm twice . . . desperately thankful for the 10-minute snooze intervals, but the resounding of the alarm soon became more annoying than the intervals were comforting. So, more out of frustration than anything, I simply turned off the alarm, content to sleep the day away if that was the Lord's will.

Truth was, I was exhausted. Not only had I played dad and host for the weekend, but on Saturday, I spent three hours cleaning the boat so that Bay and Matt could spend a little time on the water if they wanted. Then, we spent a few hours with our dear friends, John and Amy Dugger, at their lake house. John is a great cook in his own right, and he and Tom McKee channeled their efforts and maestro'd up quite the Alabama Fourth of July barbeque buffet. So, on top of working hard that morning, I ate too much that afternoon . . . and then I spent the rest of the afternoon on the back porch watching it rain. Sunday morning, we went to Sunday School and worshiped, and then after church, I hung three ceiling fans at the Cottle House, worked on my tractor, and took Banks and her little friend, Alex, to watch the fireworks on Gantt Lake.

Like I said . . . it had been an action-packed weekend, and I was exhausted.

I shook my head and squinted my eyes . . . trying to get oriented . . . "Why is it so bright in here?" I wondered, not accustomed to sleeping so late. Without true awareness of where I was or what exactly was going on, I felt next to me in the bed to see if Hannah was still asleep. The cold sheets felt good to my hand and forearm, so I sprawled out in that direction. Few inanimate things comfort me more than clean, cold, bed sheets. Amidst the comfort of the brisk sheets, I realized Hannah was not, in fact, in the bed. Had she been, I would have found nothing but molten lava and red-hot burning embers on her side of the bed . . . for I am fairly convinced that her body temperature rises to near 200 degrees when she sleeps. "It has something to do with her blue blood," I chuckled to myself, as I stretched into a full "X" across the entirety of the bed. Somehow, the fact that it was empty and I could stretch soooo far, made the sheets feel all that much better.

"Crap! I pushed 'snooze' and then turned the alarm off!" I struggled and wrestled with the once cozy sheets. They wrapped around my leg and my arm on opposite sides of the "X" much like an octopus conquering its prey. Those demon-possessed sheets now did all they could to keep me from escaping their clutches . . . I twisted and writhed until I was nearly out of breath . . . "What in the crap!" I exclaimed, gasping for air . . . finally escaping the cotton tentacles . . . "It's Monday!"

"Hannah! Why didn't you wake me up? I'm going to be late for work!"

From outside on the porch, I heard a murmured response. I had no idea what she said . . . I simply knew that my desire to sleep late was going to cost me dearly. "I can't understand you," I said in frustration. "Will you please iron me a shirt?"

I confess that the tone in my voice was something other than gratitude and humility. In the last 54 seconds, I had gone from the peaceful tranquility of cold sheets to the realization that it was Monday morning and I had overslept to wrestling a stubborn octopus to needing to figure out what in the crap I was going to wear to work. So frazzled was I that I couldn't even cypher what exactly I had on the agenda for work. "Suit? Business casual? What the crap . . ." I blurted out as I furiously tried to open my calendar on my phone.

Amongst the blaze of tension that was mounting in the house, the back door flung open . . . "I said, 'It's the Fourth of July.' You don't have work today, you dingleberry."

I stopped dead in my tracks. Still gasping for air from my battle with the eight-legged thread monster and staring stupidly at my phone . . . no doubt, I was a sight for sore eyes with one corner of the sheets still wrapped around my leg, standing there in my boxer shorts like I had shown up for school naked. "What?" I asked with an exaggerated tone in my voice, clearly indicating that I did not comprehend what she was saying.

"I said, 'It's the Fourth of July.' It's a holiday, you goose." Then she started laughing at me. It wasn't a sinister or sarcastic laugh, but rather, one of those I-love-you-because-you're-such-a-goose laughs. I couldn't help but laugh, too. After all, I looked like an idiot, and I was certain that to protest her statement that it was, in fact, a holiday, would only serve to prove that I was an idiot. What's that old saying?

"Better to keep your mouth shut and others think you're a fool than to open your mouth and prove it?

"Would you like some coffee?" she asked, gesturing upward with the cup she held in her hand. Her smile was warm and inviting, as it always was. I sort of stumbled over to her, and she wrapped her arms around me. We held each other tight for fifteen seconds or so . . . not a word was said.

"Yes, I'd love some coffee . . ." I responded, as I scratched my head and rubbed my eyes. She obliged, leaving me to put my own "fixins" of cream and sugar, as she ventured back out on the porch. The coffee smelled good, but it was still too hot. That's usually why I put milk in my coffee . . . to cool it down. But always the sugar first. Let's be honest. I drink coffee for the kick, not the taste . . . But it always smells sooo good.

"Clink-alink-alink-alink . . ." the spoon chattered against the side of the cup as I stirred. From above, I heard footsteps treading across the hardwood floor, and then feet appeared at the top of the stairs. Then shins . . . then knees . . . then thighs, and slowly, the Middle Princess made her way down the stairs. "Hey, Daddy," she said with a warm smile . . . just like her mother. "Will you take me skiing this morning before too many people get on the lake?"

"Let's see . . ." I thought to myself. "So far, I've killed my alarm clock, deveined the sheets on the bed, hollered at Hannah, and I did all of that before I even had my first sip of coffee. This is no time to make any decisions, plans, or obligations." Smiling back at her and gesturing with my cup, I said, "Let me drink a cup of coffee, sugar . . . I'll figure something out."

"Okay, Daaaadddyy." She always elongates her vowels when she is being overly sweet to get her way.

Hannah and I talked through our cup of coffee and, as I stood to get another, I texted Cape: "Okay. Ten o'clock."

A few minutes later, she replied: "Okay."

That was it . . . the warm fuzzies were over. She resumed her normal teenaged posture. We went from elongated vowels to disdain in the tone of her text. Now . . . I was bothering her.

Yosemite Sam resonated in my head . . . "Well, all the frickin' frackin' belly achin' blissen' trackin' . . ." But, I just poured my second cup of coffee and went back out onto the porch. Two monsters in one morning were simply too much for a mere mortal man such as myself to handle . . .

Hannah reminded me that the Fourth of July Parade was also this morning. Yosemite Sam made another appearance, as I had been planning all week to ride the old golf cart with all of the family in the parade. "I knew it was too soon to make major decisions," I muttered. Hannah looked at me, oblivious to the meaning behind the words that connected to my previously unspoken thoughts. "Well, you are committed now," she responded.

Curious . . . she had no idea what I was talking about, but she knew what I meant.

Twenty minutes passed as Hannah and I finished the pot and planned the day. Skiing . . . work at the lake house . . . lunch at home . . . rest . . . then fireworks tonight. That was the agenda, but it was getting tighter by the minute. Hoping to adjust the plan a little, I sent another text to Cape. "Let's do 9 o'clock instead. Can you make that work?"

"Tubing" is all the rage among kids these days when it comes to water sports. My theory is that they are too unintentional to learn any other type of water sport. So, Hannah and I told Bay and Cape they had to learn to ski before we would ever buy them a tube. Both did. And, to this day, it is an Independence Day pastime in our family to going skiing during that holiday weekend.

Five minutes passed, and I got no response. "Roger, ten four?" I texted her again, trying to provoke a response.

"okay"

This time, I didn't even get the courtesy of a capital letter or proper punctuation. But even though the devil seemed to be in these details, God was in the works. For, if I only knew what He had in store for us this Independence Day.

Part Two

An hour passed relatively quickly, and Cape had yet to make an appearance from her lair. Her boyfriend, Ethan, was sitting patiently in the driveway. "I guess that means she is almost ready," I thought to myself, trying to understand why he had yet to come inside. In the meantime, I gathered a few tools and supplies, as there was a rotten board on the pier that needed to be replaced . . . "Might as well kill two birds with one stone."

Cape came out . . . fashionable late . . . and greeted Ethan. Then, we formulated the plan . . . "Y'all go get some gas for the boat, and that will give me the few minutes I need to replace that rotten wood." Without hesitation, Cape pointed out that gas cost money, so I retrieved my worn-out wallet from my back pocket and handed her my debit card. And with that, they were off . . . "Who knows if I'll see them again today!" My sarcasm had at least a small element of genuine wonder within it . . . nevertheless . . . "Let's roll."

The lake house is only a few miles from where we live. Five minutes by car . . . one could probably hear the same whippoorwill from each house. We bought the house for $1,000 about 15 years ago. Then, we hired our old friends, Jack and Marty Odom, to move the house to a lot we bought a few years before. Seems a developer bought the house and land around it and wanted to build a subdivision . . . a 100-year-old farmhouse didn't fit the mold for his plans.

We spend a few years renovating the house, adding on a lean-to-type addition with a living room and breakfast area and completely re-doing the rest of the house. In 2010, we moved in, and we loved every day we were there. For all intents and purposes, Lincoln grew up in that house. So did Banks. We all did . . .

My mind wandered as I drove from one to the other . . . fanciful conjecture of days gone by—Cape riding the kayak down the snow-covered driveway, Bay eating earthworms, Lincoln chasing rabbits—my mind was flooded with joyful memories from the lake house. My elbow hung out the window as my hand rested on the door . . . wind fluttered through my hair and whispered in my ear as the memories ebbed and flowed like the wind pushing and pulling through the truck window. It felt like a Hallmark moment . . . an old man driving his old truck with the window down, reminiscing about the joy his kids brought to him and how much they warmed his heart . . . and they still do.

My daze was interrupted by three vehicles parked on the side of the road. "Something must be wrong," I thought to myself, recognizing that the cars were sitting precariously close to the road. People scurried about the three cars, one to the other and back again, like ants marching around an ant hill that rambunctious children just stabbed with a pine limb. Slowing to be respectful and cautious, I realized I knew several of the worker ants who scurried about. "That's Luke Philpott and his family." Luke was under the hood of his truck furiously working on something . . . He had a trailer hooked to his truck, and it was full of . . . "What is that?" I asked myself out of uncertainty . . . "Beach balls?" A second, harder look confirmed that yes, indeed, Luke had a trailer full of hundreds of red, white, and blue beach balls behind his truck.

"The parade!" Everything clicked all at once. They were on their way to Andalusia's Fourth of July parade, and something must have happened to Luke's truck. I stopped at the next driveway and drove back to them. Pulling up next to Luke's roadside truck, I stopped in the road and turned on my hazard lights. The orange ambered lights all began blinking in unison . . .

Country life has its advantages. I lived in Washington, D.C. for a little while . . . stopping in the middle of the road there—hazards or not—would surely result in a tongue lashing and prolonged horn blows. Here . . . in the country . . . people just slow, look to make sure everyone is okay, and slip around you with a gentle wave or head nod. Here . . . people react with concern, not anger. I nodded my head back to the fellow in the red Ford truck who stopped to let me get out of my truck and then walked over to Luke.

"I don't know what's wrong, Walt," Luke said, as if he thought I might be able to offer some advice. And I am a fixer . . . but I am not much of a mechanic. The fixer in me knew, though, that diagnosing and fixing Luke's truck wasn't an option . . . my watch said 9:15 a.m. The parade started at 10:00 a.m. "Five more minutes here on the roadside, and they will miss the parade," I thought to myself.

The Philpotts are an interesting clan, and yes . . . they are a clan indeed. But not "klan" in the sense that Alabamians are sometimes stereotyped as. No, they are a clan in the same sense that much of the South is. A group of people coming together to look after others . . . no matter their background. You see, Luke was born in Ireland and was raised Catholic. He converted to being Baptist after he immigrated here by way of New York City. Some years later, he migrated south to Florida, where he met his first wife. She was killed in a tragic accident . . . but God had a plan for this Irish immigrant who found himself widowed with young twin girls and a baby boy.

God brought him a second wife . . . Karen. And together, they raised a beautiful family. An Irishman and a Floridian made their way to Alabama because they wanted to live in a land where neighbors still helped neighbors . . . and then God put it on their hearts to adopt. Now, their clan is nine strong, with three sons adopted from China,

An Irish Immigrant, Luke Philpott is one of the proudest Americans I know. We'd all do well to take a lesson or two in patriotism from him!

one daughter adopted from South America, and five children of their own. And Luke Philpott . . . that Irishman with all of those immigrant children . . . well, he is one of the most patriotic, "Proud to be an American" men that I know.

"Hey, Luke, let's just unhook the trailer and put it on my truck," I suggested.

"And then you could just drive the kids in the parade, and I could stay here and fix the truck," he responded as if it was a question.

"No. You take my truck. You need to go with them. I'll get a ride." And that's what we did. I pulled my tools from the truck and grabbed my phone, cautioned Luke about the shotgun in the backseat, and gave him a hug. "Happy Fourth, old friend," I offered.

"Happy Fourth," he responded with a grin. Thirty seconds later, a trailer full of American beach balls and an all-American family was rolling down the road behind my truck on their way to show the world how proud they were . . . as immigrants . . . to be part of the American spirit.

God bless America.

And there I was . . . standing on the side of a country road with a DeWalt drill and saw, two pieces of lumber, and a box of screws in my hand. I couldn't help but laugh at myself and the places I sometimes find myself. "What will I do if Cape doesn't answer her phone?" A slight panic crept up my spine . . . but on ring three, she answered.

I waved politely to each car and truck that passed. No doubt, I caused quite the stir in the neighborhood, what with my lumber and tools on the side of the road . . . miles from anywhere. One gentleman, whom I "knew" but couldn't recall his name, stopped an offered me a ride. I politely declined, and then he hesitantly asked, "Well, do you need some help fixin' something?" He looked around after he asked, as if his eyes were saying, "I have no idea what it is you're out here trying to fix," but he was still willing to help. Grateful, I thanked him through a chuckle, and then I took time to explain my predicament. He seemed relieved at my explanation and offered me a ride again. I declined, and then he eased on down the road.

Cape pulled up a few minutes later. She was not impressed that I intended to hang lumber out the back window of her little hatchback . . . but us dads have a unique ability to embarrass our kids, don't we? Nonetheless, there she was . . . helping me, so that I could help Luke, so that he could help his kids understand what it means to be "Proud to be an American."

"Let's go skiing, baby girl," I said. She smiled at me through the rearview mirror as she whipped her car around in the road . . . and off to the lake we went. But the day was far from over . . .

Part Three

The water was warm that morning . . . July 4. Not too warm . . . not bathwater warm, but more like the third bowl of porridge that Goldilocks found. It was just right. It was also like glass. The air was still, and the only thing that disturbed the water's surface was an occasional boat passing by. "It should be good for skiing," I pointed out.

Cape nodded her head with a modest hesitation . . . "I probably won't be able to get up on slalom. It's been a year since I've been skiing."

I knew she would have no problem coming out of the water. She is a natural athlete, and her body's strength and agility rarely have any problem with athletic accomplishment. "You'll do fine," I assured her as she slipped off the back of the boat and into the water. The grin on my face let her know I didn't believe in her lack of confidence, and she shouldn't either.

She slipped her head back and under the water. As she emerged from the brown water depths, she pierced the surface with her forehead and pulled all of her long brown hair back around her ears and over her shoulders. She wiped the water from her eyes and looked up at me, standing at the boat's center console. She smiled and nodded . . . I bumped the boat into and then quickly out of gear, and the surge of thrust gave the boat some gentle forward momentum. The line drew tight in her hands, and she nodded again.

Without a word being said, I slammed the throttle forward as far as it would go. The 200-horsepower Yamaha motor screamed to life like a plowing mule that had just been whipped. The low-pitched growl slowly roared into a high-pitched whine as the revolutions of the motor surged higher and higher. The boat leapt from the water as it pulled Cape up from the depths and into a standing position . . . she was graceful and sleek as she slipped upward out of the water . . . skiing is a combination of strength, balance, and grace . . . I've often suggested that pageant contestants ought to be made to ski, not walk the stage with a pageant strut . . . for skiing is a much better demonstration of such attributes, and Cape would win every time.

She sliced through the water, to and fro, across the wake left and right, and with each pass, she gained more confidence. Her body had to "remember" how to do all of those things that it already knew how to do from years gone by . . . but time has a way of fading memories, and with a little bit too much confidence, she cut the turn exceptionally sharp and came slicing back across the wake. The ski shed water in a rainbow sheen behind her, and, for a moment . . . it was beautiful and brilliant all at the same time . . . but then reality overtook her confidence, and the ski lifted ever so slightly until it lost its edge. Her body was nearly parallel with the water when the edge came out of the water, so the first thing that hit the water was her fully exposed side.

"Ooouuucccchhh!" I said out loud when I saw her collide with the water. "Side ribs . . .

Gantt Lake in the early morning hours of July Fourth. We were the first boat on the lake.

Our family in July of 2016.

that probably knocked the breath out of her." I quickly whipped the boat around . . . we were running about 28 miles per hour, and the sharp turn brought the boat over on its edge. Ethan, Cape's boyfriend, held on for dear life as we banked like an F14 Tomcat in an aerial dogfight with a Russian Mig. As the motor roared back up to speed as it pushed the hull of the boat back up on top of the water, I searched the wake behind us for Cape. Fearful she might be struggling to catch her breath, or maybe even having suffered a broken rib, my "Papa Bear" instinct was fully engaged. But much to my chagrin, there she was, bobbing like a sea princess in the wake of a passing boat . . . her ski sticking out of the water just in front of her . . . ready to go.

Coming up alongside her, I leaned over the side of the boat and asked, "Are you okay?"

She nodded her head and grinned, "Ummm huuun," then she looked at me like I was being overly protective, and she didn't approve. Thirty seconds later, and the Yamaha screamed to life once again, and she was right back at it . . . slicing and cutting the water behind the boat like she was making a charcuterie board of meat and cheese for the creatures of the depths. Sometimes I am guilty, I suppose, of imposing the frailties of my nearly 50-year-old body onto the abilities of my much more physically fit children . . .

This time, she skied until she was tired, and she simply let go of the rope. Again, with grace and elegance, she slowed to a near standing stop before she sank gently into the water. As Ethan helped Cape back into the boat, I called Hannah. She had a few errands to tend to that morning, and I was hoping she was done and would join us. "Give me ten minutes," was her reply.

"Perfect timing," I thought to myself, and in about that same amount of time, we were all loaded up on the boat and headed back out on the lake.

Cape and I were supposed to go skiing the evening before. "Let's wait until Sunday evening," she had previously proposed. She knew that the boat traffic on Saturday of the Fourth of July weekend would be menacing, at best . . . dangerous at worst, and so, she suspected—as did I—that Sunday afternoon, there would not be many boats out. But of course, life happens, and she and I both had things interfere with our Sunday plans. So, that Monday morning when she came stumbling down the stairs at 7:30 a.m. with her baby face and pouty lips . . . how was I ever to resist? I knew Banks would be in good hands with Brenda at the parade . . . and for once, and for the love of a daughter, I would skip it.

But God is always in the details . . . for I pondered the fact that, had she not put the pouty-faced guilt trip on me and gotten me to take her skiing, I never would have found the most patriotic man that I know, broken down on the side of the road and about to miss the parade. And He wasn't done yet . . .

Thirty minutes later, and the lake was now bustling with activity. There were far too many boats to have any hope of slalom skiing, but we did have some success in pulling Ethan for his first time on two skis. He managed a hundred yards or so before he gave himself a nice enema. But for his first time up, I'd say he did very well . . . that is, until he dared suggest that I couldn't sling him off a tube. "You just screwed up," Cape said in response. That boy might as well have spit in my face . . . for there are few things that I take pride in . . . but bowing my chest like King Kong certainly occurs when I think of my ability to sling people from what I affectionately refer to as . . . "The Tube of Death."

"Ain't no way," Ethan doubled down on his previous remark.

"Get on the tube then, gunslinger," I responded. Cape tried to move to the other side of the boat. "No, no, missy. You're not getting out of this. Get on there with him," I insisted. She nervously laughed and then looked at Ethan as if she would deal with him later. For she knew . . . even if he didn't . . . that they were about to experience rocket-like propulsions, shuttle-like launches and, ultimately . . . they would both wish for death as a better alternative than the bumper-car-like crash-up-derby ride that they were about to endure.

And no matter what happened . . . they would both end up in the water.

Part Four

Cape and Ethan hung on for dear life as I turned the boat hard to the right, using the pendulum of the tube at the end of the 60-foot rope to increase momentum as they swung out wide beside the boat . . . skipping over the top of the water like Opie Taylor's skipping stone . . . And I can only imagine the g-forces they must have felt. Ethan's face bulged as he clinched both of his hands to the straps on the tube. Even from the boat, I could see a vein popping in his forehead from the amount of strain he was exerting.

Steering hard back to the left, the tube swung like a mad batter back across the top of the wake behind the boat . . . a wave cast off each back corner of the boat some 18 inches or so tall . . . and ramping them at 50 miles per hour caused that tube to soar! Launching into the air much like Evel Knievel shooting off the end of a ramp, Cape and Ethan jumped the fountain of the wake behind the boat, sometimes landing on top of the wave on the opposite side. Soaring through the air, their facial expressions would change as they experienced momentary weightlessness . . . Cape would almost smile, as she seemed to quite enjoy flying through the air. Instinctively though, both of their facial expressions would change back, almost clenching their teeth, as they anticipated the crash landing that was to come. Their faces would seize up and grimace just at the moment when the tube crashed back down into the water.

Cape's long hair flowed in the wind like seaweed in rolling breakers on the beach. One moment, her locks wrapped around her face. The next moment, they fanned out behind her like an ornate crown. Her hair flipped to and fro in the wind and the commotion. Her body bounced, her shoulders jolted, her feet and legs contorted, but, through it all, she kept a smile, and her laughter carried over the water like a seagull's song. Even through the torment of The Tube of Death, she somehow maintained her elegance . . . She truly is a special child.

I spun them through several doughnuts and a couple of figure-8s, and I have to admit that they managed to hold on pretty well. There were a couple of occasions when I thought for sure that they were done for . . . Cape was nearly off the tube, her legs and feet dragging through the water, as it spun wildly out to the side of the boat . . . Ethan dragging off the back of the tube because the g-forces were pulling him away, only inches away from having the sea monsters of the deep grab at the leg of his shorts . . . they have been known to eat plenty of shorts off the back of a tube . . . But alas, they managed to meet my every effort.

Surely, we are not headed for a draw?

Of course not! As any good, self-respecting, not-to-be-outdone-by-his-teenagers dad would do, I saved my best few tricks for last. Cutting a sharp doughnut, Hannah held fast to the console of the boat as we slashed through the water at 30 miles per hour. The tube swung hard to the right, and just as it came up alongside the boat, I made eye contact with Cape. She and Ethan both had smug grins on their faces, as if they were thinking, "Yawn . . . we've done this before" . . . so, without warning, I cut the wheel hard to the left and accelerated into the turn. The g-forces must've been tremendous as I could see each of them bulge every muscle in their arms and shoulders simply trying to hold on.

Unlike every other time where I would simply make a doughnut and then drive out into a straight line away from the wake, I stayed in the doughnuts and made two fast passes. The waves peeled off the back of the boat and fell into the doughnut hole like gobs of melted sugar piling up on themselves. What started as an 18-inch wave coming off the back of the boat compounded itself into 4-foot waves all meeting in the middle of the doughnuts. About midway through the third doughnut, Cape saw the waves building, and I think she realized what was to come.

All I had to do was cut the wheel back in the opposite direction and make a figure-8 through the middle of those waves. Mind you, the boat would dance just to the outside of the collision point in the doughnut hole, but the tube itself would come through the middle of the doughnut hole and all of that chaos. I've launched kids from the top of those 4-foot waves at 30 miles per hour before . . . it usually resembles something akin to a chicken truck overturning on the interstate. Carnage and splatters everywhere.

Cutting hard back in the opposite direction, the tube swung back through the wake, and I saw Cape's facial expression change as she realized what was about to happen. Ethan gripped desperately at the tube handles as the force and momentum tried to pull both of them off the back of the tube during the transition to the other side of the boat. I saw Cape's head turn, and I saw her mouth move as she said something to Ethan . . . and then both of them let go . . . they were smart enough to surrender.

Of course, there was some debate about who was victorious in the battle—they contended that I had not thrown them from the tube, nor did they surrender. Instead, they insisted that they had simply grown tired and bored with my less than impressive driving skills. I, on the other hand, knew full well that Cape realized what was to be when I slung them through the pyramid of waves in the middle of that doughnut, and before she was shot like a human cannonball off the top of one of those compounding waves, she wisely waved her white flag . . . and took Ethan with her. Since we could not come to an agreement, I petitioned to Hannah to be the tiebreaker . . . She declined, and so, as it was, we were each content with our own version of victory.

But they were soaking wet, and, the last time I checked, that was called evidence.

We all carried on for a few more minutes, each side insisting that it had taken the hill of victory when it came to The Tube of Death, before Cape turned the conversation and deflected from the issue by suggesting that Hannah and I should get on the tube and see if we could survive her boat-driving skills. While I had no doubt that I could survive the best that her Mario Andretti impersonations could muster, I also knew that I did not need to spend the next week at the chiropractor's office. Winning the battle but losing a war did not seem like a good plan to me . . . so, I yielded.

Such is the case too often in life, is it not? Driven by pride and emotion, sinful though they might be, we make decisions so we can win small victories. Perhaps we one-up a coworker. Perhaps we force our spouse into submission during an argument. Perhaps we alienate a friend with a singular accomplishment. So, we won the battle . . . but at what cost? Hannah and the girls suggest that I refuse to be wrong. Such arrogance can be costly. I know that, to some degree, they are right . . . I have a very difficult time accepting that my thesis or summation about a particular issue might be incorrect. And that stubbornness of opinion has won a battle or two, for sure, but lost a few wars along the way.

Take Cape, for example. She doesn't confide in me or seek my counsel nearly as much as Bay and Banks do. That's due, in no small part, to the fact that, in my younger years, I found it more prudent to be right in the things that I said, as opposed to giving her good counsel. I should have yielded. Had I done so, my bond with Cape would be much stronger than it is today. That is not to say that we don't share a bond . . . we do, and it is a good one. But it could be better.

But woe to the man who loses a war not once, but twice. That said, it is because of my shortcomings in counseling Cape that I learned how to counsel Banks. So, you might say that my failures with Cape led to successes with Banks. For that, I am grateful.

As the argument dwindled, neither side willing to accept defeat, we turned upriver to head back toward the house. It was getting on near noon, and our stomachs were starting to rumble more than our pride.

Bzzzzz . . . bzzzzz my phone vibrated on the top of the console of the boat. "Hey man," I said as I answered. It was Travis Martin.

"I just wanted to call and tell you 'Thank you' for sending Banks to help Anna," he said. Admittedly, I was befuddled, so I asked what he was talking about. "Weren't you at the parade with them?" he questioned. "I saw your truck up there."

I explained the situation with the Philpotts and that they had my truck. I then explained why we were on the lake and not at the parade, adding that Banks and her friend, Callie, both went with Brenda.

"Well, that makes me feel even better," he responded.

Still puzzled, I asked what he was referring to.

"You know Anna wanted to drive her car in the parade," he reminded me. And I did recall . . . He had spent a considerable amount of time over the previous six months or so restoring a late '60s Corvair for her 16th birthday. Anna, his daughter, loved the car, and she spent many an evening right by his side during the restoration process. The parade was sort of like the "grand entry" for the car to be revealed to the world. Pearl white and chrome, it was decorated with ribbons of red, white, and blue for the parade . . . it truly was a picture of the American Spirit. The American family . . . dad and daughter (Travis's wife, Heidi, and their other two kids helped some, too) . . . coming together to make something old new again. Good old-fashioned, American-made, American stick-to-it-iveness, American grit . . . the car represented so many good things about who we are as Americans.

"Well, it broke down about a hundred yards into the parade. The fuel pump went out, I think. Anna called me on the phone, uncertain about what to do. I told her just to push the car out of the way and that we would come get it after the parade.

"'But, Dad, I want to finish the parade,' she insisted. Her goal was to ride that car through the parade, and that was what she intended to do," he continued. "I didn't really know what to say or do, so I started trying to figure out how to get to where she was. My brother and one of his friends were with her, and I guess they just started pushing it down the parade route."

Admiring Anna's refusal to surrender, I still couldn't figure out how Banks factored into this.

"So, next thing I know, I see Banks and her little friend walk out onto the street and get in behind the car and start pushing. They pushed that car all the way through the parade route and smiled and waved and laughed the whole time."

I could hear the gratitude in Travis's voice. "She didn't have to do that. I don't think anybody asked her to help. I thought you had been there, and you told them to help, but now that I understand that you weren't there, it makes it even more special to me. Those girls saw a friend who needed some help, and they jumped in without hesitation."

"Please tell her that Anna and I said thank you. It meant a lot to Anna to be able to finish the parade."

I must admit that I welled with a different kind of pride in that moment . . . as a parent, I always pray that the values that we try to teach and instill in our children will stick like perfectly cooked spaghetti noodles to the wall. Our fear, of course, is that the lessons aren't cooked long enough, and the noodles will simply fall off as time goes on. Banks and Callie walking out into the parade route to push a car on a hot and humid July day made me think, if just for a moment, that the noodles were just right.

"Thank you, Lord."

For that is the American spirit, is it not? Neighbor helping neighbor? Friend helping friend? Red, white, and blue and never surrender? Helping the less fortunate? Bringing others into the folds of the freedom of democracy?

Yes . . . I'd say it is . . . God bless America.

For where else could you find an Irish immigrant with a quiver full of Asian and Hispanic arrows who gets teary eyed listening to Lee Greenwood? Where else would you find a blue-collar man and his white-collar friend raising their kids the best way they know how to. . . like two good ole boys? Where else could you find a community of people coming together with streamers of red, white, and blue, balloons of the same rainbow, and flags blazed in glory from every corner of their pickup truck and golf cart? Where else would you find ten thousand red, white, and blue beach balls? Where else could you find true grit? Where else would you find won't quit?

Why, right here—in these United States of America—that's where.

"'But, Dad, I want to finish the parade,' she insisted. Her goal was to ride that car through the parade, and that was what she intended to do," he continued. "I didn't really know what to say or do, so I started trying to figure out how to get to where she was. My brother and one of his friends were with her, and I guess they just started pushing it down the parade route."

T O U G H N U T S

Part One

Claude and I meet for breakfast once a week. We visit more often than that, but the breakfast meeting is a mainstay. We usually discuss the simpler things in life . . . our wives, our work, and sometimes, the job at hand. Sometimes, it's serious . . . sometimes, it's not.

He'll kill me for writing this . . . I couldn't even get him to pose for a picture, instead, having to ambush him . . . and he still turned his head away. He's still pretty quick for 80-something!

We have an unusual relationship. I usually text him the night before breakfast . . . "I'll see you in the morning if you don't die first." He'll respond with a simple, "Ok," and then, the next morning, he'll lecture me about how we shouldn't fear death. He's right, and I know it . . . "Death is just a moment in time, eternal. Bloop! And you'll be gone to the people here . . . but you'll spend eternity somewhere. If you know Jesus, you'll be alright. If you don't . . . well."

And that's just how he is. He speaks his mind, and he doesn't care if it offends you or not. Usually he is right, too. He often tells me, "I don't know why you want to eat breakfast with an old man." Well, I'll tell you why . . . because old men can teach me a lot about life that I don't already know . . . and I won't learn it unless somebody teaches me.

I once told him that I wanted to help him plant his spring garden, and that, in particular, I wanted to learn how to plant peanuts. "Why do you want to do that?" he asked . . . as if to suggest that no normal person would want to subject themselves to such.

"Because I want to learn. I want to learn, from start to finish, how to plant and harvest." I've planted before . . . as Hannah and I plant some produce plants every year, but to learn from an old-timer would be a new chapter in gardening for me.

"Why? You going to eat all those vegetables?"

"Yes, Claude . . . and put some up for the rest of the year, too. That garden can provide for me and my family for years to come."

"Well, alright. If you want to. If the rain will move on through, we'll get after it Saturday."

Saturday morning, I was up early . . . but not bright. I peered out my living room window at the grey skies, but it wasn't raining. I sent him a text at about 7:00 a.m. He said we'd better wait a little while . . . "Why?" like a dummy, I asked.

"Because it's raining at my house." Of course, I felt stupid . . . but it was a stupid assumption to make—it wasn't raining at my house, so surely it wasn't raining at his.

I think we do that a lot in life, don't we? We assume that if the sun is shining on me, then it must be shining on those around me, too. The Word tells us that God made the sun and the rain to fall on everyone equally . . . though, it's really a metaphor referring to the availability of salvation . . . but the truth is, we oftentimes take for granted that others are alright. Truth is, we don't want to know, most times, if they are not alright . . . because we are uncomfortable with helping others through their trials.

Claude asks me, "You doing okay?" almost every time we talk. I know I can confide in him. Sometimes, I do . . . sometimes, I don't. Sometimes, it's raining at my house, and sometimes, it's not . . . he always asks, and he is always willing to offer guidance to get me in from out of the rain. About 2 o'clock that afternoon, he called me. "Come on if you want to come." I was shortly on my way.

We planted Silver Queen and Golden Queen corn, and, most importantly, we planted a bunch of peanuts. Right about the time we ran out of peanuts, the thunder rolled and the lightning clapped . . . "We best get back up to the shop if we want to stay dry," he offered. So, we retreated to the shop . . . surrounded by lawnmowers and tools and grease and dust . . . the dog came and joined us, too . . . we talked for an hour or so. I was tired and sweaty. The dust of the field plastered itself to the sweat and thatch of hair on my legs. As it dried, the dust converted from a muddy paste to a mortared stucco. I felt it pull the hairs from my legs as I shifted in my seat from time to time. I had done much of the labor for the day, but that was how I wanted it. Seemed a fitting trade to me—I provided the labor, and he provided the knowledge. I don't know how many seeds I planted that day . . . too many to count. So, the cool air that came with the hellacious thunderstorm was welcomed . . . it cooled me down, and I was grateful.

I wasn't the only one planting seeds that day . . .

I planted seeds that, at best, would last a season. Crows ate some. Deer ate others. Turkeys and coons did, too. Some seeds fell too deep and did not sprout. Others were choked out by the coffeeweed and other intruders. Some of the seeds I planted bore fruit . . . and we enjoyed the fruits of that labor. But best of all . . . the seeds Claude planted will bear fruit for a lifetime.

Already, I am a better man because of his input into my life. And I pray the Lord allows me to remain humble and plowable . . . so that men like Claude can continue to plant seeds in my heart.

Proverbs 27:17, NIV says that "As iron sharpens iron, so one person sharpens another." Most of the men that I deal with at work are either so hardened that they are not plowable, or they have no one willing to invest in them. I have no idea why Claude invests in me . . . but I am ever so thankful for the time.

We planted six rows of peanuts, each about 75 yards long. The reddish-brown dirt of the Alabama soil was rich with nutrients . . . it engulfed the seeds. Surveying the

I called Claude three times to get his permission to publish this story. He never said "no." Finally, I said, "Claude, I have to hear you say 'yes' or 'no'." He grumbled a little and said, "It's fine with me. But it's only going to keep you from selling books." I told him this wasn't about selling books . . . it was about respect and honor, for I wanted to give him both.

landscape after planting is somewhat anti-climactic . . . all that work, and you don't see any immediate results. Claude was cautiously optimist as we surveyed back over the field. "If all these make, we'll have enough peanuts to fill your truck and mine." I hoped he was right, and I was excited at the prospect.

Little did I know that planting was the easy part . . . all things considered.

Through the spring and summer, we hoed. To be fair, he hoed as much, or more, than I did. For 80-something, that old man gets around pretty good. I don't much like the hoe. I never looked forward to doing it . . . though, unlike the lack of instant gratification that came from planting, it did feel good to look back across the patch and see the results of the work. Uprooted coffeeweed, dandelions, and all sorts of other unidentified weeds lay tattered and strewn . . . the peanuts and corn stalks were all that remained. It was, in fact . . . weed genocide. It was satisfying.

Weeks went by, and we continued to tend to the hoeing . . . Claude would call me every few days and give me an update. They began to be repetitive. "You need to come over here and shoot these deer. They are eating our peanuts," he complained.

"Claude, I can't. It's not hunting season," I reasoned.

"Well, so? Seems to me that if something is eating all your food, you ought to be able to kill it in self-defense. I'm an old man . . . this might be my last meal. I don't want some deer eating it before I can." It was hard to argue with his logic . . . he was right. We worked hard and poured blood, sweat, and tears into that field . . . all by hand. And the deer were eating us out of house and home. You see, we didn't have a peanut plant taller than about four inches . . . the biggest stalk of the bunch was as big around as a pencil.

The deer didn't come every day. Instead, they were patient. Like panhandlers who knew that if they asked every day, "Hey mister, can you spare some change?" you wouldn't oblige. But if they only hit you up once a week or so . . . they would fare better. The fact that they were intentional in their schedule made keeping them away difficult. I peed in a jug for about three days and then doused some old t-shirts (that I may have gotten from Hannah's drawer) with urine and hung them on stakes around the edges of the garden. I was sure the urine-soaked scarecrows worked masterfully . . . for three days, not one deer track was to be found in the garden. But they were only being patient. A few more days passed, and I checked the garden . . . I was sure that Claude had taken his riding mower and mowed the tops out of the peanuts . . . I was furious. "You dummy!" he chided, "I told you to shoot those deer." You see . . . about once a week, they would come in and literally mow the patch down. Every single peanut plant . . . to a nub.

But we were men! Not to be outdone by a few hungry quadrupeds, we doubled down on our efforts.

Claude cut up a few old t-shirts (that may or may not have belonged to the girls) and we soaked them with diesel fuel. We hung them around the perimeter of the garden . . . the loud odor of diesel permeated the air. There was no mistaking the refinery smell . . . surely, this would keep the deer at bay. Then, we bundled aluminum cans together on strings . . . like wind chimes, they'd rattle and clank at the slightest hint of a breeze . . . and we even assembled half of a real scarecrow . . . only half, because neither of us wanted to part with a good pair of pants.

We were right proud of our efforts . . . I still recall standing on the hill overlooking our little fortress of greenery and thinking, "We've done it. This will keep them away, for sure."

Apparently, sometime that night, the deer looked down that same hill at the garden patch and then drove their diesel trucks in to load up, mistaking the scarecrow for a restaurant hostess. "Buffet for four!" the scarecrow must have offered. Like bandits invading the art gallery, they would steal almost every precious morsel before they left.

And then there were turkeys.

"Claude, what is going on around here? It's like Wild Kingdom! The Summerlin Petting Zoo!" I fussed.

He shook his head . . . his answer was the same every time. "I told you . . . all you have to do is bring a lawn chair and a gun. You can fix this in one night."

"Of all the crazy places to plant a row crop," I exclaimed, pulling the hoe through a patch of weeds. A mere twenty feet away from me stood seventeen turkeys. They all walked up to the edge of the patch and stared at me . . . for at least five minutes . . . as if they were annoyed that I was in their patch! I stood my ground, not yielding an inch. I even boldly declared to the big tom that led the group that "This was my patch" as I planted the butt end of the hoe in the ground, as if it was Moses' staff. The tom strutted back and forth a few times . . . and let out a long, protracted "gobble-gobble-gobble." Looking back on it now that I am more familiar with the turkey dialect, I am fairly certain that he said, "Like MacAuthur said to the people of the Philippines . . . 'I'll be back.'"

And then he and his hens slowly eased off into the woods.

That night, I was anxious. I barely slept, for fear that the turkeys would return. I wasn't sure that any of our defenses were designed to keep turkeys out of the patch. I'd asked Claude, but he was, if nothing else, consistent: "You know what would keep them out?" He didn't wait for me to respond. "If you would just shoot the dang things."

I was up early the next morning . . . I wanted to go by the patch on my way to work. Driving up Claude's road, the patch lay on the left in a small valley between two hills. Stopping on the road and looking down at the patch, I could see the carnage. There was no need to get any closer. I could tell that many of the plants had been "scratched" up . . . that is to say that the turkeys had come in and scratched at the base of the plants to get at the peanuts that lay beneath. With many of their roots exposed and some plants completely uprooted, much destruction had set in. And for those that had been uprooted, it was plain to see that the juicy goober peas that once clung to the roots were all gone. That wild tom and his band of misfits had come in the night and plundered half of the rows.

I was beginning to think Claude's plan was best . . . "Kill them all!" I muttered under my breath . . . scanning the graveyard of peanut plants, I considered calling every turkey hunter I knew.

But deer and turkeys were not our only foes.

Rain.

I should just leave this spot in the story blank . . . a lack of discussion of rain would best aptly describe the situation we faced . . . you'd get the idea.

It was like a dust bowl. Dust swirled up from underneath each step I took every time I crossed the garden . . . tiny dust-nadoes formed around my feet as I walked. Just looking at the ground made me thirsty. The morning came that we appointed for "picking" . . . Claude drove his old McCormick Farmall down each row, and the belly plows uprooted and turned over the plants that survived the seven deadly plagues. As he turned the peanuts, a process using a special plow that digs underneath the rooty fruits and pulls them to the surface, a cloud of reddish-brown dust lifted high into the air behind him . . . almost as if the old, red Farmall breathed dusty fire from its bowels as it puttered through the field. At times, I lost sight of Claude in the fog of red . . . but he never stopped. He chugged, both tractor and breath, through the dusty haze, until every row was turned up. He wore a bandana over his face . . . a ring of red dust lay circularly over his mouth, showing the bandana has served its purpose . . . it filtered the dust as he breathed.

"I'm not sure what we just turned up," he said with disdain. "Mostly . . . coffeeweed and other trash, and then a few peanut stubs," as we called them. What the deer didn't pluck and the turkeys didn't scratch . . . the hot heat of the Alabama summer tortured. "This is the most pitiful peanut patch I've ever seen," Claude uttered. "You are a terrible farmer. Better not quit your day job . . . cause your wife will leave you for a man who can actually grow something."

Point taken.

The peanuts never had much of a chance. Most of them had one or two peanuts clinging underneath the stubbed stalks. An exciting find was a plant that grew six or seven peanuts. Between us, we didn't even harvest a gallon of peanuts.

So much for a community peanut boil!

As we walked back to the shop carrying the spoils of war with us, I said, "If we were back on the homestead trying to live off the land, I reckon we would starve to death."

He stopped, turned over his shoulder, cut a glance at me, and said, "No, we would have eaten a lot of deer and turkey."

Point taken.

I started this journey to learn how to grow peanuts. They are tough nuts to crack. And now, in my third season of growing them, I think I know how to grow peanuts . . . sort of. But in this first season . . . I learned a lot more than that along the way.

Claude reminded me later on that life is not unlike that peanut patch. As with the deer, life sometimes tries to rob us of the leaves of life that give us provision. "Maybe you lose a job, or you can't pay your bills on time that month . . . sometimes it's hard to provide for your family. They will be okay," he said. And as with the turkeys, sometimes life tears at your foundation. "Maybe you lose a loved one or suffer through some terrible illness. They will be okay," he maintained. "For, you see, as long as you keep your roots firmly planted where they can get water . . . you will bear good fruit."

Of course, I knew he was referring to the Living Water of Christ and being a tree that bears good fruit . . . I understood the lesson well. Ever since, I've always reminded myself when hard times come to be thankful that my roots were firmly planted.

"Stand firm in the faith . . . " 1 Corinthians 16:13.

What say you, old codger? Who are you investing in? There are lots of younger men like me who are eager to learn and to be sharpened. All we are waiting on is someone who is willing to invest a little in us. What say you, young buck? Are you plowable? There is much that we don't know . . . and we should take heed to the offerings of those men around us, who've seen bountiful springs and harsh winters alike. Their wisdom is life-learned and more valuable than gold.

There will never be a harvest if no one is willing to spend the time plowing the fields. And the unplowed field will likely only produce inedible fruit. And trust me . . . planting that garden will provide for me and my family . . . long after we've eaten that last ear of corn and those few peanuts.

God Bless.

Part Three

Every harvest is meant to be a feast . . . and a feast, we would have.

Driving home that mid-morning, I was disappointed. Claude and I had spent countless hours tending to those peanut plants. The deer and the turkey enjoyed most of the fruits of our labors . . . and that frustrated me. "Was it even worth the trouble?" I considered. Short-sightedly, I didn't fully appreciate the value of the time spent with Claude or the lessons learned from the toil. I was too focused on the here and now . . . the instant gratification.

I turned in the driveway to the house. Hannah had the doors and windows to the

Claude loves this old Farmall tractor. Every year we planted anything, he used it. And I have to admit, as old as they both were . . . they still did a really good job on the task at hand.

house open . . . something she customarily did several times a year to "let the house air out." It was a hot day, and I was already sweaty from the morning's work. My mouth was parched from the dust of the field . . . my cheeks had a rosy, hazed veil of dust across them . . . I whipped my hair back and forth, and red dirt fell from my longest locks. "That dust cloud that Claude pulled up was some serious business," I thought to myself. I couldn't imagine how dirty my ears and nose would be . . . "The waistline of my pants . . . my socks . . . " I knew I was a mess. I parked the truck halfway down the driveway so as to not block Hannah's car in. Carrying my bowl of wares toward the door, I lamented the fact that I would not be greeted by a cool blast of air-conditioned chill when I walked through the door. Again . . . in the matter of just a few moments, I found myself struggling with a desire for instant gratification.

Hannah met me at the door. She often does. She had an old dishrag in her hand . . . wringing her hands with it, she absorbed the residual water from her last washed dish. "Hey, sugar! What's in the bowl?" she asked from the doorstep.

At this point, I should observe that I had always remained optimistic with Hannah about the success of our peanut endeavor. Each time I would come home from working the garden, I'd complain of the invading marauders, but with confidence that only the male ego can muster, I'd assure her, "We have finally figured out a way to keep them out." So, along with the assurance of our success came the suggestion that we'd have a sizeable crop, also.

With that in mind, we had already planned our "community peanut boil." Instead of freezing the peanuts in gallon bags and eating them on occasion, we were going to invite fifty or so of our neighbors and friends over and cook all of them on the same day. Like old-timers, we'd sit around under a couple of big oaks in the back yard "eatin' goober peas" while the men swapped lies about big bucks and bigger fish and the women shared war stories about taking care of their husbands and their children . . . the former term probably being sometimes well-defined by the latter.

An old-time peanut boil is always done outside. It's a simple set up . . . a cooker, usually homemade . . . consisting of a rim off of an old truck. This rim serves as the eye of the stove, if you will. Welded to one side of the rim, but more in the bowels than on the edge, is a gas burner . . . or two. Sophisticated, fancy pants kind of folks had three burners. Welded to the other side of the rim is a tripod of three pieces of angle iron . . . they are the legs. A propane bottle from the "gas main" connects to the burners . . . fire it up, and the prettiest blue flame you've ever seen will dance up from the belly of the rim. All that steel holds the heat well, and it gets super hot, super quick. Hannah and I have a cooker. George and Brenda had another. We each also have ten-gallon pots . . . with everything lined up, we were set to have a great "community peanut boil." We'd asked some of the ladies to bring some sweet tea and lemonade . . . and they'd surely bring some tasty, sugary treats, too. Throw some salt and bunch of peanuts in the ten-gallon pots and let them slow roll in a boil for a little while . . . and we were sure to have ourselves a grand old time.

My pace slowed as I neared the back door to the house . . . Hannah's smile could light up the world. Her eyes tracked mine as she greeted me . . . "What's in the bowl?" she repeated. "Did y'all get a mess of peanuts?" she asked, craning her neck slightly as she broke eye contact to look toward the back of the truck. Bringing her eyes back toward me, she looked down into the bowl . . . I was now standing just below her at the stoop to the back door. Her eyes fell to the bowl, and she saw the half gallon or so of peanuts I held in my hand.

Right in that moment, I felt like a failure. Every man wants to provide for his wife and family. And even though this peanut crop had little to do with our edible survival, the bowl . . . to me . . . represented my effort to provide for my family. My eyes drifted down to the bowl and then lifted back up to hers like a puppy dog who had just been caught peeing on the new carpet. Her smile twitched and her mouth gaped open . . . "Is that it? Surely, y'all got more peanuts than that? You are kidding," she finally demanded, looking back toward the truck. I'm sure that, in the moment, she did think I was trying to "pull her leg" . . . it would certainly not have been the first time. But she soon realized just how serious I was when I forced the bowl into her hands and made my way past her into the doorway.

Her smile drifted down into an expression of concern . . . "Well, baby, what happened?" she asked with a tone of support that only a man's wife can convey. I knew she wasn't being judgmental . . . she sensed my feelings of failure.

"What didn't happen? Deer. Turkey. Coons. Crows. Heat . . . we never had a chance." I was dwelling in my own self-pity . . . and she quickly sensed that I wanted to wallow in it.

"Well, the Lord just wanted us to have a date instead of a community peanut boil," she offered with a twinkle in her eye. Her smile came up from its momentary lapse. "This afternoon, I am going to boil these peanuts, and we will have the best date ever!" Hannah always has a way of finding the positive . . . it is one of her best qualities. "Now . . . get out of my house . . . speaking of *Peanuts*, you look like the kid in the cartoon who always had the dust cloud following him around. Get! Get!" She popped the dish towel at me . . . "snap-snap-snap" . . . as she herded me back out the door.

I stood in the back yard and stripped down to my underwear. Red dirt fell from every crevasse and fold of skin. I shook my hair like a dog that had just come out of the water. When I finished and regained my bearings, I found myself standing in the midst of a reddish-brown cloud of fine, silty, Alabama summer dusty dirt. "Hose off with the water hose before you come back in here."

It felt like it was a hundred and ten degrees that afternoon. I don't know about at your house, but at our house during the summer, the water that comes out of the garden hose somehow magically transforms to near freezing temperatures. I hesitated as she watched from the stoop. "You just want to see me wet and naked," I suggested. "I just vacuumed this whole house . . . and you aren't bringing that cloud of dirt in with you," she retorted. She took two steps down the stoop and grabbed the end of the hose. "No . . .

"I never planned
in my imagination
A situation so heavenly
A fairy land
that no one else could enter
And in the center,
just you and me

Hear my heart
beat like a hammer
My arms wound around you tight
And stars fell on Alabama last night"

Stars Fell on Alabama, Originally recorded by
the Guy Lombardo Orchestra . . . but made
distinctively Alabama by Jimmy Buffett.

no . . . noooooo . . . " I insisted. But, with the same lightning speed as my granny mustered when retrieving a switch from the nearest bush to stripe my legs . . . Hannah picked up the hose, turned it on, and began spraying me . . . all in the blink of an eye. I ran . . . high stepping and hopping as I did . . . as if that somehow might aide in my retreat. "Get back here," she insisted. I refused . . . and I stood fifty feet out in the back yard, just out of reach of the spray . . . in my fairly wet underwear.

Then my neighbor moseyed up through his back yard . . . he looked my way and stopped dead in his tracks. He spit on the ground, nodded his head, and shoved his hands deeper into his pockets. I sheepishly raised my right hand and half-heartedly offered an embarrassing wave. He turned and moseyed back inside his house. His dog, who was following close behind, stood there and growled at me.

"Come on, now, Hannah. Put the hose down. The neighbors are out."

By this time, she was nearly in stitches . . . and she finally relented. As she gathered my clothes and whipped the dust out of them, I made my way to the nearest shower.

And there . . . in the shower . . . I washed all of that dirt from my face and ears and hair and legs . . . all of it . . . down the drain. In the solitariness of the shower, I began to reflect on the failure of the endeavor . . . the sense of dejection began to creep back into my psyche. I watched the dirt swirl down the drain of the shower and lamented the lost time and labor . . . the value of time spent doing other, more productive things . . . and fretted the waste of the effort.

The dirt from my hair trickled down my back and made a swirl of stained and clear water going down the drain.

"Lord, what was the point?" I asked sincerely.

More dirt washed off the back of my legs as I wiped them with a rag. The darkness of the swirl grew thicker. The more the dirt washed away, the more I reflected. As if the truth was to be revealed under the mask of the dirt, I began to reflect deeper . . . beyond the garden itself. I soon found myself reflecting back on the conversations that Claude and I had shared. I couldn't help but recall the laughter and the lessons. I couldn't help but be warmed by thoughts of the support of my wife, who knows me so well that she can see through the haze of the dirt . . . and she knows just what to say to wash away all of the despair. I couldn't help but realize that under all of the dirt of the desire for instant gratification, there was plenty of valuable fruit.

Just as you have to husk the shell of a peanut to get to the goodie of the goober peas . . . I had to wash the roughness of the experience away in order to find the goodness inside.

And there was plenty of good fruit . . . elsewise, I wouldn't be writing about it some years later. That might have been the most valuable crop I've ever planted . . . outside of my family. It was certainly a crop that kept producing fruit for years to come . . . and I am ever so thankful . . . for all of that dirt.

Love you, Claude. Love you, Hannah.

God Bless.

Part Four

It was lunchtime when I emerged from the bathroom, fresh and renewed. "Fresh" in the sense that all the red dirt had been washed from my crow's feet, my curly locks, and even from behind my ears. Renewed in the sense that watching all of that red dirt swirl down the drain reminded me that God has a purpose in everything we do . . . we simply must be willing to look for it and listen to Him. My labors had been less about planting peanuts and more about growing friendships. With a spring in my step, I walked into the kitchen where Hannah scurried to and fro.

"Well, don't you look all clean and spiffy," she chattered as I turned the corner. Her smile always lifts me even higher . . . wide and bright, she has a certain twinkle about her. It's not a contrived smile . . . not one of obligation, but one of celebration. When she smiles, her joy and peace ride on waves of pearly white to the target . . . and the recipient can't help but feel "better." I always do . . . even when I don't feel bad.

I smiled back, and we met in the middle of the kitchen. This time, though, instead of popping me with a dish towel as if she was herding cattle out of the house, she embraced me. We hugged and circled around the kitchen and our lips met . . . after a warm kiss, she leaned back and whispered in a soft and romantic voice . . . "There is something sexy about being married to a peanut farmer." I could feel Tim "The Toolman" Taylor conjured inside of me . . . "Arrgghh, arrggh, arrggh!" I grunted in response.

"Any man who grunts like that must be hungry," she surmised.

And I was . . . "Bacon? Is that bacon?" I dropped my hands from around her waist and sniffed the air through an imaginary trail toward the sizzling skillet of pork belly that snapped and popped on the gas burner. She laughed at my antics . . . she knew my grunts were more than just a bad impersonation of a '90s television show, and I knew that her offer of food was not a rejection, but merely the practical recognition that there was bound to be some kid roaming around the house somewhere. Men don't much concern themselves with such logistical problems . . . thank God our wives do.

A fresh, sliced tomato and a slab of crisp, green lettuce stretched across the kitchen counter. Marbled cream and brown Hull Pottery salt and pepper shakers sat at the far end. Closest to me was a fresh loaf of Bunny Bread. "I love fresh BLTs," I offered.

Hannah wrapped her hands around my waist from behind. "I know you do . . . and guess what will be a great midafternoon snack and perfect complement to a BLT?" I admit, my mind was still in the gutter . . . and my suggestion that the B, the L, and the T stood for something else . . . that more closely resembled certain parts of her anatomy . . . as if to suggest she was the perfect after-lunch snack, was quickly rejected. She pulled away from me with exclamation . . . "No! You dork! Peanuts! I'm going to boil the peanuts!"

I was a little embarrassed, but still not ready to give up the fight . . . "Oh? Is that what we are calling it now?"

"Hannah wrapped her hands around my waist from behind. 'I know you do . . . and guess what will be a great midafternoon snack and perfect complement to a BLT?' I admit, my mind was still in the gutter . . . and my suggestion that the B, the L, and the T stood for something else . . . that more closely resembled certain parts of her anatomy . . . as if to suggest she was the perfect after-lunch snack, was quickly rejected. She pulled away from me with exclamation . . . 'No! You dork! Peanuts! I'm going to boil the peanuts!'"

She slapped playfully at my chest and quickly got me back in line . . . "Shut up and fix your sandwich."

"Yes, ma'am," I finally relented.

We sat under the midday sun of the big windows at our breakfast table and enjoyed the Southern summertime staple, but we also enjoyed each other. The sun burst forth through the windows, cascading down on Hannah's face, showering her right side with rays of adoration. At the same time, the bright light cast a shadow on her left side . . . and that shadow was the perfect platform for her smile to radiate from.

I don't know why, but the sun always seems to shine brighter when Hannah is nearby.

I was . . . and still am . . . smitten.

After lunch, we cleaned up the kitchen, and she audibly went through her "to-do" list for the day. She was about to head out for a few errands . . . life in south Alabama is not complete on the weekend without at least one trip to "Momma's house and the Dollar General." By now, I had grown disinterested. If we were not going to do something that involved B, L, or T . . . I wasn't overly concerned. I started to mentally wade through my own "to-do" list. Hannah's voice resonated in the back of my eardrums like Charlie Brown's teacher. I turned the old, tarnished brass knob on the back door and headed to my shop to start my projects.

"Are you listening to me?" she quipped as I pulled the door open.

"Of course, I am. Every word!"

My insistent tone persuaded her . . . "Okay . . . now don't forget."

"I won't," I assured her . . . though I wasn't entirely sure what it was I was promising. "No matter," I thought to myself. "She will ask me again." I was confident that forgiveness would be the better plan . . . no man ever wants to admit to his wife that he wasn't listening.

I tinkered in my shop and waved as she backed out of the driveway. Cape was in the back seat. "I'm taking her to town, and I'll be back. Don't forget now!"

"I won't," I yelled, blowing them a kiss with my right hand as they pulled out onto the quiet street. I recollected that Bay had spent the night off, and I dropped Banks off earlier that morning when I went to pick peanuts . . . I now had the peace of knowing I was alone. And peaceful it was . . .

Being alone is part of what draws me to working with my hands. I am a poor woodworker. I am an inept carpenter. I am a sad excuse for a mechanic. But I love working with my hands . . . I build. I construct. I craft. I turn. I repair. All the while . . . I am only thinking about the "thing" that lay before me. Woodworking forces my brain to let go of the murder, mayhem, and tragedy that I see on a daily basis. Working with my hands is a cleansing of sorts . . . it allows my mind to drift.

As I measured once and cut twice . . . my mind thought of peanuts. I recollected Uncle Pickens' tale of renting the big field across the highway—the one you might recall that I wrote of in "The Lincoln Chronicles"— to "a carpetbagger." I'm not sure why Pickens called the fellow a carpetbagger. I suppose he was a "Yankee" . . . though he never actually said that. Perhaps it was because he wasn't a farmer either . . . you see, Pickens rented the near-50-acre field to the fellow to plant peanuts. After a near perfect spring and gorgeous summer growing season, the man's peanut plants were as green as emeralds and as vibrant as the sun glistening in the morning dew. "I've never seen peanut plants that pretty," Pickens said. "Before or since," he added for emphasis.

"One day, that fella came to the house and was near about in tears. I asked him, 'What's troubling you?' and he said, 'The whole crop is a bust.'" Pickens recalled the tale as if it had just happened yesterday. "He said he searched nearly every plant in that field and couldn't find one dad-blasted peanut. Said he had spent every dime he had to plant those peanuts and wasn't going to be able to pay the land rent." Pickens said, "It was the beatenest thing. So, I walked on over to that field and grabbed the first plant I came to. I pulled hard on the meaty stalk until the earth finally let go beneath it . . . there were more peanuts on those roots than I had ever seen on a plant in my life. It was like peanut gold—I tell you what!" Pickens felt sorry for the carpetbagger . . . I suppose he went on the explain to the man that peanuts were a root crop—a fact that fellow clearly didn't realize. Pickens always got the biggest howl from telling that story . . . that man surely didn't know much about peanuts.

Drawn back to the task at hand, I realized my craftsmanship skills were still lacking, as the board I had cut was too short for its intended purpose. "That table might wobble," I chuckled to myself. Sawdust clung to the sweat on my forehead, and I squinted my eyes to keep them from catching any of the dust as it fell from my hair. The measurements grow harder to read with each passing day . . . I keep telling myself it's the squinty eyes from the sawdust. Surely it is. I also keep having to remind myself that I am not forgetful. And I oftentimes reflect back on things Hannah told me . . . just to prove that I listened. I pondered all of these apparent frailties as I recut the last leg of the table . . . out of the corner of my eye, I noticed Hannah pulled back in the driveway.

She had Dollar General bags draped over her arms like they were a poor woman's mink coat. She did that awkward waddle-walk that we all do when our arms are so loaded down with grocery bags that it throws our center of balance off. I put down the table leg and dusted my hands . . . headed to help her.

As I made it to her car to grab the last of the bags, she opened the back door of the house. "Oh my gaaawwwddd!" Her yell was panicked. The shriek captured my attention, and I pivoted, expecting a snake or some other critter. Instead, smoke rolled out of the door of the house. I dropped my bags and ran to the door . . . as I arrived, she came out with a pot of blackened and scorched vegetable matter. Black smoke billowed up from the now ruined pot . . . "What on earth?" I barked as I fanned the smoke. She sat the pot down in the yard, and I proceeded to open most of the doors and windows to the house.

Fit to be tied, I intended to lambast her with every ounce of my being for her carelessness. Marching like I was the drum major at a high school football game, index finger extended . . . I was armed and ready. "What in the sam-fire-hell happened?" I demanded with authority. She paused, took a deep breath, and smiled as wide as the Mississippi. It was hard to stay mad when confronted with such majesty . . .

"Those were your peanuts," she offered quietly. Her monotone, yet stern voice, suggested to me that perhaps there was something amiss. "You can either explain that you are deaf and didn't hear me tell you to turn the peanuts off after five minutes and let them simmer . . . or you can tell me that you are too senile to remember to turn the stove off. But whatever you do, you better not tell me you weren't paying attention or that you forgot." By now, I knew that not only was the Great Peanut Boil of 2019 going to be cancelled, but I feared we'd be having cooked goose for supper . . . namely, mine.

I furled my brow to indicate I was intimately paying attention. As she "Wanh, wannnhhh, wahh, wahhh, waaa'd," I nodded my headed to make sure I was intentionally demonstrating I was responsive to her emotions. And when I was quite convinced that I was absolutely responsible for nearly burning down our house and ruining our meager crop of peanuts, I clasped her hand in mine, looked deep into her eyes, and said, "I sure would like a BLT."

Woooooo!

Just remember, friends, that laughter is a great medicine. Prayer is better, but laughter is good. Most of this story is true, and Hannah and I still have a great laugh about it even to this day. God was so faithful to us through those peanuts . . . in so many ways . . . and we never ate a single one.

Sometimes, the blessing is in the calamity. Everything about the peanuts that year was calamity. But here I am, years later . . . writing about the blessings that came from them.

Have an awesome day!

WARMTH IN A COLD WORLD

Last night was the coldest night of the season . . . the low was forecast to be 37 degrees. Yesterday, I purged the air from the gas lines and made sure the gas logs were working properly. I brought in Hannah's fancy fern . . . I can't remember the name of it, but I know it is fancy. I moved a few other of her plants under the porch. And lastly, I pulled out Lincoln's yoga mat—Hannah got him a blanket, too—and made him a pallet on the floor in front of the gas logs.

As I make my way into the living room this morning, I find him sleeping soundly on his pallet. We turn the gas logs off during the night, but he is still warm and cozy inside the house . . . the upper sixties is much preferred to the upper thirties . . . even for a dog. He raises his head and thumps the hardwood floor three or four times . . . his way of saying, "Good morning." I scratched behind his ears and whispered, "Good morning, buddy." Releasing his ears, he laid back down. The gas logs fired to life, and the heat chased the chill quickly away. Lincoln repositioned himself to catch the heat . . . he thumped the floor three or four more times in celebration of the warmth. I stood on the hearth, as if a rotisserie, warming my bones as I turned. The heat was good to me, too . . . soothing and comforting.

Within a minute or two, I am hypnotized by the flames . . . I break my hypnotic state, shaking my head and wondering, "How long have I been standing here?" I laughed at myself and started making my way to the kitchen . . . Lincoln is snoring obnoxiously.

Through the window, I can see that Jack Frost has paid us a visit . . . a thin veil of ice covers the ground. Everywhere, except under the trees, that is. The trees catch the dew as it falls, so dew never accumulates under a tree. The tree shelters all that resides below it. Otherwise, though, the ground looks milky white out across the back yard. Silver streaks of frost zigzag their way around the edges of the trees and completely envelope the open spaces.

I imagine the "crunching" sound one often hears as they walk through thick frost in the pre-dawn morning . . . staring out the window, I see where a deer, no doubt, foraging the massive buffet for breakfast under the white oak tree, has already crunched her way through part of the yard. I traced her tracks from the woods, through the yard,

Even the warmest fires eventually fade away.

and to the white oak tree. Patiently, I gaze . . . and, soon enough, she reveals herself. A young doe . . . hiding in the stillness under the canopy of the tree. No doubt, the frost-less ground there is more comfortable... and she certainly is enjoying the smorgasbord of massive acorns that the tree provides to her.

A big brown squirrel joins her under the tree. In fact, he almost appears aggravated with her. She is, after all, eating "his" acorns. He stands on his hind legs glaring at her . . . reaching down and picking up an acorn with both hands, he begins to eat. Then he chatters at her . . . she stops eating herself and turns her head to him. As if to say, "There is plenty for all of us under the tree," she shakes her head and then resumes her feast. The squirrel gnaws at his acorn furiously . . . still aggravated with the deer . . . but he knows that this tree and its provision are the best to be had.

After a choice glance, he rests . . . "Enough for both of us, there is," he must have agreed. And they both enjoyed the shelter and the provision.

The sun, too, is trying to find its way into the yard . . . the slightest hint of a fireball peaks through the trees at the horizon. For a moment, my eyes squint as they adjust to the piercing light. Soon, the rays will stretch across the yard, finding everything in its place and dissolving the ice. For now, though, there is a battle for balance . . . the frost holds firm to the grass blades . . . clutching tightly against the sun's encroachment. And try as it might, even the frost knows it cannot prevail . . . for even the coldest of darkness must always give way to the warmth of the light.

I turn my attention to the coffee pot. A mainstay in our house, I get up every morning . . . most times before the sun . . . and make the coffee. The aromatic Columbian flavor permeates the house . . . drifting from room to room and enchanting my nose with its seduction. Hannah always prefers to have her cup warmed . . . I run hot water over the cup until the cup itself is hot. That way, her coffee doesn't waste its heat on the cup . . . instead, the heat of the coffee is preserved . . . to warm your insides. I run water through my own cup until it is hot, and then I pour my first cup. Standing in the kitchen window, watching that same deer . . . the coffee cup warms my hands. I press my lips against the cup and find comfort in the warmth from its brim. And then, as if a grand finale on the Fourth of July, I sip the warmth into my mouth . . . and the trickle down my throat warms my soul.

From my perch at the window, I can see Hannah, still sleeping, in our bed. She is nestled in a cocoon of sorts, wrapped up in the sheet and blanket and down comforter . . . she is warm and cozy within her layers. The air in the house is still cool. Though the gas logs do heat well and give off a romantic glow . . . they are slow to heat the house. "It is still cold in here," I think to myself, taking my next sip of coffee. "But I know she is warm," I chuckled to myself.

I've never known anyone who can sleep like Hannah can. Sleep is not just her friend; it is, perhaps, her best friend. If Hannah lays motionless for more than a minute or two . . . she is asleep to the world. And she doesn't wake easily either . . . most mornings, I have my coffee and write, all before she ever tosses for the first time. Her body is nestled within the layers such that the only thing I can see of her is her face . . . barely poking out from the cocoon, one might liken her to a turtle who is considering sticking her head out to see what is in the world. Yet, instead, she sleeps soundly . . . safe within the warmth and comfort of the bed.

Lincoln is warm by the fire.

The critters are comfortable under the tree . . . fast away from Jack Frost.

The sun and coffee warm my body.

Hannah is warm in her cocoon.

It's the coldest day of the fall . . . but take comfort . . . it is Sunday.

He has provided for you, too . . . He has given you warmth and shelter, food and provision . . . despite the cold, there is plenty of shelter for all of us. His provision knows no bounds . . . and His Light will always prevail.

"Come to me, all you who are weary and burdened, and I will give you rest. Take my yoke upon you and learn from me, for I am gentle and humble in heart, and you will find rest for your souls. For my yoke is easy and my burden is light." Matthew 11:28-30, NIV.

As for me and my house . . . we will bask in the warmth of His love this morning. We will shelter under the tree of His provision. We will feast at His table, and we will find warmth wrapped in His arms. As for me and my house . . . we will serve the Lord.

If you are cold and weary this morning... seek Him, and he will give you rest. Join Him in His house . . . or yours . . . but join Him, nonetheless.

Have a beautiful day . . . God is good.

True warmth comes from Jesus and from the love of family, frends, and a faithful dog. As you bring yourself nearer the end of this journey, I pray you have warmth . . . and that this book helped warm your soul . . . even if but for a moment.

——— C L O S I N G   T H O U G H T ———

It's been nearly ten years since I began the journey that is Shepherding Outdoors. Three books and hundreds of stories with hundreds of thousands of words . . . and still, I don't feel the season changing.

As I type these last few words, though, fall is setting in south Alabama. Nighttime temperatures are dipping into the 50s, and the air seems slightly crisper . . . the sky slightly bluer . . . and the stars slightly brighter than they were just a few months ago. The heat of summer always clouds not only judgment . . . not only the sky . . . but also the mind. That is, after all, why dogs dig holes in the dirt driveway . . . to escape the clouded swelter of the dog days of summer.

Parenting is sometimes not dissimilar. Frustrated and confused, sometimes the parental temptation is to lay down and surrender to the swelter. No longer resolved to fight, but simply content to lay in the cool of the rut . . . refusing even to move for the next oncoming car. I've had three dog days in my life. And maybe I've been a part of even more.

But that dog better get up and out of the driveway, elsewise he might find himself on the wrong side of a Goodyear radial. Such is life, too . . . parenting is not optional. Even on the hardest of days, get up. Don't surrender. Don't quit.

For my girls, it seemed that somewhere around their age of 12 or 13, we began to dive into the dog days. Those days when, according to them, everything I said was wrong, and I lost all ability to compose a decent thought or have a good idea. If you don't believe me . . . just ask one of the girls. Met with eye rolls and huffs at the simplest of greetings, Hannah and I clearly became public enemy number one.

And no one ever warned us that these dog days were coming.

So . . . know that they will come. You will be stupid. You will feel defeated. You will feel like a failure. But know that you must press the fight . . . for the enemy hopes you will lay there in the dirt driveway . . . for the heat in the kitchen is simply too hot. And if you do, he knows he can do the thing he came to do . . . "Steal, kill and destroy." John 10:10.

"Train them up in the ways of the Lord," even on the hard days. He will take care of the rest.

God bless.